I0214179

Emotional Intelligence

4 In 1 Mastery Guide

(4 Manuscripts In 1 Book)

Emotional Intelligence Mastery

Learn To Spot And Avoid Manipulation

The Procrastination Fix

Cognitive Behavioral Therapy

Jacob Greene

This is dedicated to all the people

who have contributed

to my craft one way or the other

Thank You

© Copyright 2018, 2019 by Jacob Greene - All rights reserved.

This document is geared towards providing exact and reliable information in regards to the topic and issue covered. The publication is sold with the idea that the publisher is not required to render accounting, officially permitted, or otherwise, qualified services. If advice is necessary, legal or professional, a practiced individual in the profession should be ordered.

From a Declaration of Principles which was accepted and approved by a Committee of the American Bar Association and a Committee of Publishers and Associations.

In no way is it legal to reproduce, duplicate, or transmit any part of this document in either electronic means or in printed format. Recording of this publication is strictly prohibited and any storage of this document is not allowed unless with written permission from the publisher. All rights reserved.

The information provided herein is stated to be truthful and consistent, in that any liability, in terms of inattention or otherwise, by any usage or abuse of any policies, processes, or directions contained within is the solitary and utter responsibility of the recipient reader. Under no circumstances will any legal responsibility or blame be held against the publisher for any reparation, damages, or monetary loss due to the information herein, either directly or indirectly.

Respective authors own all copyrights not held by the publisher.

The information herein is offered for informational purposes solely, and is universal as so. The presentation of the information is without contract or any type of guarantee assurance.

The trademarks that are used are without any consent, and the publication of the trademark is without permission or backing by the trademark owner. All trademarks and brands within this book are for clarifying purposes only and are the owned by the owners themselves, not affiliated with this document.

Table Of Contents

Emotional Intelligence
And How To Achieve Mastery

25 Proven Ways To Improve Your People Skills And Boost Your
EQ For Work And Life

Jacob Greene

Emotional Intelligence
And How To Achieve Mastery

Introduction

Ever been in one of those days where you just seemed to be getting on the wrong side of everyone? Heck, you might have even felt that you were getting on the wrong side of yourself! Being angry, seething with rage and frustration for the whole day. That does not sound very good does it?

Now picture this, what if you got out of bed feeling a little down and out of sorts. Maybe it's that big project dateline looming or that fearsome meeting with the Boss. Or it might just be the after effects of that hurricane like argument you had with your partner last night. Whatever it is, you know in the pit of your stomach that this mood really has the potential to ruin your day. It might end up like what happens earlier – stepping on everyone's toes and clipping your own wings. Or it might be a case where you actually know what is going on, and are able to masterfully handle your own emotions.

You have just defused a potential time bomb, and it all came down to your knowledge and understanding of your very own emotions.

How would you like to at least have a chance to know what to do, and how to do it whenever emotions threaten to boil over and actually start impacting your business and personal relationships? With this book, you are actually well placed to begin exploring how to do that.

You are probably quite a logical person. You may know what two and two equals, but how emotionally intelligent are you? Do you feel that you are in control of your emotions, or do they sneak up on you when you are not prepared? What about the emotions of other people? Are you capable of handling them and calming situations? If you can do either of these, then you are heading toward emotional intelligence, although many cannot do this balancing act. They are too self-absorbed and let their emotions rule their lives, or they are intolerant of others and lack empathy.

Imagine a manager in a business. He has to have a certain amount of emotional intelligence to be able to get the most from his workforce. That means being able to do the following:

- Able to use active listening

- Able to diffuse difficult situations

- Able to control his own emotions

Bosses who do not possess these abilities are not very good bosses and we all know them. These are people who are too egoistical or who don't keep staff very long because their only view toward colleagues is that they are at work for a purpose and nothing else. They forget that people are also human beings with emotional responses. However, when you find entrepreneurs these days that do well for themselves, what you find as well is that colleagues and friends are happy to praise those bosses who inspire them. I remember seeing an article once where people who work with Richard Branson were telling readers about the positive energy they were able to get from his leadership. He himself said in the same interview that he employed people who were energetic and clever because it allowed him to place trust in others who could do specific jobs better than he could. Thus, one can see that emotional intelligence means being able to understand the needs of employees and balance them with the needs of the business. On a personal basis, people who exercise emotional intelligence will show the following traits:

- They will listen to others

- They will know how to empathize

- They are genuine people who can be trusted

There's something else that sets emotionally intelligent people apart from those who do not have this gift. Emotionally intelligent people are aware of their own strengths and weaknesses and can use different emotions to advantage. For example, a poet may be aware that he writes better when he is upset. A mathematician may realize that his powers of analytical investigation are better when he is depressed.

Emotional intelligence helps in so many ways because it makes the path through the maze of life easier and if you can foster this kind of emotional intelligence and make it part of your life, you will not only get on better with people, but you are also likely to put yourself in a direct line for promotion and be able to achieve more than those around you who don't have this gift.

It is not something that gains you qualifications, but it is something that gains you a quality of life. Those who have a high IQ are different from those who have a high level of EI or emotional intelligence and, in the coming chapters, you will be able to test your abilities and try to improve upon them, using your emotional intelligence to help you.

Emotional intelligence keeps you in control of your life in a good way. You will find all the triggers that start your emotions stirring are within your control when you have analyzed them and knew how to control them. The chapters that follow will help you to be able to not only control your emotions but enjoy them as well because you will be more positive in your life and your approach will be very different. In fact, you may enjoy seeing the positive person that you are becoming.

You will learn how to control your emotions and how to judge the emotions of others so that you can respond to them in an appropriate way, instead of letting your emotions take control of you and your potential actions toward others.

Chapter 1: What Is This EQ All About

How does emotional quotient differ from intelligence quotient? The simple answer is- they measure different forms of intelligence. Your technical acumen or technical skills is a direct result of a high intelligence quotient. You've mastered your skills well, which is a reflection of well-developed cognitive abilities. However, is intelligent quotient enough to determine your success when it comes to dealing with people (unless you are cooped up on a remote island all yourself, you have to deal with people)?

While intelligence quotient measures your technical expertise, emotional quotient evaluates your ability to manage your and other people's emotions in your work and personal life. You know where every employee stands when it comes to technical prowess but do you really understand their thoughts, actions and feelings to be able to better manage your and their behavior in sync with these emotions. When we gain insights into the underlying emotional patterns of people, it becomes easier to relate to them and channelize more productive behavior. This is a fundamental difference between intelligence quotient and emotional quotient.

Ever wondered why some of the cleverest people hit a blank in their professional lives and just can't seem to climb the corporate ladder, while the less knowledgeable and inexperienced folks smoothly sail their way to professional success? We all know of people who don't exactly possess the slickest technical skills yet surprisingly manage to reach top management positions. What is it that sets them apart from their more technically competent peers? Emotional intelligence is the key. It is their ability to recognize and control their and others' emotions to build more productive relationships that helps them score.

A person's intelligence quotient demonstrates their core technical competencies, cognitive development and unusual abilities, their emotional intelligence determines their ability to identify emotions and deal with others. Your emotional quotient determines how you will deal with stress, difficult people, bullying, high pressure work situations, conflict within the team, and differences in relationships.

Intelligence is an indicator of your cognitive prowess such as logical thinking, analytical reasoning, memorizing information, solving problems, verbal abilities, creative thinking and much more. Emotional intelligence is controlling your and others' emotions for creating optimally positive circumstances. Starkly different from your ability to comprehend words and numbers, emotional quotient helps you develop healthy interpersonal relationships in your personal and work life.

Emotional intelligence can include stress management, intuition, emotional flexibility, empathy, honesty and more. Emotional quotient highlights your and others emotions with respect to changing circumstances and people, while intelligence quotient is all about cognitive abilities.

While intelligence quotient can determine your success during your academic stint, emotional quotient is vital for all round success in life. You may excel as a student if you possess a high intelligence quotient. However to attain overall success in life, you need a high emotional quotient.

Research has indicated that there are five fundamental skills that distinguish the star performers from low performers. These skills are empathy, self-awareness, assertiveness, problem solving and happiness. Potential recruits who score high on these five attributes are 2.7 times likelier to succeed than folks who bag low scores.

So, why is emotional quotient so closely associated with a person's chances of becoming successful in life? The answer is – awareness of emotions and ability to express themselves confidently. Emotionally intelligent people are experts in gauging people's emotions and altering their pitches/presentations accordingly. Little wonder then that emotionally intelligence is so vital for people in sales, customer service, counseling and other industries.

For instance, a study closely followed the recruitment of sales personnel for cosmetic giant L'Oreal based on their emotional skills. It was observed that these emotionally competent sales people outdid other salespersons by a whopping $91,370 to amass a net revenue growth of $ 2,558, 360. In another research, a national insurance firm discovered that salespersons who were low on emotional skills like initiative, confidence and empathy sold far less policies (average premium of $54,000) that agents who scored high on emotional skills (average premium of $114,000). You get the picture, right? When you show high emotional competencies by being proactive, self-confident and empathetic, you are able to connect to potential buyers and help them buy rather than simply sell.

In the workplace, intelligence quotient helps for analyzing, connecting the dots and undertaking research and development. Emotional intelligence is about forging a strong team spirit, leadership, building successful professional relationships, collaboration, service and initiative. Emotional quotient can be gained and enhanced as opposed to intelligence quotient, which is a more inborn and hereditary characteristic.

The goal for businesses isn't to simply hire people who are intellectually competent, but lack emotional or people skills. Today's competitive and social interactions dominated world demands workers who are smart (that's a given), and endowed with more thoughtfulness. The ideal candidate is a combination of emotional intelligence and general intelligence. Since all candidates applying for a position possess more or less the same technical competence, emotional intelligence often becomes a clinching factor when it comes to selecting people for important roles.

Standford-Binet, Woodcock-Johnson Tests of Cognitive abilities and Wechsler are some popular intelligence quotient tests, while Mayer-Salovey-Caruso Test and Daniel Goleman model score test are popular emotional intelligence assessment tests. An Intelligence Quotient test generally involves a collection of standardized questions where participants are assigned precise scores based on their answers. These scores are evaluated with respect to average scores within the age group to establish a person's intellectual capabilities.

Emotional quotient tests, on the other hand, are more challenging to administer because feelings and emotional skills are tougher to depict numerically. While intelligence quotient questions have a definite answer for every question, emotional quotient tests tend to be more subjective and require greater evaluation effort. Unlike IQ tests, there aren't any right or wrong answers. Respondents may not answer questions honestly simply to rank high or may adjust their responses according to what they are currently experiencing, which makes these results more skewed. There may be a tendency on part of the participant to say exactly what the evaluators want to hear rather than responding truthfully.

People possessing a high intelligence quotient are excellent at conducting tasks. They are quick absorbers of new skills and information. However, if they have a low emotional quotient, they tend to overlook their and other's feelings. For instance, when something doesn't turn out according to the way they wanted, these folks tend to lose their temper and lash out at people. While someone who is high on emotional intelligence will learn to control their emotions and get along with people around them. They are extremely effective when it comes to working as a team or working in a leadership role.

The concept of emotional intelligence has gained such a strong momentum that it has impacted a large a large number of areas including the corporate world. Several top organizations have now made emotional intelligence tests mandatory as part of the hiring process, along with intelligence quotient.

In personal relationships, 90 percent of the issues arise due to lack of emotional intelligence. Everything revolves around empathy, self-awareness, awareness of the other person's emotions, understanding, communication patterns and the likes, which are all components of emotional intelligence.

Emotional quotient is not the antithesis of intelligence quotient. They aren't mutually exclusive. Some folks possess both in huge quantities, while others possess neither. Psychologists are keener to explore how the two attributes balance each other. For instance, how your ability to deal with stress impacts your ability to focus or learn new information.

The Three Models of Emotional Intelligence

The CEO of a tech company happened to stroll along the halls of his building, and he came across two developers with whom he wasn't impressed. He lashed out at them, and the two developers – a man and a woman – spent the rest of the day feeling terrible. When they each went home after work, their kids happily mobbed them. The woman was receptive to her kids' joy, but the man quickly dismissed his kids.

One thing stands out here: the woman was in a position wherein she can control her emotions; the man wasn't. He literally took out his frustrations with the CEO on his kids. Thus, we can infer that despite the man and woman having about the same intelligence quotient, considering that they work in a similar capacity, the woman has a higher emotional quotient.

Emotional intelligence is primarily the capacity of an individual to be aware of their emotions and the emotions of other people. An individual with a high emotional intelligence may discern between different feelings and control both how they express their feelings and how they react to other peoples' feelings.

The term "emotional intelligence" was first coined by a researcher named Michael Beldoch in 1964, but it became popular in 1995 when a science journalist named Daniel Goleman published a book titled Emotional Intelligence.

Today, emotional intelligence is categorized into three main models:

- Ability Model

- Mixed Model

- Trait Model

Ability Model

Peter Salovey of Yale University and John Mayer of the University of New Hampshire came up with the Ability Model. They define emotional intelligence as "the capacity to think about emotions, and of emotions, to enhance thinking." This includes the capacity of an individual to recognize emotions, to access and produce emotions for thought purposes, to understand feelings and the emotional language, and to be in control of their emotions to advance both emotionally and mentally.

The Ability Model considers emotions to be an important source of information that helps an individual understand the world that they live in. According to the developers of this model, people have different capacities to process information that carries emotional undertones, and their ability to relate discernment of emotions to cognitive potential also varies. Here are the four main abilities that this model postulates:

•   Perceiving emotions. This deals with a person's capability to spot and decode emotions in various things, people, and most importantly, yourself. The mere ability to recognize emotions is critical because it enhances the processing of any emotional information.

•   Using emotions. This is about a person's capacity to tap into emotions to enhance cognitive functions like problem-solving, creativity, and critical thinking. Emotional intelligence enables a person to make the best of their situations based on the emotions generated.

•   Understanding emotions. This relates to a person's capacity to understand the language of emotions. An individual with a high emotional intelligence is able to comprehend the emotional weight in every message. They are even proficient at detecting how emotions change in response to varying conditions.

•   Managing emotions. The last one is about our capacity to regulate our emotions and respond appropriately to the emotions of other people. An individual with a high emotional intelligence is in a position to control himself and to give an appropriate response in the face of other people's feelings.

This model has received both praise and criticism in the research community about its effectiveness.

Mixed Model

It is so named as the "Mixed Model" because it contains qualities of emotional intelligence and other personal traits that have no connection to emotions or intelligence. The Mixed Model is based on Daniel Goleman's idea of competencies and skills that drive performance. Some of these competencies include self-awareness, teamwork, motivation, service orientation, and initiative. Emotional competencies are not inborn. Rather, they are abilities that any person can develop with enough commitment and practice. Goleman proposed five categories where various emotional competencies fit.

- Self-awareness. This is the ability to recognize your general emotional traits. A self-aware person has a strong sense of how to perceive and experience emotions. This is critical because it helps them make informed decisions. To be self-aware, you have to be confident first. An individual who is not ashamed of who they are gains a clear understanding of their emotions.

- Self-regulation. This is the ability to rein in oneself. When emotions are involved, logic is likely to disappear. Having this ability means being able to control yourself so as not to arrive at an undesirable outcome. Besides self-control, you also need to be honest and practice integrity, as well as to learn to adapt to various situations much quicker and utilize your creativity when you're in emotionally-volatile situations. Self-regulation also fosters the capacity of an individual to take responsibility for their actions.

- Motivation. This is the ability to pursue the various goals that you set for yourself. A motivated person harbors a lot more positive thinking and eliminates negativity. Even in the face of obstacles, a motivated person sticks to their goal and always takes the initiative. A motivated person is in perpetual search for tactics to improve their lives.

- Empathy. This is the capacity to discern other peoples' emotions and figure out the appropriate response. Empathy mainly stems from having political awareness and being willing and ready to be of service to other peoples' needs. An empathic person makes decisions that are aimed at connecting with other people and building them up.

- Social skills. This is the ability to relate to other people and establish relationships. Some of the competencies involved include collaboration, cooperation, influence, communication, conflict management, and building bonds.

Trait Model

This model postulates that emotional traits and emotional self-perceptions are ingrained in a person's personality. Therefore, emotional intelligence is how a person perceives their emotional abilities and behaviors. The key distinction is that this construct is not based upon any scientific basis but upon the individual's evaluation of oneself. This model is relatively new, having been published in 2009 by Petrides and his colleagues, and it is considered the answer to the ability-based construct. The Trait Model has received its fair share of praise and criticism as well.

Benefits of Emotional Intelligence

As discussed earlier, emotional intelligence is our ability to manage our and other's emotions by discriminating among these feelings, and using the information to guide our words, thoughts and actions. To cut a long story short, emotional intelligence is an aggregation of your mental and emotional skills. Emotionally intelligent people enjoy a multitude of benefits in all spheres of life including relationships, career and social life. Here are some ways in which your life can be impacted or benefited if you consciously focus on developing high emotional intelligence.

Greater Compassion in Personal and Work Life

One of the best benefits of high emotional intelligence is your ability to demonstrate more compassion for others both in the personal and professional sphere. This compassion allows them to connect with people at much deeper levels to forge meaningful relationships. Compassion can be manifested in several ways, including helping someone dealing with a personal issue by taking on their responsibilities or making small everyday decisions for the comfort/convenience of your employees.

Compassion helps you meaningfully connect with people both in your personal and professional life. You are able to reach out to people efficiently, forge more mutually fulfilling relationships and create an atmosphere of harmony and productivity. Emotional intelligence awards you greater compassion in dealing with people in various personal professional and social scenarios.

Fine Communication Skills

People with a well-developed emotional quotient are more efficient when it comes to expressing themselves. They possess the ability to listen attentively to other people's verbal clues, while also tuning in to their nonverbal communication. They know exactly what to say to channelize people's strengths. They use the right words and nonverbal signals to help people feel at ease. There is little scope for misunderstanding whilst communicating with a person who has high emotional intelligence.

Emotionally intelligent people are well aware about the most compelling emotional triggers of the people around them. They know exactly how to inspire people to act. People who are able to communicate by emotionally connecting with are far more effective than technically competent folks who fail to demonstrate empathy while communicating with people. Emotional intelligence awards you better response skills.

Lower Chances of Addiction and Other Emotional Disorders

Addictions are generally a direct result of our inability to cope with emotions. People who struggle to come to terms with their emotions use addiction as a mechanism to avoid the more underlying and deeper prevailing issues. When you fail to recognize and manage negative. emotions, there develops an unfortunate pattern of dependency on external factors such as food, nicotine, substance, alcohol, porn and the likes. Addiction is just a means to escape from emotions you aren't willing to deal with.

Emotionally intelligent folks are lesser prone to addiction because of their awareness of their emotions and the ability to manage these emotions. They have a solid understanding of their feelings, and do not struggle to deal with it. Since emotional intelligence makes you happier, more confident and balanced, there is a lesser propensity for dependence on destructive coping mechanisms. They adapt more easily to challenges and changing scenarios in life. Emotionally intelligent people are competent in resolving differences and coming up with more positive solutions. Since they display such a high understanding of their and other's emotions, it becomes easier for them to deal with conflicts.

Emotionally healthy people are less prone to be victims of drug abuse or binge eating disorders, which predominantly originate from much deeper psychological issues.

Coping With Life Challenges

Don't you sometimes look at some people and wonder how they are able to stay afloat through the most challenging situations and emerge even more successful than before? Chances are, these guys score high on emotional intelligence. Emotionally intelligent folks have the ability to calm their body and mind to view things from a clearer and more objective perspective. Their acts are more mindful and less panic stricken.

Greater calmness, objectivity and clarity award you more resilience where life's challenges are concerned. Think about the kungfu fighter who can take on the most powerful opponents by constantly working on martial arts skills. Emotional intelligence equips you with those skills to take on the toughest challenges life throws at you with resilience.

Stellar Productivity

Emotional intelligence has a high correlation with an individual's work performance. Research has revealed that emotional intelligence is twice as crucial as technical/cognitive abilities even among professions such as engineering. Emotionally intelligent managers, supervisors and leaders are way more effective in managing teams, motivating people and negotiating.

They create a more positive atmosphere with happier workers, who are an asset to any organization. Happier workers translate into higher morale, low absenteeism, reduced attrition rate and higher productivity. This leads to happier customers, more sales and higher profits. Thus emotional intelligence is an invaluable trait when it comes to success at the workplace. Whilst everyone within an organization possesses more or less the same technical competency and educational qualifications, only a few rise up the corporate ladder because of their ability to manage people and their emotions.

An emotionally intelligent leader who understands the true value of identifying and managing emotions can empower his/her subordinates with these skills on a daily basis. Discipline or self regulation is essential when it comes to keeping your emotions in check, avoiding panic, remaining calm and being an asset to the team. Emotionally intelligent folks have little trouble in recognizing and managing potentially destructive emotions that can create stress and lower productivity. The approach is calmer, more confident and efficient. Rather than experiencing a more touchy view, these folks depend on their ability to possess a more realistic view of themselves and others.

Boosted Leadership Skills

Emotionally intelligent folks possess a highly evolved ability in recognizing and understanding factors that drive others, which makes them amazing leaders. They are able to make the most of this invaluable information to strengthen their loyalty and forge stronger relationships with people. A competent leader is intuitively tuned in to the most compelling aspirations and desires of his followers. He knows the "hot buttons" of his employees and exactly how to channelize these "hot buttons" to increase overall productivity and positivity within the work environment.

Emotionally intelligent leaders know how to channelize this information for extracting better performance/productivity from people and keeping them happy. People with a high emotional quotient excel at recognizing the strengths and weaknesses of people and harnessing an individual's virtues for benefiting the team.

High emotional intelligence creates better leaders who are able to inspire greater faith and loyalty by using their team's or follower's or emotional range. They are more aware of their emotions, which allow emotionally intelligent folks to create a harmonious environment. Practicing emotional intelligence makes you a better leader.

Did you know that 67% of all competencies said to be fundamental for high performance in the professional sphere is emotional intelligence? Take the example of the world's most successful CEOs. Amazon's Jeff Bezos passionately talks about getting right into the hearts of his customers in a 2009 YouTube video while announcing the company's Zappos acquisition. When Howard Schultz of Starbucks was a child, his father lost a health insurance claim. This turned him into one of the most empathetic CEOs, who is well known showing his employees thoughtfulness by offering generous healthcare rewards. Little wonder then that these folks are as successful as they are. They understand the emotional pulse of their employees and customers to keep them emotionally gratified.

Emotional intelligence helps in building emotional maturity, boosting social intelligence, preventing relationship problems, enhancing interpersonal communication, helping control emotions, dealing with stress, influencing leadership, helping authorities make sound business change decisions, supporting staff and controlling resistance to change.

Boosted Employee Morale and Lower Attrition

Morale may be an intangible concept in the corporate world but its effects are highly measureable. You may not realize the value of a high morale when it's there, but you will definitely know when it's missing. Think about the lateness, early departures, attrition, sick leaves your company suffers from. When leaders take the time to build emotional intelligence and connect with their team members, it reflects in the employee morale.

Emotionally intelligent leaders who build stronger emotional ties with subordinates witness improvement in the team's morale, lower measureable absenteeism, a higher team spirit and a greater desire to contribute to an organization's success. The emotional intelligence skill building cost can be minimal. However, the return on investment can be extremely high.

Let's get real here and call a spade a spade. Employees do not really quit roles, they quit senior managers. It is about escaping people and not positions. Emotionally intelligent leaders, who recognize emotional triggers, quickly pick up emotional clues of their team members and "customize" their approach to each member's unique emotional make-up and motivation will experience greater success in retaining employees. This should not be mistaken with not doing justice to one's own voice or feelings. It simply means, presenting an accurate emotional response towards each team member to treat them with greater compassion, respect and empathy.

The problem with most managers who do not understand the concept of emotional intelligence is that they use a one size fits all approach for dealing with all employees, without understanding the emotional framework, motivators and goals of individual team members. This one size fits all approach does not produce flattering results because personalities vary. Some people are more intrinsically motivated, while others thrive on extrinsic motivation. Some folks are quick to reveal their emotions; others aren't very comfortable sharing their feelings. Once you understand the emotional make-up of people, it becomes easy to deal with them more efficiently.

Chapter 2: EQ And Why You Want It

Social intelligence is characterized by the ability to build successful social relationships and overcome challenging social environments. It is our ability to connect with and deal with other people in a social set-up scenario. As a society, we are obsessed with intelligence and academic smartness. However, our relationships play a much bigger role in our overall development and well-being. Of course, you need to be academically sound to enjoy professional success but you also need to be socially smart to lead people and build strong relationships.

However, have you wondered what happens when you are not socially adept or intelligent?

Lack of Understanding of Other People's Emotions

A person I knew (let's call her Anne for this example) was exceptionally good where technical knowledge, ability and potential were concerned. Anne was able to get things done and drive commendable results. However, her approach to getting those results wasn't very favorable and didn't find many takers, which made her an unpopular manager. Anne was known to demean others, display impatience and sport a rather dogmatic attitude. She left a lot of people disappointed and unmotivated, which didn't go down well in her feedback. When confronted about the feedback others gave against her, Anne was shocked. She didn't see it this way and was surprised others found her dictatorial.

For Anne, she was only getting people to perform according to the demands of the projects. This lack of self-awareness and lack of understanding about how she impacted other people's emotions led to Anne's downfall. Imagine an otherwise ace professional struggling with lack of self-awareness and a sense of empathy.

What Anne was saying was, "At the end of it all, it is about results and getting stuff done." What her team and subordinates were interpreting was, "I don't care about anything but results, and in the process, if I hurt your feelings, it doesn't matter." There was a clear gap between what Anne thought she was coming across as and what she was actually coming across as. This disconnect is what caused her professional downfall!

Socially and emotionally intelligent people can identify not just their own feelings but also the impact they have on other people's emotions. They can recognize and perceive other people's emotions and manage them in the best interests of everyone involved. Unlike Anne, they know the impact their actions or emotions have on others and therefore, alter their own emotional behavior to positively influence other people's actions.

You may have all the intelligence, academic excellence and experience in the world, but if you don't know how to deal with your emotions and other people's emotions, you aren't going to get far in your professional and personal life.

Signs that you lack social and emotional intelligence:

•	You often think people are being too sensitive to your humor or jokes and are overreacting.

•	You jump into any conversation with absolute assertiveness and refuse to budge most of the time. You are also quick to defend your stand with gusto should anyone even question it reasonably.

•	You think social popularity and being liked in your workplace is grossly overrated. As long as you do your work and deliver results, it shouldn't matter whether people like you or not.

•	You have extremely high expectations of yourself and others, many times bordering on unreasonable and impractical.

•	You get irritated and frustrated when others expect you to understand how they feel. Your thought process is, "How am I supposed to know or understand someone else's feelings without them talking to me about it?"

•	Most of the time you feel like people don't understand your point or know where you are coming from, which makes you annoyed and upset.

•	You always find yourself blaming other people and circumstances for your shortcomings and failures. You seldom accept responsibility and accountability for your acts, and you pass the buck elsewhere.

Of course, it isn't just limited to these signs. There are many other indicators of low social and emotional intelligence, though these are typical signs that most people with low emotional and social intelligence display.

Not Being Flexible or Agreeable

Be honest and answer this. Do you like people who always take the high road around you? Nope, no one does really! These are people who are extremely rigid about their views, are not open to suggestions, don't believe in working out a way to meet in the middle, and don't appreciate even constructive criticism from others. It is either my way or the highway for them. If you are one of these people, you are sooner or later going to struggle with social relationships. A huge component of emotional and social intelligence is being open, agreeable and flexible.

If you are a rigid and closed person, people may pretend to be nice to you on the outside but deep on the inside, they don't really appreciate your tendency to dictate terms all the time. Before you know it, they'll start avoiding you and minimizing interaction with you. Social intelligence is about accepting and respecting other people's perspectives even if it is different from your own. It is about being flexible enough to identify and incorporate the good in other people's suggestions. It helps you gain a different perspective and puts you on the same page as the other person to connect in a more harmonious manner. People will appreciate having you around them and listening to your perspective in an open and agreeable manner.

Social Anxiety and Social Triggers

People who lack social intelligence often become increasingly anxious in a social situation, which hinders their ability to connect with people.

What are the triggers that are causing this social anxiety? As a child, you may not have had many people attending your birthday party. This has been firmly embedded in your mind even though you've grown up now, and things have changed a lot. Today, you may have plenty of people who would willingly attend your party but disappointing and negative thoughts about your childhood birthday party prevent you from inviting your friends to celebrate with you.

Identifying your social triggers can help combat social anxiety.

- What are the types of social situations that make you anxious?

- What type of interactions make you want to quickly escape from the place?

- When do you get a feeling that you can't really be yourself?

Socially anxious people find it challenging to conduct themselves in social scenarios, to fulfill social relationships and professionally network with people from within their industry. They are basically operating in isolation which doesn't help them leverage the power of social contacts and belonging in a community.

Lack of Empathy

Imagine a scenario where a person who is not socially intelligent comes to you and tries to offer condolences on the death of a family member. You get his or her phone call to offer condolence. They talk about how sorry they are for your loss but you get a feeling they don't really mean it and are doing it more out of a sense of obligation. You can hear them speaking to someone else in the background and typing on a keyboard—basically, they are preoccupied with something else and are only offering their regret about your loss as an obligation without actually empathizing with you. How do you end up feeling after the rather insincere, ice cold and mechanical condolence? It makes you feel even worse than you felt before they called.

Socially unintelligent folks lack the ability to empathize with other people and their troubles, which makes it challenging for them to form strong and mutually fulfilling bonds with others.

How Emotional Intelligence Affects Your Personal Life and Career

For the longest time, people hadn't been aware of the importance of emotional intelligence. The emphasis had been on IQ. People believed that IQ was the biggest – if not the only – requirement for achieving success.

Thanks to researchers like Daniel Goleman, the evidence has been dug out that emotional quotient is every bit as critical as intelligence quotient. People who have a high emotional intelligence enjoy a much rewarding life than their low-EQ counterparts. This is tied to their ability to understand and manage their feelings as well as the feelings of other people.

Personal Relationships

The most important relationship in society is the family unit. It takes a special kind of partnership to live together harmoniously and bring up a family.

Emotional intelligence is one of the vital ingredients of a stable family. For one, it allows you to lead by example. Children are highly impressionable; they never do as you tell them – they do as they see you do. A parent who leads by example acknowledges that they shoulder a huge responsibility towards their children. In this way, the children would have a good role model to imitate. You might also attempt to practice your values such that your partner would follow. For instance, if truth-telling is one of your values, you should see to it that you always tell the truth. In this way, you will challenge your spouse into always telling the truth as well.

Emotional intelligence promotes forgiveness. When two or more people form a relationship, one thing is to be expected: conflict. If the parties to that relationship have low emotional intelligence, they are likely to fight between themselves and may end up throwing away what they have. But if they have high emotional intelligence, they will surely give compassion a chance. Only emotionally strong people can afford to forgive.

Emotional intelligence strengthens relationships through honest communication, and communication is not just about opening your mouth and saying something. It encompasses verbal and nonverbal aspects, and most importantly, it must be honest. Both partners should be free to state their needs, wants, and problems.

Career

One of the areas where emotional intelligence makes a big impact is in your career. If you're like most people, your job must be demanding. The average employee calls it "stressful." But sadly, your success rate will be measured according to your ability to adapt to these unfavorable working conditions. And so, it takes emotional intelligence to survive in an environment that keeps you on your toes. Without emotional intelligence, you would likely become an underperforming employee, which makes you dispensable.

If you can achieve results in a high-stress environment, it is indicative of a high emotional intelligence. It doesn't mean that you cannot feel the stress, but it means that you acknowledge the stress and are not ready to let it bog you down. On the other hand, a person with low emotional intelligence tends to let every minor issue derail them. And the output of such an employee is going to be greatly affected. Keeping in mind the benefits of emotional intelligence, it is easy to see why a person with high emotional intelligence would receive a job promotion over a person who lacks it.

When you're working alongside other people, there will be instances when they will need you to be the bigger person. It's called the practice of empathy. As an empathetic individual, you have to show concern for your colleagues. Sometimes, they may be unable to deliver on a set task for whatever reason, but it is upon you to respond appropriately instead of criticizing them. When you show your colleagues empathy, you come across as being charismatic. And in such environments, having social capital is critical in advancing through the ranks. A person with low emotional intelligence would hardly notice a colleague in need, let alone offer empathy. They are unable to understand the feelings of another person.

Emotional intelligence also promotes problem-solving skills. In a work environment, you can expect controversies, arguments, and fights. Obviously, such conflicts should be resolved as quickly as possible because they hold back the workers from adding value to their time. It takes emotional intelligence to stop conflict and prevent similar outcomes in the future.

Creativity goes together with emotional intelligence. Creativity has a role to play in an amicable conflict resolution. Creating options when you resolve a conflict lessens the damage, if not eliminating it altogether. The only downside is that the success of your method greatly depends on the behaviors of the other parties. But even if you're up against non-cooperative colleagues, you can still be in control of your emotions and respond appropriately.

Emotional intelligence helps you make great career decisions. Well, you're always going to have to make decisions that impact your career. What is your basis for gauging the perfect job for you? Is it the salary, working environment, the boss, or the nature of the work? When it comes to career advancement, the stakes are high, and one wrong move could potentially ruin your career. So, you have to depend on your emotional intelligence to make the right choice.

The important career decisions are not only those that involve migrating jobs but also the decisions that touch upon skill improvement and team building. If you're low on emotional intelligence, you will hardly identify opportunities to advance your career. And in the instance where you have alternatives, you're likely to take the option that will flop. This is because of your one-sided inclination as opposed to taking all factors into consideration. For instance, if an employer A and an employer B offered you $100,000 and $150,000 salary respectively, you might be tempted to rush to employer B, failing to question other important factors.

Chapter 3: Those Things You Can Do For Your EQ

After gaining a thorough understanding of emotional intelligence and its benefits, the million dollar question is – is it really possible to improve one's emotional intelligence or emotional quotient? Is it possible from struggling to cope with your and other's emotions to being a rockstar at understanding emotions?

With all its advantages, who wouldn't want high emotional intelligence? Who wouldn't want greater professional success, business potential, leadership skills, relationship gratification, humor, good health, positivity and happiness around them? Think about an antidote that beats stress, helps you form rewarding relationships with people and much more.

Take any coaching intervention program, and it will generally highlight some aspect of emotional intelligence in the name of interpersonal skills or social/soft skills. The most compelling reason for this is that, while intelligence quotient is tough to change, emotional quotient can be acquired with training and consistent practice. So, the good news is that even if you do not consider yourself very emotionally evolved, there is plenty of scope to boost your emotional quotient with practice, training and conscious effort.

 The best part about enhancing your emotional intelligence is that it can be practiced in your everyday life. For instance, if you are short tempered, start by showing greater empathy or being a more considerate listener.

Respond Rather Than React

Reacting is a more unconscious and uncontrolled process that is a result of an emotional trigger. For instance, you snap when someone annoys you or you are already stressed due to another reason.

Responding, on the other hand, is more controlled and something you choose to do. You decide exactly how you behave in the given situation. For example, explaining to someone that you are not feeling too good and that this isn't the best time to interrupt you, and that later you'd be in a much better position to give them a good hearing. You've simply chosen to deal with the situation in a more productive and less impulsive manner by taking control of your emotions.

Evaluate how your actions will impact others before acting. If your behavior will affect others, try and place yourself in their shoes. How are they bound to feel if you say or do something? Would you like to go through the experience yourself? If you have to take a particular action, can you help people in coping with its effects?

Emotional Quotient Is Not Rigid

Though our capacity to recognize and handle our and other's emotions is largely determined by childhood experiences, heredity and other factors, it isn't rigid. We can alter our ability to comprehend and manage emotions over the long term with the right coaching and dedication. You can change of course, however, the question is do you want to change? Are you willing to put in the effort required to be more emotionally intelligent? Sometimes, while you may successfully be able to manage your external emotions, you may still grapple with emotions you do not manage to display on the outside.

While some folks are naturally positive, calm and social, others can be plain grumpy, egoistic, shy or insecure. However, no trait is unchangeable. If you truly want to change an aspect of your personality, you can. Emotional intelligence naturally increases with age, without any intervention. This is the rationale behind the popular belief that people gain more maturity as they grow older. Overall, yes it is possible to improve your emotional quotient over the long term with intervention, guidance and regular practice.

Some Methods Work More Efficiently Than Others

Some techniques for boosting emotional intelligence such as cognitive behavioral therapy for better psychological flexibility can work better than other methods. Since emotional intelligence is linked to human behavior, it can never be an exact science. The dynamics of human behavior, motivation, communication and feelings will keep changing. You have to identify and evaluate what works for you. While behavioral therapy works wonderfully well for some people, others may find meditation or deep breathing more effective in calming their emotions.

Here are some tried and tested tips for being the ultimate emotional intelligence ninja.

Accurate Feedback

One of the most crucial aspects if you want to enhance your emotional quotient through any coaching intervention or self practice program is accurate feedback. People generally do not realize how others perceive them, especially people in senior management positions in organizations.

Though these folks are increasingly motivated, responsible and high on technical skills, they rarely take the time to pause and assess their behavior. In a nutshell, we do not possess a very accurate notion of how nice we come across as. Wishful thinking, misplaced optimism and overconfidence can be factors contributing to this blind spot.

Generally people tend to over evaluate themselves in the niceness department. They believe they are nicer than they actually are. Any effort at increasing your emotional quotient must begin with gaining a thorough understanding your strengths and weaknesses. Use valid and genuine assessment techniques like personality tests or accurate feedback to determine your success with developing a higher emotional quotient.

Pay Close Attention to Your Behavior

You can only manage your emotions more effectively if you are consciously aware of it. It starts with paying very close attention to your emotions and their impact on your behavior. Emotional awareness is one of the cornerstones of EQ.

Start noticing how you act when you experience specific situations, and how it affects your everyday life. Do these feelings impact your productivity? How about your communication with other people? Do your emotions pose a threat to your overall well-being, including your physical and emotional health? How do you react when you are extremely angry, happy or sad? Once you are consciously aware of your reactions to emotions, you will be able to wield better control over them and channelize them more productively.

Use Your Mental Pause Button

Use your mental pause button each time you find yourself on the verge of speaking or acting. Take a moment, breathe deeply and think before you respond. Whenever you feel tempted to type an elaborate mail in rage, stop and think if it is going to help resolve the issue or only make it worse. Each time you feel like screaming at someone or making a combustible comment on the social media, apply the pause button.

When you consciously work on pausing before you speak or act, you get into the habit of thinking before acting or speaking in a manner that can worsen any situation. You learn to manage, control and tackle your emotions to handle any situation in a more constructive manner. When you learn to use this technique, you realize that the button to your feelings and emotions is in your hands.

When you sense a challenge in controlling impulses, deal with it by quickly diverting your attention. Distract your thoughts by counting or concentrating on a pre-planned diversion thought. Your mind can be trained to shift thoughts or conversations fast.

Emotional Intelligence Can Be Developed

Our emotional intelligence pathway originates within the brain going right down to the spinal cord. The primary senses are involved here and must go to the brain's front portion before you start thinking logically or rationally about an occurrence. Emotions are generated in our limbic system, which is why our emotional response to an incident occurs before the rational mind gets involved. Emotional intelligence is based on efficient communication patterns between the brain's logical and emotional points.

Have you heard of plasticity? It is a term used by neurologists for describing the brain's ability to keep evolving and changing. The brain keeps growing newer connections as we acquire new skills. The change is slow, as the brain keeps developing more and more connections to boost its efficiency.

When you use various strategies for boosting emotional intelligence, you are actually letting the microscopic neurons (billions of them) lined between the emotional and logical centers of the brain to branch into smaller arms that touch other cells. This simply means, one cell can form more than 15,000 connections. The chain reaction signifies that it is simpler for the brain to adapt to this new behavior in the long term. Once the brain is trained with the help of emotional intelligence strategies, it becomes a habitual behavior/thought pattern.

Be Open to Feedback

Boost your emotional intelligence by being more receptive to feedback. While you may disagree with the criticism/feedback, sometimes being open to others' views can help you identify behavior patterns that may be having an effect that you didn't intend. Healthy feedback can guard you from blind spots and adjust your behavior.

The more you exist in denial mode about destructive behavior, the more challenging it may be for you to develop a high emotional quotient. Acceptance and awareness is the key to increasing your emotional intelligence.

Read Body Language

Try to gauge people's innermost emotions by tuning in to their body language. Pick up clues about their emotional health by observing their body language. Sometimes people say something while their expressions and gestures convey the opposite or a deeper truth they aren't comfortable revealing. When you practice being more mindful of their body language, you tap into their true emotional fabric to adapt your responses and reactions. Sometimes people resort to less conspicuous ways for communicating their emotions.

For instance, a person may try saying something reassuring but the high tone of their voice may defeat those words and indicate high stress. These are small yet powerful indicators of people's behavior patterns and reading them correctly will give you the power to unlock another's emotional framework.

Be Positive and Happy

How would you rate your happiness quotient on a scale of 1 to 10? Emotional intelligence originates from being happy and vice versa. They aren't simply happy because good things are happening to them but because they are great at managing and taking control of their own happiness.

Happiness originates from within. A person who is capable of managing his emotions efficiently wakes up joyfully each morning. These people encounter challenges too, just like everyone else. However, they do not let these issues dampen their zest for positivity. Develop greater emotional intelligence by keeping your mind clear, avoid getting caught in destructive self-pity and take charge of your happiness. Emotional intelligence comes with being more positive and solution oriented.

Happy people gain more appreciation and following from people to help them tide over tough times. They spread more happiness, live longer and come up with constructive solution. It is a misconception that happiness is a result of material possessions. Genuinely happy people are those who can manage their emotions well, spread happiness, and most importantly those who focus on giving rather than receiving. Emotionally intelligent people know that it costs zilch to be happy and yet the returns are invaluable.

Avoid Labeling Your Emotions

All your emotions are valid, including the not so positive ones. Avoid assigning labels and judging your emotions. When you judge your feelings, you inhibit your ability to experience them. When you cannot fully express or experience something, you prevent yourself from using these emotions more positively.

Each emotion you experience is a vital piece of information closely linked with what is happening around you and how it affects you. Without information about your emotions, you'd be left clueless about how to react to your emotions and manage them more effectively.

Connect negative feelings to events but avoid judging them to gain a better understanding. For instance, if you feel envious, try and figure out what the emotions is conveying to you about the situation. Learn to experience positive emotions so you recognize each opportunity to feel them to the fullest.

Practice Empathy

Empathy is all about trying to understand why someone feels or acts in the way they do by putting yourself in their shoes. It is also being able to communicate this understanding to them more effectively. Empathy can also apply to your emotions and feelings.

Each time you notice yourself experiencing a specific emotion or behavior, try and think why you feel the way you do. You may not be able to figure it out at the onset but pay close attention and you'll start receiving various answers that you didn't notice earlier.

When someone is experiencing a rather strong feeling, ask yourself how you would feel in a similar scenario. Always be interested in what people say to respond in a more sensitive manner. It is always a good practice to ask questions and summarize what people say so you are clear, and people know you are actively listening to them.

When you put yourself in the other person's shoe, you reduce reactivity. For instance, if your child is resisting something you are telling him/her, try thinking it isn't easy for them to deal with peer pressure and academics. Think for a moment how it must be to be a young kid in the current competitive age.

 If your manager is being demanding and difficult, think about the pressure of performance expectation they are dealing with at the hands of senior management. When you start thinking more objectively by considering where the other person is coming from, understanding and conflict resolution become much simpler.

Managing other's emotions requires maturity, skill and tact. It starts by being aware of exactly where you want the person to go? Do you want to lead them to feeling happier, calmer, more aware, secure, vigilant or cautious, for instance? Once you realize how they are feeling and how to lead them there, you will know what to say and do.

We tend to forget how particular experiences feel; even we've lived through it ourselves. You can only imagine how much perspective limiting it becomes if we've not experienced what the other person is going through. What is the best way to bridge this gap? The nucleus of empathy lies in understanding the "why" among other things. Why does this person feel the way they do? What are they dealing with that I fail to see? Why do I experience different feelings than them? Explore your "whys" and you will be well on your way to better understanding the feelings of others.

Being kind, considerate and helpful is one of the best ways of practicing emotional intelligence.

Be Assertive

Emotionally intelligent folks know the importance of setting appropriate boundaries to let people know our stand. You have the right to disagree with people without acting in a disagreeable manner. Learn to say no and refuse without feeling guilty when you are not up to something or you find people taking advantage of you. Set your priorities and safeguard yourself from stress, harm and duress.

Rather than using "you" followed by the accusation and putting people on the defensive foot, try making them more open to listening to and understanding your point. For instance, instead of saying "you should do this" or "you are xyx", try saying, "I feel really uncomfortable when you expect me to do this over my priorities" or "I strongly believe that I deserve recognition from the organization based on my consistent performance and contributions." See what we did there? We aren't putting people on the defensive by pointing a finger at them and saying, "you did this" or "you are like this." We are being assertive and talking about our feelings without blaming anybody.

Accept Responsibility for Your Feelings and Actions

This can be one of the most challenging yet productive tips for boost your emotional quotient. Your emotions originate from you and therefore you are completely responsible for them.

People around you may be responsible for creating certain situations but it is ultimately you who are in charge of your reaction to those situations. You may not always be able to control how others around you speak or behave. However, the way you react to their words and actions is something you have control over.

If you are hurt by someone and lash out, you are the one responsible for it. Get out of the mindset that "someone makes you do something." No one can make you angry; you are responsible for your anger. No one holds the strings to your emotions. No one makes you do or feel anything. Your reaction is completely your own responsibility. Your feelings can offer you important guidelines about your experience with different people along with your own requirements and preferences. However, your feelings and actions are no one's but your responsibility.

Once you start accepting responsibility for your feelings and behavior, it becomes simpler to manage it for impacting all spheres of your life positively.

If you hurt people, be gracious enough to accept it and apologize. Ignoring the person or not accepting the responsibility for your behavior is not a sign of high emotional intelligence. Your relationships will be much more positive and people will forgive you more easily if you make an honest attempt to set things right rather than live in denial land. Accepting your mistakes, apologizing and moving on is a sign of high emotional intelligence.

Practice Being More Light Hearted

When you are more light hearted and optimistic, it is simpler to capture the goodness of everyday situations and objects. Positivity results in greater emotional happiness and increased opportunities. People are forever looking to be around optimistic folks who come up with positive connections and possibilities. When you become more negative, you only concentrate on what can go awry rather than building a stronger resistance to the torrid periods in life.

People with a more evolved emotional quotient know how to utilize wit and humor to make everyone feel happier, positive and safer. They know the art of using laughter to tide over tough times.

Practice Deep Breathing

Strong emotions impact us physically too. When we are stressed or anxious, our bodies respond in a more evolutionary instinctive manner like we're face to face with a nature based threat. The physical reactions include constricted blood vessels, shallow breathing and speedier heart rate.

When we learn to consciously manage our body's reaction to anxiety, the emotional attribute is lowered. Each time you feel nervous or tense, practice slow and deep breathing. Concentrate on the flow of the breath and the abdominal cavity. You will invariably feel better and calmer once you relax and create more space in your mind.

Mindfulness or mindful breathing is another way to achieve stillness of the mind by completely immersing yourself in the present non-judgmentally. When you get into the habit of identifying your thoughts and emotions without judgment, you boost your awareness and gain greater clarity rather than operating from a judgmental and assumption laden point of view. Mindfulness reduces your chances of being overtaken by negative or destructive emotions.

Decrease Negative Personalization

When we feel negatively impacted by someone's behavior, do not rush into a conclusion. Tempting as it is to ascribe a negative reason for their behavior, try to gather a more holistic perspective of the circumstances before reacting. For instance, it is easy to think a friend isn't returning your call or message because he/she wants to avoid you.

However, they may also be busy or ill or in a dire situation. When we avoid ascribing negative reasons or personalizing people's behavior, we view them more objectively and with less hateful/judgmental emotions. The ability to overcome negative personalization of people's behavior is critical for boosting your emotional quotient.

Develop Flexibility

Sometimes we get stuck in our own monotonous traps and become rigid and inflexible, which may impair our emotional intelligence. People with a highly developed emotional quotient know when to adapt and keep pace with newer techniques rather than getting stuck in an increasingly unproductive cycle. They know when how to adapt and manage their emotions according to the situation. Emotionally intelligent folks know when to adapt and shift perceptions.

Those who possess a highly developed emotional quotient are always open to newer experiences, challenging opportunities and a variety of adventures. Be open to change and shed the uneasiness and inhibitions attached with change.

Learn to decipher the consequences of your words and behavior. Emotionally intelligent folks pick their battles very selectively. They realize that peace and relationships are more valuable than being right.

When you learn to evaluate the consequences of your words and actions and demonstrate more flexibility and adaptability in your actions/words, you display high emotional intelligence. This isn't to be mistaken with letting people walk all over you. By all means, be assertive. However, know that it's not about being right or winning arguments all the time. Emotional intelligence is also about having the perspective to realize what is worth fighting for and what is worth giving up.

Practice Active Listening

During arguments or disagreements we often listen not to understand but to react and respond. When the other person is speaking, we are almost mentally constructing out own arguments to answer back or give back to them. This leads to even more conflict.

Dealing with conflict becomes more effective when you tackle issues in an assertive yet respective manner, without being defensive. When you listen empathetically, your own thoughts and emotions are taken into account. Listening actively and empathetically can help you shed toxic feelings building up in you.

Be assertive by all means, but also practice active listening to find that one point that can lead to resolution. Problem solution only happens when you understand where the other person is coming from and what they want. You can find a middle ground only when you tune in to the words, feelings and emotions of the other person, not just to give a fitting reply but also to resolve the issue. Listening is all about putting the other person's words, thoughts and feelings first.

Your opinion about people or events may not change. However, the time spent listening to the other person may just calm you and help you come up with a more positive or constructive response. It may help you see things from a different perspective and analyze the situation more objectively.

Resolve Conflicts Like a Boss

One of the best tips for developing high emotional quotient is mastering conflict management skills. Conflict resolution actually puts your emotional intelligence to practical use. Resolving differences and conflicts involves many aspects including identifying feelings, clear expression of thoughts, active listening, staying calm and coming up with a solution that diffuses the situation rather than escalating it. When we struggle to understand and control our feeling, we experience a sense of irritation, depression and erratic behavior patterns. Conflicts only get magnified, making it all the more stressful for anyone to deal with. Once you recognize yours and other's emotions, and learn to manage them, you enjoy a happier and more balanced life.

Be Emotionally Honest

Be emotionally honest and transparent. You are not communicating genuinely if you shut yourself off from expressing emotions. If you say you are alright with a sorrowful face, you are being dishonest in your communication. When you practice being more real about emotions, it is easier for people to read it. It is always great to be able to be yourself and share your real feelings. It helps people know your feelings and understand where you are coming from. They trust you more, which sets the base for more rewarding relationships.

By all means manage your emotions so as to avoid hurting others but misleading others about your emotions or denying real deeper emotions is not a sign of high emotional intelligence.

Stop Complaining

One of the first steps towards boosting your emotional intelligence is to stop complaining. Shed the victim syndrome and know that the solution to your problem is well within your grasp. Emotionally intelligent people rarely blame others or their circumstances for the challenges in their life. Instead, they search for matured ways to dissolve a relationship or talk to people who've wronged them in private. They also have a steady stream of effective coping mechanisms such as yoga, meditation, nature trips or simply venting their feelings by writing.

Listen to Physical Clues

Some of the best indicators of our emotional condition are the physical signals our body gives us. You can develop a greater awareness of your emotions simply by tuning in to your physical sensations. You may feel a knot in your tummy while commuting to work, which can be a sign of high stress.

Similarly, when you are with someone you've recently started dating, and experience a too strong to ignore flutter in your heart, it could be an indication of having found the person who'd like to spend the rest of your life with. Our body is constantly trying to communicate emotions we may not be aware of through physical sensations. Listening to these feelings and emotions signaled by the body helps process our emotions and reactions more efficiently.

Tap Into Your Subconscious Mind

How can you gain a greater awareness of your subconscious emotions or feelings? Apart from deep breathing and mindfulness, let your thoughts wander freely and evaluate where they go. Pay close attention to your dreams. Are there any recurring symbols that can be closely connected with the current events in your life?

Keep a journal and pen next to your bed and write down the details you can recall about your most compelling dreams as soon as you are up. Analyze the emotions and patterns of these dreams, their symbolic references and the message they are trying to communicate. When you gain a thorough understanding of the emotions that dominate your subconscious mind, it becomes simpler to train your subconscious mind to guide your actions.

Sometimes, our conscious minds are unable to come with solutions we are faced with, which is why the phrase "sleep over it" originated. Our subconscious mind's functionality is at its peak when we are asleep. Ever wondered why many a times the solution to our problems strikes us when we are asleep? Or we wake up with a totally different perspective or solution much to our surprise? Our subconscious mind is ticking overtime when our conscious mind is resting. By tuning into our subconscious mind, we are tapping into our inner most emotional reserve to uncover our deepest feelings.

Boost Your Social EQ with These Powerful Verbal and Non-Verbal Clues

We've established earlier how emotional intelligence is the master key to effective leadership and social skills. By tuning into other people's emotions or by empathizing with how they feel, there is a higher chance that you will respond appropriately to create the desired positive result. Thus, our ability to connect with our own and other people's emotions can be a powerful tool in social and leadership situations.

Understanding other people, helping overcome stress situations, motivating your team, negotiating business deals, and building a close-knit social circle becomes easier when you can use the emotional information you have about them as leverage. It increases situational awareness and our ability to read people, thus helping us make the most positive decision.

Here are some verbal and non-verbal factors impacting social-emotional quotient, or our ability to read and deal with people:

Verbal clues

A person's choice of words can say a lot about what they are thinking and feeling. Words are symbolic of our thoughts and feelings which, when combined with non-verbal clues, give us a comprehensive understanding of their emotional state.

The human brain is a miracle, really. When we think, or process rational and logical thoughts, we tend to use nouns and verbs. Conversely, when we attempt to express our thoughts or feelings in a verbal or written format, there is a tendency to use more adverbs and adjectives.

Any basic sentence features a subject and a verb. For example, "I walked." When a person adds more words to it, they can indicate their feelings or personality. For example, "I walked fast," can indicate a sense of urgency, fear, or insecurity. There are clear reasons why people use specific words over others.

Similarly, there is a hidden meaning behind what people say. Through their choice of words, people reveal emotions left unsaid.

Let's say you booked a table to take your family out for dinner at one of the fanciest, fine dining restaurants that recently opened in your neighborhood. The server greets you courteously and directs you to your table. What follows is an amazing dining experience.

The waiter introduces each of the seven courses in an informative yet engaging style, while you dine and enjoy wine in an upscale ambiance. After you enjoy a hearty meal and call for the tab, the waiter inquires if you enjoyed the food. You reply with, "The entrées were good."

The waiter doesn't look very delighted, even if what you said is a compliment in your opinion. Those four words you uttered reveal your real opinion about the food. It implies that other than the entrées, everything else was pretty average or the only thing that stood out during the entire meal were the entrées.

Did you actually say everything else other than the entrées was average? No. Then why did the waiter look crestfallen at your statement? It is obvious, people convey a lot not only through what they say but also through what they leave unsaid. Gather the hidden meaning or subtext behind what people say to tune in to their inner feelings. Notice how sometimes people will say, "You look very lovely today." It can either mean you look plain every day (which is a more passive-aggressive kind of statement), or you are looking exceptionally good today compared to other days.

Another powerful clue about what people are thinking or feeling is noticing how they talk about other people. In a research published in the Journal of Personality and Social Psychology, headed by Peter Harms and Simine Vazire of the University of Nebraska and University of St. Louis respectively, it was discovered that merely asking participants to rate positive and negative traits of three other people revealed a lot about the participants' social competence, general well-being, other people's perception of them, and their mental health.

It was observed that an individual's inclination to view other people in a positive manner was a strong indication of their own positive emotions. There is a strong link between seeing others in a more positive light and being emotionally stable, happy, productive, and enthusiastic.

On the other hand, viewing others in a negative light bears a strong correlation with a general sense of dissatisfaction, low self-esteem, anti-social behavior, and narcissism. People who hold plenty of negative emotions tend to perceive other people in a poorer or more negative light. This can also be an indication of emotional issues, mental health conditions, or a personality disorder. Again, emotions aren't good or bad but are reflections of how you are feeling. If a person experiences more negative emotions for others around them, it can be a clue to how they really feel about themselves.

If a person says that they 'made up their mind' after plenty of deliberation, the phrase indicates a mindset that is high on logic and rational thinking. The individual may be more contemplative and practical by nature. He or she may consider all the available options before making a decision. These are not your likely contenders for a snap of the moment decisions.

Do you know what meta language is? It is the intended words behind the words you speak. You don't say something directly but reveal it through the words you use. For example, notice how when people want to get someone to agree with what they've said, they'll always place yes, done, or okay followed by a question mark at the end. For example, "I can't hand in the project today. I'll submit it tomorrow, okay?" It is like manipulating the other person to agree.

To further increase your social-emotional quotient, pay attention to the sounds people utter, other than coherent words. Moaning, grunting, sighing, etc. can reveal a lot. Sometimes, these sounds will complement the words the speaker is using to make the message even more persuasive. However, at other times, there may be a mismatch between the person's words and sounds.

For example, someone may say, "I am having a really good day," followed by a sigh, which can indicate they are simply being sarcastic and are in fact having a bad day. You can even understand more about what a person really means when you observe their words and other miscellaneous sounds they make.

Environmental clues

A person's immediate environment says a lot about their emotional state. For instance, a messy, unclean, or disorganized space can indicate a lack of clarity of emotions or thoughts. Of course, everything has to be analyzed within a context. Someone may have an unkempt house because he or she is too busy to tidy it up and doesn't have housekeeping help.

All of us have certain spaces around us that are inaccessible that we don't really bother cleaning or organizing (space behind the cupboard or under the bed). These are spaces that we wouldn't normally clean. If such spaces are immaculately clean or organized, it can indicate anxiety or a disorder (obsessive-compulsive disorder).

Well-organized and clean spaces can indicate clarity of emotions or control over one's emotions. The person tends to be more reflective and introverted by nature. Similarly, people who are outwardly focused, or extroverts, tend to be surrounded by chaos.

This isn't pop psychology, but it is based on clear principles of how the environment around us is created through our actions, which themselves are directed by our subconscious thoughts and emotions. For example, using bright, vibrant, and bold prints in your décor or attire can be a sign of confidence, emotional self-assurance, and independence of thought or opinion. Likewise, a home with brighter and more vibrant colors is an indication of being bold, emotionally expressive, and outgoing. These people are not afraid of taking risks and are more than capable of understanding the needs and feelings of other people. More subtle colors imply inward directed emotions, or an introverted personality. These people may not be too receptive to another person's feelings and emotions.

People who hold on to old objects or hoard various objects can be excessively emotional, sensitive, or sentimental. They find it tough to move away from their past emotions or are still ridden by feelings of shame, regret, and guilt related to the past. These are people who latch on to old memories and can't release the emotions that hold them back.

When you use these verbal and non-verbal principles to understand people, your social-emotional quotient invariably increases.

Tone

The tone, volume, pitch, and emphasis of a person's voice can help you decode the hints that can help you tell what they are feeling. For example, if you notice plenty of inconsistencies in the tone of their voice as they speak, they are probably very angry, hurt, excited, or nervous. Ever notice how your voice shakes when you speak in a rage or are nervous about something? It can also be a sign the person is lying.

Similarly, if a person is speaking louder or softer than their regular volume, something may be amiss. Again, a person's tone is a dead giveaway. Sometimes people say something that sounds like a compliment. However, upon examining their tone closely, you realize the sarcasm and the condescension with which it was uttered.

The tone in which an individual ends their sentence says a lot about what they are trying to convey even with similar verbal clues. For example, if a person completes their sentence on a raised note, they are doubtful of something or are asking a question. Similarly, if they finish the sentence with a flat tone, they are pronouncing a statement or judgment. Watch out for how people end their sentences to get a clue about their inner feelings.

Again, the words people emphasize can help you uncover their true feelings. For example, if a person says, "Have you borrowed the blazer?" while emphasizing 'borrowed,' it indicates their doubt over whether you have borrowed, stolen, or done something else to the blazer. However, if the emphasis is on 'you,' they aren't sure if it is you or someone else who has borrowed the blazer.

I also like to look at pauses between phrases to know about the person's attitude, emotions, and intentions. For example, if a person pauses after saying something, it could be because what they just said is extremely important to them, or they truly believe in it. Sometimes, a person pauses to seek validation or feedback from others. The speaker wants to gauge your reaction to what they said since it is important for them.

When people are in a more emotionally unstable or negative frame of mind (angry, hurt, or upset), their voice tends to be higher pitched or squeaky. They are most likely losing a grip on their emotions or aren't able to regulate their emotions effectively. Notice how, when people are very angry, their voice becomes more screechy and squeaky, as if they are about to cry.

The speed of a speech

A person's emotions clearly impact the speed of their speech. Notice how you start talking much faster than your normal rate of speech, or words per minute, when you are angry or upset. A rapid speech can convey lack of organization, uncertainty, or lack of clarity. The person is not very comfortable with speaking and is just trying to finish throwing his or her words. Again, a slower than usual pace translates into low self-confidence, inability to express emotions, inability to come to terms with one's emotions, lack of emotional reassurance, and other similar feelings.

Body language

Research reveals that body language accounts for 50 percent of our communication. You'd wonder why there were words in the first place if body language accounts for half the communication process. Tuning in to a person's body language will help you pick up important signals related to their emotional state and subconscious thoughts or feelings.

Here's a quick cue sheet to reading people's feelings through their body language:

•   Crossed arms and legs are signals of people creating a subconscious barrier. They are emotionally closed, suspicious, or do not subscribe to your ideas. They aren't open to listening to your views or are disinterested in the topic of conversation. You may have to emotionally open the person up a bit by changing the topic and then get back to the original topic. The physical act of uncrossing their arms and legs will make them more subconsciously receptive to your ideas.

•   How can you tell a genuine smile from a fake one? Simple, it's all in the eyes. Observe that there's crinkled skin near the person's eyes forming crow's feet. People often present a happy expression to hide their true feelings. However, if their smile doesn't cause the skin around their eyes and mouth to crinkle, they are most likely not as happy as they are pretending to be. Artificial smiles create wrinkles only around the mouth, while genuine smiles create wrinkles around the sides of the eyes.

•   When people constantly take their gaze away from you while speaking, they are most likely not being very honest or trying to hide something. Similarly, if a person speaks to you without taking their gaze away from you for long, they may be trying to threaten or intimidate you with their gaze. It is alright to look away periodically. However, shifting gaze constantly is a red flag.

•   When you are addressing a group of people, closely observe the ones who are nodding excessively or in a more exaggerated manner. These are the people who are most concerned about your approval. They are anxious about making a positive impression and want to be in your 'good books'.

• People who are nervous or anxious tend to fidget with their hands or objects. Other signs of nervousness also include excessive blinking, tapping feet, and constantly running one's hand over the face.

• When an entire group walks into the room, how do you analyze who the leader or decision maker is? Quickly observe everyone's posture. The leader will most likely walk with a straight posture, with shoulders pulled out. Subconsciously, they are trying to occupy maximum space to convey authority over their team. Standing straight and pulling back shoulders increases a person's physical frame. It makes them come across as much bigger than they actually are. This is why people in power love to keep this posture to show their influence over a group or place.

• Expressions are the windows into a person's emotional state. When a person is amazed or surprised, their eyebrows are raised, and the upper eyelids widen. Similarly, the mouth gapes open. Expressions can often overlap, so watch for micro expressions that can reveal precise emotions.

• For instance, raised eyebrows can also reveal fear. Look for other micro expression clues to determine the exact emotion. If a person is experiencing fear, the eyebrows will be raised and pulled together with tensed lower eyelids, while the two corners of their lips will appear stretched. Similarly, a person's surprise is expressed by eyebrows pulled up and a lowered jaw. Learn to read the entire face, especially micro expressions, if you want to learn more about how a person is feeling.

• Since micro expressions occur in fractions of seconds, they are virtually impossible to fake. For instance, notice how when people are being deceptive, their mouths will slightly angle differently. Similarly, their eye movements become more rapid, the nostrils flare a little bit, and they purse their lips together (a subconscious gesture signaling their lips are sealed, or they won't reveal the truth). Since these split expressions are driven by the subconscious, this makes them involuntary, and it is almost impossible to manipulate them.

• Enlarged pupils reveal intense emotions such as excitement, elation, delight, surprise, and interest. When a person is attracted to you or truly delighted to see you, their pupils will involuntarily enlarge.

• The direction of a person's feet can also determine what's going on in their mind. Since feet aren't the first thing on anyone's mind, it's harder to manipulate body language related to legs and feet. If a person's feet are pointing away from you, they are subconsciously signaling their need to escape. However, if their feet are pointed towards you, they are interested or in agreement with what you are saying.

•   Typical signs of frustration and stress are clenched jaws, wrinkled eyebrows, and tensed neck. The person's words notwithstanding, if you observe any of these signs, he or she may be undergoing a stressful situation that they are trying to conceal. The trick for reading people's emotions accurately is to keep an eye out for a clear mismatch between verbal and non-verbal clues.

•   Observe a person's walk to tune in to their feelings. People with a heavier gait along with low gravity while moving their legs are most likely hurt, stressed, frustrated, or depressed. People who walk with a slower and more relaxed pace are reflecting upon something. Notice how confident, happy, and goal-oriented people walk swiftly in one direction.

•   Observing a person's eye movements is a near accurate way of gauging how he or she is feeling since our eye movements are connected to precise brain functions. Our eye movements have an established pattern depending on the brain function or type of information we are trying to access. For example, when a person is caught in an internal conflict or dilemma (to speak the truth or lie), they are more likely to look in the direction of their left collarbone. Darting sideways from one side to another can be a red flag that indicates deception.

•   Proxemics is a subtopic within body language that talks about how people reveal their feelings and emotions through the physical distance they maintain with other people during the process of face-to-face interaction or communication. It is a very useful non-verbal signal for understanding a person's thought process or state of mind.

Psychologists and body language experts believe that the amount of physical distance we maintain while interacting with a person helps establish the dynamics of our relationship with them or reveals our emotions about them.

A person who isn't standing very close to you may not be emotionally open or receptive to you. They may have a tendency to closely guard their emotions or give only a little of themselves to the interaction. Such people may be more emotionally guarded and closed. You may need to make extra effort to get them to drop their guard and feel less intimidated. It may be a defense mechanism against being emotionally hurt or vulnerable.

On the other hand, if a person is leaning in your direction, they may subconsciously convey being emotionally open, or they trust you with their feelings. They may also be more interested in what you are speaking about.

Yes, when you listen keenly to people, empathize with them, and try to understand things from their perspective, it paves the way for healthier and more rewarding relationships. We must understand that emotional intelligence is not a static skill that we acquire and will last a lifetime. It is a lifelong process and skill that keeps evolving as we navigate various relationships. However, there are a few established tips that will help you sharpen your emotional skills and help you relate to other people more effectively, thus helping you build strong relationships. Here are a few tips for using the power of emotional intelligence to build healthy relationships:

Avoid Complaining

Complaining is a huge sign of low emotional intelligence. It happens when a person believes he is victimized and that the situation is beyond his or her control. They will pass on the blame to the next person or situation before thinking it through.

Emotionally intelligent people think in a constructive manner to resolve the issue rather than blaming someone else or complaining. They operate from a mindset that seeks to resolve the problem rather than working from the perspective of just making complaints.

Complaining is a huge sign that people believe they are mere victims of a situation and that the solution is beyond their reach. We consider ourselves victims of other people or circumstances and therefore are unable to find solutions to pressing issues. We believe that the solutions to the circumstances enveloping us are beyond our realm of control. An emotionally intelligent person seldom believes himself or herself to be a victim. They rarely feel that problem resolution is beyond their control. In place of blaming something or someone, they approach the matter in a more constructive manner and look for a solution quietly. Emotionally intelligent folks will peacefully contemplate an issue and look for a resolution through reflection and consideration of all possibilities in lieu of the current circumstances. There is a sense of maturity in their thinking and manner of approach.

The next time you are tempted to blame your alarm clock for waking up late and showing up late at work, resist the urge and focus on what you can do to wake up on time each morning. Can you cut down on post work partying? Can you watch less television and go to bed early instead? Can you set the alarm on two clocks, so you have a back-up if one conks out? There are many ways to resolve the issue if you get out of the victim zone and start looking for proactive solutions that are within your control.

Sonja Lyubomirsky's research has suggested that 50 percent of our happy state of mind is influenced by factors that are beyond control (genes, personality, temperament). The other 50 percent is influenced by a combination of multiple factors such as attitude (over which we have full control). Practice celebrating joy even in the most seemingly adverse situation.

Open Yourself Up to Establish a Connection

One of the fastest and most surefire ways to build a connection with people is to listen to their experiences with empathy and link it with a similar experience you've undergone. This exchange of similar experiences strikes the right chord in people and makes them open up to you. Don't be afraid to open up a bit and share a similar experience when the other person is sharing theirs. For instance, someone may talk about how painful it has been to grow up in a single parent home. You may be tempted not to share that information about yourself too early on or open up before knowing the person really well, but it can help establish a connection. You can add how you completely understand how it feels because you had been living in a single parent home all through your teens. This is a quick way to set the foundation for a lasting relationship.

Develop a sense of curiosity when it comes to strangers. Emotionally intelligent folks are intrigued by strangers and always have an insatiable hunger to know more about them and understand their lives and views. They make an attempt to understand how the opinions and perspectives of these people are different from theirs. You know what to do next time you're on the train or at the airport. Immerse yourself in a different culture by traveling to various destinations whenever you can. It broadens your understanding of people and cultures. Sometimes, the only way to have an open mind is to go to a different destination and establish connections with locals.

Focus on How You Say it

What you say is important, but how you convey it is even more vital. There are multiple ways to say the same thing or handle a situation. Non-verbal communication can have a massive impact on how you are perceived by people.

Eye contact, voice, tone, expressions, and body language all contribute towards creating an impression about you among other people. It conveys to others how you are thinking and feeling emotionally. Think whether your body language and emotions complement each other. Are you able to articulate your emotions or feelings without offending the other person?

Keep in mind that there are not many things which destroy an individual's morale quicker than an overly critical person. Think of different ways to say something without affecting the other person negatively. I always recommend learning something about the other person or understanding them before attempting to communicate with them. For instance, if someone is particularly sensitive, they may not appreciate a direct, straightforward approach. You may have to get your point across in a more diplomatic and tactful manner.

Similarly, straightforward folks may not appreciate you beating around the bush. You may also have to employ a more frank and forthright approach. Thus, knowing an individual's personality will help you communicate with him or her in a more effective manner.

How you say it makes all the difference while communicating, especially on slightly tricky topics. For example, let's take a scenario where you think an employee is not suitable for a specific department and has consistently underperformed there despite receiving the best training, development, and mentoring.

As a manager, it is your responsibility to inform him that he or she is going to be shifted to another department. Now you are placed with the conundrum of telling them the truth without affecting his or her morale. What approach would you take as an emotionally intelligent person to accomplish the same?

Instead of telling the person that he or she isn't good in 'XYZ' department and that he or she is being shifted to another department, you can focus on the positive of the situation and change the angle or approach to give it a more positive twist. You can say something like, "We think you have the ideal skills for (new department) and that your skills or qualities will be utilized to the fullest there." You are still telling the employee that he or she will be transferred to another department, but you are putting across your point in a manner that doesn't offend them or lower their morale. You are simply telling him or her that their skills aren't being utilized to the fullest in the current department instead of telling him or her that their skills are not good enough for the current department. The words, body language, and approach make all the difference.

Also, active listening is a huge component of emotional intelligence, especially during conflicts. Often, while arguing with people, we have our responses ready even before the other person finishes speaking.

During heated discussions, arguments, and conflicts, we only listen to reply but not to understand the other person. How many times have you heard the other person out to truly understand them and not to prepare your response to what he or she is saying? Resist the urge to come across as too overpowering during a disagreement and try to understand where the other person is coming from. Deal with issues in a respective, productive, and assertive manner, without an element of defensiveness. When you actively and empathetically listen to the other person, you are also creating a space for your feelings and emotions to be heard.

When you listen intently to the other person's views, you drain all the toxic energy from the situation and instead focus on arriving at a beneficial solution.

I always recommend practicing your non-verbal skills at home to make yourself even more clear and transparent in social situations. Start at your home because it is a space that doesn't make you feel overwhelmed, unlike an alien setting. Make a video of yourself interacting with a friend or relative.

Watch it so you can know what areas you can improve in when it comes to non-verbal signals. Another super way is to practice before a mirror. Pretend that you are interacting with a person and watch yourself in the mirror. Enlist the help of trusted folks when it comes to gaining valuable feedback. They can offer helpful insights about your voice, posture, expressions, and more. You'll be in a more private, low-stress setting, which reduces your shyness and preps your confidence for more important interactions. It's actually enjoyable to try out multiple gestures, expressions, signs, and postures.

When you can read non-verbal signals passed by others, you can quickly spot the disagreement in their feelings or emotions and words. Even a subtle mismatch in verbal and non-verbal signals will help you understand the other person's feelings and behavior.

Notice how sometimes you pick up some clue and call it a "hunch" that something isn't right about what the person is saying. What we like to call or think of as a gut feeling, or hunch, is actually a subconscious notice of the mismatch between the person's body language and words. The person didn't intend to communicate it, but we tuned in to their body language and "listened" to it.

Spend Time Away from the Social Media

Though this is the age of the social media, try and balance your online time and connections with offline relationships too. It is important to maintain face to face relationships with people since it paves the way for developing better social skills. Don't go messaging people. Instead, meet them over dinner or drinks and have a real, face to face conversation. Emotional intelligence goes beyond social media confines and needs real-world connections. Our ability to identify, process, and manage emotions is impeded by instant messaging and social media. Emoticons don't build emotional intelligence. It expands when we actually get out there and interact with people face to face. Staying in the constricted space of social media doesn't allow you to experience real emotions that can increase your emotional perception and intelligence.

Isolate One Skill

If you are looking to improve emotional intelligence and social skills, rather than trying to be good at everything, isolate one skill that you want to develop at a time. For instance, you may want to work on your listening skills or develop greater empathy. Don't try to work on too many aspects at a time. Identify one component of social-emotional intelligence and observe someone who is particularly good at it. If you know a friend is really good at listening to people and making them feel comfortable, try and observe how they manage their emotions, react, and speak. How does their body language reveal that they are keenly listening to the other person? How do they acknowledge what the other person is saying? What are the usual words they use to make the person feel comfortable? This technique has been suggested by none other than the father of the term "Emotional Intelligence," Daniel Goleman himself.

Reduce Stress and Practice Staying More Lighthearted

Stress rears its ugly head in all ways of life and completely consumes us following a range of negative emotions. From relationship breakdowns to being laid off from work, there are plenty of emotions that can overwhelm us. When you are stressed, it is challenging to behave reasonably. It will be tough to be emotionally intelligent when you are under tremendous stress.

Find what your stress triggers are and make a list of everything you can do to relieve yourself of that stress. What is it that helps decrease your stress? A long lonesome walk in the midst of nature? Listening to soothing music? Talking to a trusted friend? Having lunch at your favorite café?

Enlist the help of a professional therapist if it feels too overpowering to handle it by yourself. A psychologist, counselor, or therapist can help you cope with the stress in an effective and professional manner, while also helping you raise your emotional quotient. It is easier to establish rewarding interpersonal relationships with people when you are not under stress.

I personally love to combat stress by maintaining a lighthearted atmosphere at work, home, and other social scenarios. It is simpler to appreciate the joy and beauty of life when you take on a more humorous or lighthearted approach. It makes others around you feel less stressed too. Optimism and positivity not just lead to better emotional health (for yourself and others) but also more opportunities. (Who doesn't like being around a positive and optimistic person?) People are naturally drawn to optimistic, lighthearted, and positive people. Negativity, on the other hand, builds defenses. People with high emotional quotient use lots of fun, jokes, and humor to make the atmosphere for others (and themselves) safe, joyful, and happy. Laughter is indeed the best medicine to get through challenging times in our life.

Practice Assertiveness and Expressing Challenging Emotions

An essential part of being who you really are is asserting or being able to speak frankly and openly about things that truly matter to you or are important in your life. Practice taking a clear position on where you stand when it comes to vital emotional issues. Draw clear lines about what is acceptable and not acceptable in relationships.

Setting boundaries in relationships is also a huge component of emotional intelligence. It isn't restricted to being empathetic and being nice to others. Emotional intelligence is also about being fair to yourself.

Set clear boundaries so others can know more about your position which leads to lesser misunderstandings in relationships. This can include anything from disagreeing with someone about establishing priorities, to saying no, to protecting yourself from physical harm or mental duress.

Use the "I feel...when you" technique to assert yourself in tricky situations. For instance, "I strongly feel that I deserve a promotion from the organization based on my performance and contribution."

Similarly, when you are not comfortable doing something for someone over your own priorities you can assert yourself saying something like, "I don't feel comfortable that you expect me to do everything for you over my tasks and priorities." When you feel disappointed that someone doesn't follow through or listen to your instructions, you can articulate it with something like, "I feel really upset or disappointed that you didn't update me about the project despite being instructed to do so."

The trick is to say how you feel when something happens. Refrain from beginning your sentence with "you." It makes you sound accusatory and judgment. The moment the other person hears "you," he or she will subconsciously slip into a defensive position. You are quickly allowing the listener to assume a defensive position, followed by a bunch of excuses. If you want people to listen to you, talk about how you feel when they do something.

Learning not to Judge

During the course of our lives, we tend to judge people because we have a set of standards and these are imposed upon us by our parents and upon them by their parents. Then there are standards set by peers and the standards of society in general. The problem with measuring everything by these standards is that it limits who you are because you are not making a decision based on something that has any solidity. You are basing it upon unwritten rules and that's not a very emotionally intelligent thing to do.

If you want to learn to use your emotional intelligence, you need to be able to let go of judgment and one of the best ways to do this is to learn to meditate. The process of meditation hones in on learning how to let go of thoughts or to see them and not judge them and it's a hard lesson to learn. If you take lessons in meditation or learn to do it yourself, you will find that the mind slows down a little and that when things are said that you would normally judge, you tend to step back a bit from them and don't judge. You simply use the information and quietly deduct whatever you need to in order to help the situation, rather than add complexity to it.

The first place to start is learning to breathe correctly, in through the nostrils and out to a counting system. You count eight as you breathe in and then as you breathe out and as thoughts come to you, you acknowledge them and then dismiss them. They are not appropriate at the time when you are meditating, so you learn to be able to let go of them. If you practice even for as little as fifteen minutes a day, every day, you find that you are not one that judges situations too hastily and this also helps to calm down the emotions and be able to solve things without going through all the negative feelings that people who judge have to endure.

Try it and I am sure that you will find this to be so. Every time that you pass judgment on something, what you are doing is putting up barriers. These barriers make you biased and biased people don't have much emotional intelligence at all. They are too busy building barriers against the world that doesn't fit in with their ideals. The tramp on the corner of the street may just have something valid to say. Don't ignore him because he is a tramp. The preacher in a church may just say something that helps you to see the end to a problem. Even if you are a non-believer, don't put up walls without waiting to hear what is being said. Whenever you do this, you make your emotions snap into judgment mode and that's the unhealthiest state of your mind.

I remember being told that one particular child in a class was trouble. The fact was that the teacher passing this information on wasn't very emotionally intelligent. What the truth of the situation was, as it came to light later, was that she didn't have the teaching abilities to deal with this particular child's problems. Usually, when the pieces don't go together right during the course of your lifetime, there is another reason other than blame and blame doesn't help anyone.

Emotionally intelligent people will be the first to forgive others because they know that circumstances differ for everyone and there may have been reasons why someone did what they did. The world at large is much bigger than what goes on in your head and emotionally intelligent people know this. The reason I suggested meditation as the first step toward emotional intelligence is that it helps you to see things in perspective, slows down your anger and negative feelings and helps you to be able to assess each individual situation using something people don't seem to use much anymore – intuition. When you unlock your intuition, you can trust it because it is there to safeguard you and it helps you to be able to see beyond the obvious.

People who have a high level of emotional intelligence will be calm people who are not quick to judge others, who are able to forgive easily and who understand that their own actions actually dictate the outcome of a situation. They tend not to blame others but instead look into themselves to see what could be done to improve any given situation. That's the difference between them and ordinary people whose level of emotional intelligence is low.

Learning to Gain Confidence

If you want to gain confidence, emotional intelligence will help you to achieve this. Instead of feeling unsure of your actions and hesitating, hesitate for the right reasons. This hesitation is simply your way of being more certain that the response you give will be one that is considered. Learn to look at your face in the mirror and ask yourself questions that you fear answering. Then, look at the facial expressions that you use when these questions are posed.

The changes in your facial body language come because your emotions kick in whether you want them to or not. Ask people around you questions and you will be able to recognize doubt, lying, unhappiness and all kinds of emotional responses, but that's something that can help you. As you gain confidence in recognizing these things, by using your intuition, you actually start to understand your own reactions better and are able to stem those actions that let you down.

Mary was always upset about the way that people treated her as if she was incompetent. However, when she did this exercise, she suddenly realized that her own reactions were what fueled this opinion in people and she was able to change that. When your emotions turn to confusion or anger, you have a habit of changing your facial expression and your body language. Try it again with the use of a mirror. Shock yourself if you have to because all of this trains you to respond in a different way. When Mary stopped looking in a blank way at people giving her instructions, they started to trust her more with the tasks that they had given her. She was able to develop trusting relationships as well because people didn't know what to make of her expressions and she could see clearly in the mirror what was causing all of this negativity in people who communicated with her.

In fact, you can also make a mental note of times when responses have not been the way you wanted them to be and note down what the questions were and what the responses were so that you are better able to analyze reactions and adjust the way that you put yourself over as a communicator. Look at people who communicate well and who appear to have confidence and their body language is what you need to aim for. The head back, the smile, the shoulders back and the confident stride all help you to be seen as different by others, but they also help you to use your emotional intelligence in a more effective way.

It may be worthwhile keeping a journal. Before you go to bed every night, write out your worries or your doubts and try to come to some kind of conclusion about how you will face them with a smile or at least in a positive way. The things that get in the way of emotional intelligence are:

- Negative thoughts

- Negative self-talk

- Negative emotions

You can look at your own behavior over a given period and try to change your way of handling situations. Instead of negative thoughts, replace them with positive ones. Instead of negative self-talk, start to praise the things that you know you can do well and gradually improve upon the things you find difficult. That feeling that a cyclist gets when he/she first learns to balance on a bike is unforgettable because it's so positive and if you can convert your life into a series of events that all have positive outcomes, you will feel that buzz and people around you will also pick up on your positive energy.

When you find that you are talking negatively to yourself, replace that thought as soon as it comes with breathing exercises that bring you into the moment because these help you to move forward and to realize that you have this habit of talking negatively to yourself. You can even have a song that you can sing quietly in your mind to get rid of these negative thoughts. Emotional intelligence immediately recognizes when a positive input is needed and that's what you are aiming for.

Try and be more empathetic as well. This means being able to place yourself in the shoes of someone else. Instead of thinking negative things about others, try to understand where the negativity or emotional reaction they give comes from and you will find empathy will help you to feel better about them and also about yourself. This helps you to gain confidence and to feel better about being you. Give a beggar a sandwich or try to imagine what it's like for the homeless and do something voluntarily with absolutely no strings attached because when you do, you show your emotional intelligence and will find that voluntary actions actually fuel confidence in yourself.

Learning to Listen to your Body and Learn to Listen to Others

Although the above quotation relates to talking with someone else, it also applies equally when you talk to yourself. Often you don't listen sufficiently to give reasonable answers and that's where emotional intelligence comes in. When you learn to listen to your body, this means that you are able to slow your life down a little and remember the importance of being aware of how you feel. If you were to stop people in the street and ask how they feel, chances are most people would shrug the question off and ask what you mean. The fact is that there are clues in the messages we receive from our bodies that help us to feel better or to feel more positive, but often we throw the answers at them before we have actually taken the time to be logical and to examine why the body is sending those messages in the first place.

Let me try to examine this in detail so that you can see the sequence of events. If your neck hurts, you may start to feel irritable. You may even shake your head to try to get rid of the ache or swallow a pill hoping that the neck ache will simply vanish. An emotionally intelligent person doesn't tend to do either. They take the time to listen to their body and are able to distinguish from the symptoms what they need to do to ease the pain. Perhaps posture hasn't helped. Perhaps the ache is as a result of sitting in the same position over an extended period. When you don't listen to your body and your aches persist, what happens is that you begin to feel worse and that eventually changes your humor and your emotional well-being.

However, if you examine why your body is sending the messages, you can do something tangible about it, so that the body doesn't have to send those messages anymore. For example:

- Change your posture to avoid the pain

- Change your seat, so you don't suffer any more

- Work out what's going on with your body and do something to relieve the pain

Negative people tend to rely on the messages from their body to justify their negativity. However, motivated people with a good sense of emotional intelligence don't do this. They simply work out the problem and do not allow the messages from the body to turn into negative messages that make them feel worse. There's absolutely no benefit to feeling negative about your neck ache. When you feel negative, your emotions jump in and you are snappy and not very nice to be with. When you allow emotional intelligence to step in, you find solutions and thus never reach the point where emotions are able to take over.

It's very much the same when you are listening to people. Really listen. Don't cut into the conversation and assume that what you have to say has more credence than that said by others. When you do, you miss opportunities to get to know people and to learn things. People who do this think very highly of themselves and think their opinions are more important than the opinions of people they are listening to. This makes them emotionally draining. Have you ever met someone who does this? You may know the know-it-all character that visits you and who doesn't listen to anything that you have to say. Do you want people to see you in that way? If not, the only way out of a situation like this is to be patient. Listen with all of your attention.

Breathe before you reply. Think out your answers and bear in mind that others are entitled to have different views.

Emotionally intelligent people are those who are open to learning. They not only listen to their own bodies, but they listen to other people and make those around them feel like they are important or liked. That's a very important element because when you stop feeling that way, you actually alienate people and can find that your emotional lows are as a result of your own actions, rather than of the actions of others. Listening to kids can really help you to learn to use your emotional intelligence. Sometimes they come out with amazingly astute ideas that maybe you have left behind you as you have grown up. Embrace the child inside sometimes because we are all entitled to. Those who are able to do this have great imaginations, can see others' points of view and also know that the reason their bodies are complaining is because there is just cause. Emotionally intelligent people find the cause and work on it so that they have a more enriching experience in the future.

If you are not prepared to listen, you will learn nothing at all and your emotional intelligence will be stunted. Hear the laughter of children. Feel the magical feeling of emotional freedom and enjoy experiencing that laughter with someone else who needs it and you will find that your emotional intelligence quota will improve.

Chapter 4: Connecting The Dots

There are times in your life when you feel bad about life or when your emotions go into overdrive. This is quite normal as long as you don't let the emotions dictate the outcome. People who are emotionally intelligent are able to look back at situations that provoked the same kind of emotional response. When they do that, they are also able to see that it was only a matter of time and circumstance that took them out of those negative emotions and back on track. People without emotional intelligence are unable to do that.

For example, if you are drawn to tears of frustration when things go wrong, your mind will analyze the situation and you can join up the dots. You may be saying to yourself that the last time you felt that bad, you managed to move forward by being patient and seeing what the outcome was, rather than assuming the worst. The problem is that people in an emotional state of mind often don't bother to look back and see similar situations where things were solved. They are too busy being unhappy. The emotionally intelligent person knows for example that frustration of this kind triggers an emotional response. They, therefore, understand where the emotional inadequacy comes from and can rationalize it.

The next time that you feel emotional, instead of acting on that emotion, try to analyze it. If you can remember the last time that you felt that way and look at what the outcome was, this helps you to remain focused even though your emotions are trying to take over. Don't let them. You are the driver and when you analyze these things, you make better sense of them. Let me demonstrate.

Kate felt an overwhelming sense of being out of control and was feeling tears running down her cheeks. She could have become even more emotional but chose not to. Instead, she looked at her current circumstances and then looked back to another time in her life when she had felt that bad and was able to see quite clearly that there was a reason for the emotional response. She was then able to calm herself knowing that this response was normal and that there was nothing wrong with her or that response. When you can rationalize your response, it doesn't do as much harm because you don't take it out on the first person that comes along. Instead of doing that, you look inwardly and find your own conclusions.

If you find that you are emotional, try to spend a little more time alone and analyze your feelings and work out why they are happening. The elements to keep out of the picture are:

- Blame

- Jealousy

- Hate

- Anger

These all taint your results. For example, Kate could have blamed her coworker for the way that she was feeling. She could have said that her coworker was throwing too much work at her, but that wasn't, in fact, the case. Although, to an outsider, it may have looked that way, what Kate was actually crying about was that things at home were not the way that she wanted them to be. When she separated these facts from work facts, she was able to get back on track and then tackle the home situation with a fresh outlook, which helped it rather than aggravate it. Someone with less emotional intelligence may have spent the day grumbling about her husband and tried to get people within the office to take sides with her. All this does is fuel a fire and that fire may not actually be necessary. Don't use others to stoke your fires. When you do, things get out of control and your situation becomes worse, rather than better.

If you analyze your feelings, you can then walk away from them because you are able to give them a name or put logic into the situation that doesn't involve others, but merely examines the thoughts and emotions that you have going on in your head and recognizes these from past events. You will then take control of your emotions, knowing and trusting that these negative feelings will pass and that the problem is not as large as your emotional mind is making it out to be.

The Chain of Goals and Intentions

Here's how you can differently use the Chain of Goals technique not only to solve your internal conflicts, but also to work on many other things. It could be your procrastination, getting angry in certain situations, your laziness and stress recurring at specific times or fear of meeting new people. It must be something that is inside you, something about which you have an internal representation. Don't work on things and issues that are dependent on other people.

You can also pick something that is not a problem per-se, but needs to be improved. It could be motivation to do something, being more passionate about your project, waking up early, etc. The choice is yours.

Specify the thing you want to work on in one sentence as a concrete action or behavior (e.g. "I'm always getting angry when…I always procrastinate when…I'm stressed out in situations like…" etc.). Then take these steps:

1. Imagine a situation in which the problem or behavior specified by you takes place. Take a moment to relax and visualize this situation.

2. Think about a part of your body in which this piece of you being responsible for this action or behavior resides. Locate this spot.

3. Turn to this spot in your body where this part of yourself is and ask it, "What do you want? What precisely do you want to achieve by doing that?" Wait for the answer and then write it down on a piece of paper. This answer is your first intention. Say "thank you" to this part for giving you the answer.

4. Now, feel how it is when this new intention is entirely fulfilled, when you have fully obtained what this part of you wants to accomplish by this initial behavior/action you're working on. Do as much as you can to feel it deeply and ask yourself this question, "Once you have and fully feel (intention number 1 or further intentions) what you want to achieve by doing what you are usually doing, what's even more important now?" Wait for the answer and write it down. This is the next intention.

5. Create your chain of intentions this way, repeating step four, every single time feeling the further intention in the chain and asking yourself what's next. Do it until you can't answer the question from step four. It means that you have discovered the "original condition" or "core state": the ultimate, most important intention/goal you want to achieve.

For example, the whole process could look like this:

Problem: I'm totally stressed out before exams!

Question: What exactly do you want to achieve?

Answers: Prepare myself thoroughly. -> Intention 1: Pass the exams. -> Intention 2: Achieve the feeling of safety. -> Intention 3: Achieve the feeling of clearance. -> Original intention: Deep peace of mind.

The original intention is usually connected to a deep feeling of something, in a sense, a state of being: e.g. peace of mind, total calm, love, unity, presence, happiness. That's the state the part we are working with is following. It wants to achieve it by the action or behavior you want to change.

It's interesting as somehow this part of you concluded it will achieve that goal by acting or behaving like this, but in a large majority of cases the outcomes are totally opposite. By discovering that, you can change it.

The last step of this exercise is getting into that original intention fully and deeply. Now, thinking about each of these intentions from your chain of goals, starting from the end, think how having the Original Intention (and still feeling it at the same time) changes or enriches having each of these intentions.

So, for example, having the instance above for consideration, you should first access the state of deep peace of mind (by physical exercise, visualizations or meditation, preferably using all three of these ideas) and then think about how having this peace of mind modifies or enhances the feeling of clearance. Give yourself a moment to feel and imagine it, then proceed to the next intention (feeling of safety). At the end, think about how having the Original State/Intention will influence the behavior or action you are working on. Try to fully feel every single intention, while being entirely in the Original Intention, and imagine for a moment how it changes every ring/step in your chain of goals. At the very end, pay attention to how your approach to the behavior or action you are working with has changed. You are probably looking at it differently now.

Remember, resistance may appear during the process. Your subconscious mind may protest at some point, for example, saying, "But you can't be entirely happy!" Then, see this objection as a part of yourself and ask it what precisely it wants to achieve by this protesting and start this exercise over again, this time with this new part. Once when you're done with it, go back to the place where you've previously stopped.

I'd like to note that this isn't a typical intellectual or logical process. It's mainly about exploration and examination of your interior. When answering the questions in this technique, listen to your intuition, not your logical mind. It's very important as we are working with your subconscious and what's sitting deep inside of you, not with your rational thinking.

Some people, on the other hand, are not sure if they are going to get any answers using this method. Don't worry about it—when you're turned towards your interior, you will get your answers quickly. Sometimes they will come to you as a premonition, sometimes it will be an image or symbol, sometimes a memory, internal dialogue or a sound. Set yourself to listening and something will surely appear. Only then will you verbalize it and write it down on a sheet of paper.

Regular practice of this technique will enable you to go through it quickly and easily. You can also print the steps of this technique and use them only when you feel you need them.

How to Increase Your Self-Awareness

How well do you understand your character, emotions, motivations, strengths, and weaknesses? Self-awareness helps us understand what we are and what other people see in us. It also helps determine how similar or different we are from others.

Emotional intelligence promotes self-awareness. Some of the advantages of being self-aware include:

- Finding yourself

- Expressing yourself

- Understanding others

- Practicing empathy

- Having positive relationships

- Having clarity of mind

You get to develop your self-awareness through introspection. This is all about questioning your motivations – why you act or think in a certain way. Some of the questions you may ask yourself include:

- Why do you value certain things?

- Are you living responsibly?

- Are you moral or immoral?

- Why do you love certain things/people?

- Why do you hate certain things/people?

Here are some of the tips for increasing your self-awareness:

Try new things

When you seek new experiences, you're definitely going to learn a thing or two about yourself. Sometimes, it takes a change of environment, or a change of routines, to gain a new perspective on your strengths, weaknesses, emotions, and overall character. Exploring new things is a way of stretching your limits and stepping out of your comfort zone. One of the commonest methods of seeking new experiences is traveling. When you travel, you get to meet people from different cultures, and their way of life might force you to look at yourself in a new light. Traveling also has a calming effect on your mind and can promote clarity of thought.

Keep a journal

Get in the habit of writing down the various emotional states that you go through during the day, as well as their triggers. This will help you assess your emotional nature, and more importantly, it will put a timeline to your emotional states.

Meditate

A favorite exercise of yogis, meditation is truly a great practice for increasing your self-awareness. The premise behind meditation is that achieving a calm mental state multiplies your odds of reaching your goals. The classic yoga pose is made by sitting on a firm surface and placing each foot on the opposing thigh. Then you have to perform a breathing exercise that is aimed at eliminating the noise off of your mind. Meditation increases your ability to focus on your internal facets and thus helps you attain a clear understanding of the person that you are.

Know your strengths and weakness

Having a clear understanding of areas that you're weak and strong in is a great step towards increasing your self-awareness. This is important because after knowing your strengths, you can seek more ways to capitalize on it. On the other hand, knowing your weaknesses can encourage you to do something about it. For instance, if you have a weakness for binge eating, and it is showing in your waistline, it may affect your self-image. And so, through introspection, you might be able to identify the link between your binge eating and your self-esteem issues and perhaps cut out the binge eating and turn to healthy meals and workouts to get the body that you want. Finding out your weaknesses and strengths is a continuous process.

Know your emotional triggers

Emotions are merely the brain's way of trying to pass across an important message. There are certain things and events that cause the brain to activate the correlating emotion. It is critical to understand the various causes of your emotions. If you have gone through trauma, obviously you are emotionally scarred. Whenever you come across an event that is even loosely associated with the trauma, the bad emotions come rushing back. For instance, if you were once sexually assaulted on a dark road at night, you might find yourself getting anxious every time you're walking along isolated and lightless paths. Becoming aware that this anxiety is merely a warning that your brain is trying to send might help calm you down.

Reflect on your life

Get in the habit of taking stock of your life. This practice should be done on a daily basis. For instance, you may elect to reflect upon the day's events before you sleep. This will help you identify the areas where you have performed well, underperformed, or outright tanked. It will grant you the insight to sharpen your weak areas and capitalize on your strengths.

Avoid being narrow-minded

A narrow-minded person hardly sees the sense in what other people say, thus closing off any chance to expand their knowledge. However, if you want to increase your self-awareness, you must learn to open up your mind. There are various things you can learn about yourself if only you're open-minded. This is critical especially when it comes to accepting parts of yourself that you consider unbecoming. With an open mind, you also get to change your way of thinking and free yourself from frustrations.

Ask for feedback

As much as you may not want to admit it, sometimes people see things in you that you cannot see yourself. And so, you may want to hear what these people think about you, but take care that you ask people who have your best interests, people who want to see you make progress. When you solicit people's opinions, you make yourself vulnerable because their feedback might hurt you. But you should be open-minded enough to allow criticism, as this is the only way to grow. With the right feedback, you will realize the areas that you have to work on.

Set boundaries

You have to learn to set boundaries to develop your self-awareness. Setting boundaries is a way of respecting your time and showing people that you have goals to achieve. It regulates your behavior and guides you in the best manner possible. Setting boundaries and following through with the implementation takes courage and the support of other people. It is one of the critical things in understanding your limits.

Chapter 5: How To Get The Best Out of What You Have Learnt On EQ

In the 60s, renowned psychologist Walter Mischel did an experiment to observe how four-year-olds controlled their impulses. He put the children in a room and offered each a marshmallow. But there was a hook. He stated that he'd be going out to run an errand and that when he comes back, he will give another marshmallow to the children who don't eat their first marshmallow; however, it was still okay if they choose to not wait for him and eat their first marshmallow anyway.

After he stepped out, most of the kids started feasting on their marshmallow. But a small percentage of the children resisted the urge to eat their marshmallow and chose to wait for Mischel to come back and give them another. In the meantime, these kids performed various activities to avoid temptation, like walking around the room, covering their eyes, putting their heads down, and singing.

Many years later, when the children were in high school, remarkable differences were found between the two groups. The kids who had shown restraint over their impulses seemed more socially confident and well-adjusted compared to their low-willed counterparts. On the side of academics, the kids who held out scored an average of 210 points higher in their SAT.

What can be inferred in this experiment is that there's a huge correlation between delayed gratification and achieving success.

Motivation

In today's society, there's too much noise. Everywhere you turn, someone is trying to get your attention and distract you from what you're doing. Most people find it hard to stay "hungry" for their goals. They get carried away by other thrills. But a person who can manage their urges is in a position to keep fighting for their goals, as they know too well what they stand to gain. Since they have an understanding of this pleasant feeling and the sense of fulfillment that awaits them on the other side, it motivates them to carry on in their pursuit of success.

Good leadership

Success doesn't have to be one-dimensional. For a leader, the real measure of success is not when they reach their goals – it's when their followers reach their goals. As a leader, you have to be able to set good examples. This calls for great self-awareness and consideration on your part. When you set a good example, your followers can adapt to your ways and thus create an enabling environment for accomplishment. It takes a person who can delay gratification to lead by example.

Gratitude

It can be difficult to show gratitude if you're used to instant thrills and taking the easy way out. Actually, people who like having it easy tend to be entitled. On the other hand, people who can delay their gratification tend to show gratitude to both themselves and other people. This is because they achieve their goals by making plans and putting in the effort. For instance, such people tend to have a great appreciation for their money, and they ensure that they are careful about the things that they buy. They also appreciate people who commit resources to their projects, e.g., employees.

Sense of fulfillment

If you constantly make poor decisions, it doesn't necessarily mean that you're not aware of what you're doing. Most people are. For instance, if you decide against paying your child's school fee so that you can acquire your favorite item, you obviously know that you have done poorly. These bad habits tend to compound, and the resultant guilt can crush your soul. But a person who can control their impulse is careful about the decisions they make, financially or otherwise. In the end, it gives them a sense of fulfillment just knowing they took the best decision that there was.

Hard work

In this era of seeking instant thrills, it can be hard to get anyone to invest the time and resources required to achieve a desired outcome. Many people tend to seek the easy way out, and this usually leads to mediocrity. However, a person who can reign in their impulses is much more likely to invest the time and resources to achieve the desired outcome.

Learning to keep from gratifying your every want will instill in you a sense of discipline. For instance, when you challenge yourself into making the best of your income opportunities, you will have an appreciation for your money, and you might be able to see the advantage of saving over mindless spending.

Hard work teaches you how to prioritize and set goals. When you work within that framework, you tend to achieve more and become mindful of your habits. It takes a combination of various productive habits to eventually realize success.

Healthy lifestyle

If your health is failing, it can be difficult or outright impossible to achieve your goals. While deteriorating health is caused by factors both within and without our control, taking your health in your hands is a major step that asks for commitment on your part. For instance, if you have an alcohol problem, it can be difficult to give it up, and it will thus keep compromising your health. But if you have it in you to delay gratification, you will understand the long-term importance of giving up your alcohol habit. This mentality sets you up for success.

Improved finances

Most people lack financial discipline. That is why they spend their hard-earned money on things that they don't really need and end up burying themselves in debt. Poor financial decisions obviously affect the quality of an individual's life, and there's the possibility of what we call, "Financial ruin." However, a person who's mastered the art of delaying gratification will prioritize their needs. Their money only ever goes into what they really need, and such habits shield them from getting bogged down by debts or straying into financial graves. People who have a hold on their feelings are in a much better position to advance financially.

Guidelines on Managing and Expressing Your Emotions

Emotions are powerful biological forces that we cannot manipulate consciously. Once emotions get involved, things become complicated. Here are some important tips to adhere to to manage and express your emotions appropriately.

Master the art of timing

When you are pressed emotionally, being considerate is the last thing on your mind. You are simply dying to let the other person know what you're feeling. Emotions have a way of pushing all our wrong buttons, causing us to become impulsive in our decisions, and before we know it, it is over just as quickly as it began. Then we are stuck with the consequences. But, to communicate your emotions meaningfully, you have to ensure that the timing is right.

For instance, if your boss has done something that has triggered you, the last thing you should do is to storm into his office when he's in the middle of a meeting with other high-rank officials. You want to make sure that the environment in which you're communicating your emotions is an enabling one. This increases your odds of achieving the outcome you had planned.

Have a healthy outlet

In as much as you have to practice restraint where your emotions are concerned, it is also important to have an outlet lest you become an irritable person. When you bottle up emotions inside, you risk having it burst out one day, and woe unto the person on the receiving end. Obviously, this would defeat the purpose of practicing restraint considering that you have overreacted. One of the best outlets for your emotions is engaging in a physically-taxing activity like exercising and training.

Spend time in nature

Our environment has a big effect on our emotional states. If we live or work in chaotic places, our emotions are more or less going to take on that tone. Taking time to be surrounded by nature has a calming effect on your emotions. You could take walks in nature parks, hike, or hunt in the forest. This could help raise your spirits and release all the bad emotions.

Keep the big picture in mind

If you fail to get a handle on your emotions, you run the risk of throwing the baby out with the bathwater. Sometimes, you may get stuck in an unpleasant situation and feel like letting your emotions explode. Try to be wise enough to keep the bigger picture in mind. First ask yourself, what's your agenda? And how are your actions helping that agenda? For instance, say your teenage daughter is driving you up the wall. If you become hostile with her, she may end up cutting off ties with you, thus killing off any chance of you getting to guide her through life.

Learn to distract yourself

An emotionally intelligent person is aware of his emotional makeup; i.e., how their body responds to various stimuli. At the onset of an unpleasant emotion, rather than entertain it, learn to distract yourself. For instance, if you were working on a serious academic project and a very attractive person of the opposite sex stumbled by, you might get aroused and experience passionate feelings. Well, sexual emotion is not bad in and of itself, but considering that you're doing an important academic project, you might want to banish that sexual emotion.

You can achieve that by distracting yourself – engaging your mind in other activities. You may not have the ability to decide which emotion to experience, but when you pay less attention to a particular emotion, it tends to subside. However, if you lend your attention to a particular emotion, you tend to fuel it and end up increasing its potency.

Never react immediately

Whenever you experience a massive emotional trigger, be careful not to give an immediate response. This will give you time to assess the real situation and come up with the perfect plan.

When you give an immediate emotional response, chances are the outcome will be less than desirable. For instance, if the actions or words of a person have triggered your anger, don't erupt in an outburst. This will get your aggressor worried about your next move. Meanwhile, you can be devising your comeback plan, or choose not to do anything at all. When you're consumed by an overpowering urge to give an emotionally-charged response, both your heartbeat and breathing rate will go up. Learning to control your breath can help in regaining your calm.

Communicate well

It doesn't matter what your intentions are, but if you cannot get around to communicating well, you'll have little chance of making progress. For instance, if you are agitated and have to face someone to resolve an issue, your verbal and nonverbal cues will play a critical role in how your message will be taken. Use a pleasant tone and ensure that you engage in active listening. Regardless of how powerful your emotions might be, there are always the right words to capture perfectly what you feel.

Practice honesty

Honesty is indeed the best policy. What's the purpose of expressing yourself in the first place if you're not going to be honest about how you feel? You should at all times ensure that you communicate your emotions in a manner that's as honest as possible, simply because that is the best way for you to get an honest reply. For instance, if someone at work did or said something that left you with a bad taste in your mouth, you might want to walk up to them and express how their actions or words made you feel. How they react is not in your power, but when you take the initiative, you will at least be on the right path to making things right again.

Practice mindfulness

Learn to stay aware of what is going on in your environment. This can only be achieved through mindfulness. When you get in the habit of being interested in other people, you create avenues for channeling positive emotions. We live in a world of pain, and so many people are in need of kindness. It is through mindfulness that we get to show our positive feelings to the world.

Chapter 6: The Past With Its Anchors On EQ

Take a moment to reflect on your past. What do you see? Is it a source of strength and useful experiences for you or rather a source of recurrent pain and suffering?

We often hear confessions like, "These memories keep returning." "I regret what I did a few years ago." "How do I stop thinking about it?" Luckily, there's an effective way of dealing with your memories.

How old are you? Even if you're still young, you've surely been through a lot in your life already. Some moments were great, magnificent, worth remembering, whereas you would surely be eager to pay lots of money to have forgotten some of those less fortunate moments. Which of these memories take up most of the space in your mind?

There are people in this world who focus all their attention only on the unpleasant memories from their past. The more they want to forget about them, the bigger impact these thoughts have on them, and the more frequently they return. They experienced something unpleasant once and then they experience it again, again and again, ad infinitum, spending crazy amounts of time every day thinking about these past events and situations. They spend their entire lives thinking about the past.

It's exactly as if someone was driving a car looking in the rearview mirror all the time—not only is it impossible to reach the destination that way, but also, it's extremely likely to cause some serious accidents. The rearview mirror is very useful, indeed, but only to look at it occasionally to find what's necessary at the moment. Still, you have to look at what's in front of you all the time. That's the only way to drive your car safely to your destination.

Remember what you were doing yesterday at this hour? This recalled memory will probably come together with a certain image. When did this image appear? Here and now. So, does the past exist anywhere else other than outside of your head? NO. The past is nothing more than your imagination—a mind creation, collage of images, sounds and feelings. Just like a video recording. Is what you see on the recording real? Is it happening? No. It is only a reflection of reality. Not reality itself.

Let's state this again: the past does not exist. It is only a record in your head, in the form of multi-sensory memories. Why should you be worried so much about something that doesn't exist anymore? Why would you waste your life away focusing your attention on a videotape, on a stretch of reality which is recorded?

Think how many useless video recordings you keep in your head that do nothing but hold you back. Put them aside or you will go through all these negative emotions again and again, doing to yourself again what already ended a long time ago.

You can look at your past from many different perspectives. You can define it as a heavy burden you must bear until the end of your life or as very useful baggage of experiences, from which you will reap the wisdom just when you need it. Even the worst experiences can be viewed as a source of priceless teachings, which will provide you a helpful hand and direction sign on a desert in every difficult life situation.

When I sometimes work with people, I often come across those who regret what they have done in the past. I ask them, "Would you want to be in some other place in your life, different than you're in right now?" In most of the cases the answer is "No." Then I tell them that every single element of their past life contributed to the fact that they now are where they are. It's like in the movie The Butterfly Effect. Appreciate every single experience from your past, because even the unpleasant ones can prove as a useful source of skills and knowledge to you.

I recently talked to a businessman who told me a story of how once he lost huge amounts of money when his own co-worker robbed his office. He couldn't get over it for a long time and he couldn't let go of his anger and resentment. He really wanted his revenge, but finally, after some time, he decided to change his point of view to cease his suffering. He told me he now looks at this unfortunate situation as one of the most valuable lessons in his life. He's even grateful he got cheated, because now he pays more attention when picking new co-workers and cares much more about the safety of his business, thanks to which his new company grows much faster.

You can reframe every single memory like that. Everything is a matter of your perception. Looking from an entirely different perspective, you will feel totally different emotions. Always choose the perspective that is better for you. Change your view of certain situations and you will free yourself from excessive suffering.

Ask yourself these questions: Was what happened definitely a bad thing? Even if it was, what good can it bring into my life? What lesson have I learned? The answers will surely come and that's the moment when you start changing your detrimental perception of your past.

Mind you that liberating yourself from unpleasant memories doesn't mean erasing them from your life. They are, in a way, a part of who you are. You don't need to forget about where you came from and how you became the person who you are now. Your task is only to gain distance from what has happened, so that you can free yourself from the negative impact of these memories. It's about you learning how to look at the past situation without thinking, "Man, that was so horrible!" Instead, think, "What can I learn from that?" Once you get rid of the negative impact, it will be much easier for you to reap reward from the experiences you gathered during all those years.

Once you have come to an understanding of that, you will suddenly realize that all people's chances are equal. Their past doesn't really matter that much. It's not about where you came from, it's about where you're heading. Where you grew up, what kind of childhood you had, what parents you had and which school you attended doesn't have to affect your future at all.

It is extremely important for you to know your past doesn't have to equal your future.

The decisions about your future are always made here and now. Always make them taking your past experiences into consideration, but, before all, consider who you want to be in a month, one year, five years, etc.

There's one NLP exercise I'm going to show you that will help you to finally deal with all your negative memories. You will be able to start over again, leaving all your burdens behind and finally looking ahead with your chin up.

To begin, take a sheet of paper and start with writing down all the memories you can access in the form of keywords. Gather all the thoughts about your past that keep returning and inflicting bad emotions.

Then, pick one at a time and apply the NLP technique presented below. It is very important that you work on every single bad memory, once and for all, liberating yourself from all these returning thoughts about your past.

Perceptual Positions

Perceptual Positions in NLP refers to considering a situation from the first, second and third-person perspective.

The first position is your regular, daily experience about any event or experience. In the first-person perspective, or first perceptual position, you are completely connected with the experience through subjective filters. It is a personal, subjective experience that is free from another person's perspective.

The second-person perspective, or second perceptual position, is when you assume things from another person's point of view. Typically, salespeople, negotiators and counselors are remarkably good at the second perceptual position. They are processing information from the other person's perceptual experiences. This is done to empathize with the other person or understand their mind map.

The third-person perspective, or third perceptual position, is when you assume the role of an objective observer and consider perceptual experiences from an objective point of view or that of an external observer, much like watching a movie.

How do You Assume a Third Person Position?

Perform an activity, and during the activity move to a position that offers you a clear unobstructed view of the space where you just performed the activity. Take on a straight, upright position with shoulders pulled back. Imagine watching yourself in the performance space. Doing it this way, you can give unbiased feedback. It is like watching a movie or theatre performance.

How Do You Assume a Second Position?

The second position is the position of modeling, learning and absorbing. It is like activating neurons in your nervous system that are dormant within the observer but boast of the same neuron functions as the neurons in the person you are modeling after.

The next time you find yourself in the company of a person you want to emulate, try these helpful tips:

• Clear your mind completely.

• Try to match your breathing rhythm or pattern with the person you want to emulate or empathize with.

• Practice micro muscle mirroring. For example, if the other individual moves their legs, move your leg muscles slightly as if you are about to move your legs. Feel your leg muscles moving before lifting them. Practice this with full body movements.

The objective of the practice is to experience the world as if you are the other person. Imagine yourself assuming their body, so you become them.

Visualization

Since this book tells you to use visualization very often and because that's something some people have trouble with, I decided to add this chapter to help you better see your mental images. Again, it contains three practical and very effective exercises that will help you visualize better, with bigger intensity and the ability to take your visualization techniques to the next level. Visualization is a key to many tools, not only connected with NLP, but also with effective learning, goal setting, maintaining motivation and positive thinking, so it's worth it to establish this skill on a decent level!

Self-development can be defined as a pursuit of the desired condition. Since the state you want to achieve lies somewhere in the future, your ability to see what you want to achieve is one of the very crucial parts of the bigger picture.

Without a preview on how our lives should look like in the future, it's much more difficult to make real changes in the present. That's why rich and colorful visualizations that can totally devour you are so important. When you add sounds, smells, flavors and feelings, the references created in your brain can be so strong your subconscious will automatically focus all its attention on achieving your goal and will maintain that state for a long time.

Whether you have trouble with seeing the internal images at all or they get distorted and unclear, regular use of these exercises will enable you to create sharp, clear and detail-saturated visualizations.

Exercise I

·   Go to a silent place, ideally your room, with doors closed. Close your eyes and recall any situation from your life, preferably a nice memory. Don't try to see the images at this point, but focus on hearing sounds which accompanied that memory. Take a moment to listen to what happened there. What sounds are there? Is anybody saying anything? What's the manner, tempo and volume of their speech? Hear what you heard then.

·   Now, add a sense of touch to this. In your imagination, touch something that was there, any object, piece of clothing, whatever. Feel the surface of this object, its texture, temperature, weight. Get into that memory…

·   Now, add all the scents that were there. Feel the smell of the air… and then…

·   What do you see? See the images that appear. Maintain it and enjoy the view. You've just fully created your visualization.

This exercise is about activating any other senses than sight at first, which makes it much easier to bring back the image associated with that memory. It happens because every piece of information is saved in different parts of the brain. Not only does the information about memories contain visual data, but also auditory, sensory, etc., so that the increased activity in other parts of the brain helps you activate the sense of vision in your imagination and put it all together.

Exercise II

·   Choose any object from your room. It can be a phone, computer screen, book or anything else. Put that object somewhere close to you, so you can look at it freely. Observe it thoroughly for about five seconds.

· After that, close your eyes and visualize exactly what you have just seen. Keep the image of this object as long as you can. If the image goes away, it doesn't matter. Open your eyes and start again.

· After a few series, choose another object and repeat the same process—observe it for five seconds, then close your eyes and visualize it thoroughly.

· Do this exercise five minutes a day, every day.

Practiced regularly, this exercise will give you the ability to create clear and accurate images on demand. It's just a matter of training—you will see that day after day the visualizations will be becoming increasingly natural for you.

Once you master bringing back the images of objects you normally see around you, modify it and create imaginary things in your mind.

Create abstractions of various kinds and keep them in your imagination as long as possible.

Exercise III

· Open a book, preferably a fiction story you like. Randomly pick a page and start reading.

· After a few lines, stop reading and close your eyes.

· Start imagining what you have just read about. Try to notice as many details as possible: people who are there, environment in which they are, the words they speak.

· Create this visualization for a minute, then go back to reading.

· After another few lines, close your eyes and start creating inner images again. Repeat this for about five minutes.

· Practice daily.

Literature is often rich in colorful, detailed descriptions that many times help improve imagination. The fact of reading about what's in the picture automatically creates the picture itself. In this exercise, you will additionally be able to consciously focus on that visualization, seeing many more details.

You can use the exercises above together or you could also pick one or two of them, the ones that suit you the most. Remember to practice regularly. It's like riding a bicycle —once you learn it, you will always be able to do it, as it will become perfectly natural to you. The ability to get into rich visualizations is a key that opens many self-development doors. You will finally be able to visualize a successful future, get rid of bad memories using NLP, remember difficult things using memorization techniques and do many other useful things.

Change of Personal History with NLP

1. Identify the memory you want to work on. If it's a situation you experienced more than once, pick the memory of the time when you experienced it for the first time. Close your eyes and imagine this situation as thoroughly as you can. Then, get into that memory as deeply as you can, feeling all these emotions that you then felt. Proceed to the next step once you're already immersed in that situation.

2. Now, break the state—do and think about something totally unrelated to that situation for a few minutes. Check your e-mail, cuddle your cat, count fruits in your kitchen or do anything else.

3. After five minutes, return to the technique and think what resource you'd need in that situation to make it a satisfactory experience instead of an unpleasant one—resource being an emotional state, skill or a certain belief. Maybe it could be the feeling of trust, being loved, self-confident or certainty that the other side had good intentions? Choose the resource that would entirely change your perception of that bad situation.

4. Focus on remembering if you had any situation in your life when you had this resource, fully and entirely? For example, when you really felt loved or self-assured? Pick certain memories that will bring you the desired emotional state. Close your eyes and bring back exactly what you then saw, felt and heard. Get into that memory and recall all the emotions that were there. Once you can feel them fully, create the so-called "anchor" for the state—you need to establish a stimulus that will be connected to that feeling in your mind. I prefer kinesthetic anchors. You can, for example, touch the back of your hand with your fingers, grip your wrist a little bit or lightly pinch your ear. It should be unique, something you're not used to doing daily, such as scratching your nose.

5. Once you do this, break this state again. Then, close your eyes and go back to the negative memory, but this time see it as "dissociated", that is from the spectator's perspective (as a "third person"). Launch your anchor with the positive resource and watch yourself and the whole situation from aside. See how your entire behavior changes once you achieve the state you needed. See how the whole situation is changing along with the other people's behavior and your perception of that situation. Anchor that feeling.

6. Now go back to the beginning of that situation and watch it again, this time "associated"— from your own eyes' perspective. Launch the positive anchor again and see how the situation is going once you've obtained the necessary resources. What is different in your perception of this

situation? How's your behavior and other people's behavior changing? Give yourself the time to watch this situation until the end, then establish an anchor.

7. Check the effects. Bring back the feeling without launching the anchor and observe how the memory had changed. If you're still not satisfied with the change, go back to step 3 and go through the process again, this time choosing a different resource. If the negative emotions are gone—congrats!

Once you have worked through every single unpleasant memory, you're ready to take the next step. If you really want to bring back your memories, only go through the positive ones, the moments that give you joy and happiness.

The best solution is to move most of your thinking to the present and future. This kind of approach will give you more power and motivation and much more pleasure from living every day!

Dealing with Your Past

If you are still living in painful memories or carry any emotional baggage from the past, you are not paving the way for an emotionally healthy and balanced future. You'll have a hard time creating a happy and positive life ahead of you if you are still wrestling with the past. When you accept the past rather than obsessing about it, and deal with it, you are creating avenues for a more rewarding life.

Here are a few brilliant tips for dealing with the past and living a more positive, balanced and emotionally fulfilling life:

Acknowledge Past Challenges

Unresolved experiences of the past can create not only lasting physical damage but psychological consequences as well. Don't let these destructive emotions of shame, guilt, regret, revenge, etc breed inside you for long. Learn to come to terms with these emotions so as to not let your present or future be affected by them.

Don't pretend that you are not affected by these events. You won't be in a position to get over it if you pretend that it didn't happen. Try to acknowledge and allow yourself to feel everything that you felt in the past (and still feel).

For instance, if you feel an overpowering emotion triggered by memories of the past, instead of curbing the feeling, step away for some time. Use this time to reflect on your emotions and how they impact you. Once you are done reflecting upon and feeling the emotions, get back to what you were doing. The consequence of past actions can be very powerful, especially if you are without a support system.

At times, the trauma from past actions is so overpowering that it impacts our relationships. Past trauma can also prevent you from fulfilling your goals. This affects not just your present perspective about life but also your ability to deal with challenges in life.

Understand that There's No Way to Change the Past

There is nothing you can do to change the past. As much as you wish to, you can't do anything to change events or people. The best way to manage a painful past is to tell yourself that it can't be changed now, accept it and change the way you perceive it.

There are many things that are outside our circle of control. However, the way we react to them is something that is still in our hands. We can either live in the past and ruin our present and future, or we can choose to learn from the past and move on. Even though plenty of circumstances are beyond our control, accepting these events as being a part of life is something that is completely within our realm of control.

The past cannot be revisited, but perception about it can be changed. If you don't stop obsessing over the past, the hurt will spill over and damage future experiences.

Direct your efforts towards accepting the past and offering forgiveness to the ones who have hurt you. You don't do this for them; you do it for your own peace and well-being. You give forgiveness to let go of the past and move on. Feel the emotions you want to feel and then let go after a point.

Try to remind yourself that hanging on to these destructive emotions will only end up harming you. Acknowledge the negative emotions and seek compassion for others as well as yourself. Gather all the strength to forgive everyone who harmed you.

Don't expect this to be an overnight process. It will differ from person to person and may take time.

Spend Time with Different People

Spending time in the same setting with the same people where you experienced negative past emotions will only trigger more of the same reactions. Instead, change your setting or spend time with a different group of people who are supportive, inspiring and positive. A powerful social support system can safeguard you from damaging experiences.

Support other people around you who are feeling low to derive strength from their situation and support them. Volunteering is one of the most wonderful ways to let go of a painful past and build a positive and constructive present which will serve as a foundation for a good future. It will also be a great way to interact with a new set of people. When you see other people's vulnerabilities, you become more thankful for your blessings and learn to cope with your troubles.

Seek the Help of a Professional

If you are feeling overwhelmed by your past and nothing else seems to work, seek the help of a professional counselor or therapist. There are instances when experiences can be devastating and can threaten to change your entire life ahead. In such cases, professional intervention is required. Talk to therapists who will help you with a series of therapies to move on from the past.

If nothing else, simply talking to a professional will help you see things from a more objective perspective.

Examine Your Social Circle

Consider moving away from friends who compel you to live in the past. Your immediate social environment will play an essential role when it comes to helping you let go of the past. It also defines who you are and affects your experiences. An encouraging, positive and supportive social circle that doesn't make you stay in the past can change the way you look at things.

I would recommend spending time with people who make you laugh or help you feel good about yourself. Stay away from folks who encourage negative habits or make you feel miserable about yourself. These are the type of people who will only stop your emotional growth or development. For instance, friends who constantly try to put you down or keep reminding you of the past may not be good news. Try making new friends in a different setting. This will get you out of your comfort zone and facilitate personal growth.

Try new hobbies with new friends. Join a hobby group on social media or a local hobby club where you can interact with people who share similar interests. Fresh directions in life can open avenues you hadn't thought were possible earlier.

Systematic Desensitization

Systematic desensitization is a technique through which you are gradually relieving yourself of a potentially destructive situation with a series of relaxation techniques. The objective is to be at ease while exploring different stress relief methods.

Start with simple relaxation techniques such as deep breathing, exercising and meditation. Each time you find yourself exposed to a situation that stresses you as it reminds you of a past experience, you can practice these relaxation techniques to stay calm. The idea is to progress at your pace without rushing yourself to eliminate the pain. You should be able to engage confidently in situations that cause you distress over a period of time

For instance, if you had a terrible experience while addressing an audience on the stage earlier, you may avoid all opportunities to speak on stage. A past experience comes to haunt you each time you think of going on the stage. Get past this by actively opting to address an audience. Start with a small group of friends or co-workers in a meeting room or your home.

Employ relaxation techniques each time you find yourself being a bundle of nerves before speaking. Gradually, go with a bigger audience. There will come a time when you will be completely confident about addressing an audience without any fear. Keep going slowly, steadily and consistently. It may not be easy in the beginning, but eventually, you'll gather the confidence to master the art of speaking to an audience without being nervous.

The Art of Forgiving People

Forgiving people is important for emotional and spiritual growth. Your negative experience of how someone has hurt you is nothing but a negative energy you carry in your mind. These feelings of anger, revenge, hatred, rage and more gradually take away your power to focus on constructive and positive things by occupying space in your mind. When you release it, you will award or gift yourself more peace. Here are some tips for practicing forgiveness and letting your mind be occupied by more positive emotions:

Learn to Let Go like Water

Don't be forceful or try to one-up people in pointless ego battles. Rather be like water that just flows. Be soft, accommodating, tolerant and flexible of other opinions rather than forcing your views on others. Instead of focusing on telling and talking, concentrate on listening. When someone says something that is contrary to your argument, say something like, "I've never thought about it like this before, thank you for introducing me to a new point of view. I'll sure think about it."

Don't Actively Seek Occasions to be Offended

Don't keep looking for opportunities to be offended. Many people spend a huge amount of energy looking for occasions to be hurt. It can be a discourteous stranger, a person swearing around you, someone disagreeing with your views on social media or just about anything that ticks you off. Become a person who isn't offended by the tiniest of things or a series of circumstances.

Focus on Being Kind Instead of Being Right

When your mind is consumed by revenge, you are actually digging a grave for yourself too. Resentment is destructive for you. The world isn't always hunky dory. People behave the way they do because that's just how they are. That's how they believe they are supposed to behave, and there's nothing much you can do about it unless it's a legally punishable offense. However, processing your reaction is something you can choose.

Get rid of the need to prove others wrong or to reinforce the idea that something bad has happened to you.

Think of a scenario where someone hurts you by saying something offensive. Rather than harboring feelings of resentment, you just disconnect or remove yourself from the situation and choose to react with kindness. You choose to send energies of joy and forgiveness rather than reacting in a negative manner. This is something you can do to maintain your internal balance and harmony. Focus on being compassionate more than being right.

Don't Sleep Angry

Before going to bed, don't spend valuable time reviewing anything negative that you don't want to be reinforced in your subconscious because as we discussed earlier, the subconscious is the most active when we are asleep. Focus on positive and constructive thoughts just before going to bed rather than harboring hatred. If you have had an argument or disagreement with someone, talk to them and clear the air before going to bed. Focus on ending it on a positive note even if you don't wish to associate with the person in future.

Be grateful and peaceful in aligning with your values and who you are as a person. Associate with people who possess the same beliefs and ideals as you. You are in control of how your mind is programmed just before going to sleep, which means you should only focus on positive thoughts.

Think About How No One is Perfect

Think about the person who has hurt you. He or she is a human with his or her own strengths and shortcomings. They are acting from their own limited beliefs and personality traits, for which you don't have to punish yourself. Their frame of reference may not be the same as yours.

While you were feeling hurt, the other person is trying to meet their own needs. What was the need of the other individual? Why do you think they behaved in a hurtful manner towards you? This will help you consider things from their perspective or be empathetic towards their situation despite being hurt.

At the end of the day, when we learn to handle our own emotions, our capacity to love and to also forgive will grow as well.

Chapter 7: Commonly Asked Questions and Answers

The following are questions set to determine the emotional intelligence and social skills of an individual.

If you started a company, what would be your values?

This question is aimed at finding out your ideals. Company ideals are just as important as company goals. Come up with values that are all-inclusive and that reward excellence. Show that you understand the critical role that values play in the success of a company.

What inspires you?

This question is aimed at digging the sort of person you really are underneath your casual look. Your source of inspiration pretty much sums up what kind of person you are. It tells the world if you're a serious person or a joker. Thus, always select an individual or a cause that is closest to your objectives.

How would you create a more rewarding life?

This question is aimed at challenging your creativity. The underlying assumption is that life isn't great, but it has to be made so using only the materials at your disposal. You might want to take a close look at your suggestions to make sure that they are workable ideas. Write down the steps of moving from an unrewarding life to a rewarding one.

What angers you?

The question is about finding out the various things that push your buttons. Everyone has them. But be careful not to come across as an extremely sensitive person. You want to mention a couple of things that irritate other people as well and use some creativity to include other bad behaviors and attitudes.

What is your idea of fun?

Even the top managers of fortune 500 companies have a fun side to them. When answering the things that you consider fun, ensure that you don't sound cliché. Try to be a little bit more creative and mention activities that are not quite in the mainstream. It lends some mystery to your image.

What are your thoughts on asking for help?

This question seeks to understand your perception of team work and collaborative efforts. Try to come across as being in favor of collaboration. Many hands make the duty light. Many minds make the problem small. The input of other people is critical to the success of an activity.

What are your achievements?

This is not your chance to toot your horn like never before. Mention the cool things you have done with your life, but ask yourself if your achievements are truly important or whether you're the only person that considers them important. It could save you a great deal of embarrassment. Also, be careful not to come across as someone who thinks he's better than everybody else.

How do you react to frustrations?

Nobody is safe from feeling frustrated, but everyone has their own way of dealing with it. This question seeks to gauge your capacity to withstand frustrations. You should come across as someone who keeps your head in spite of challenges. Don't indicate any negative behavior you usually engage in every time you're frustrated.

What are your goals?

This question aims to find out your ambitions. Try not to sound like a person who lives in a fantasy world. Your goals should sound achievable, and your goals show what kind of person you are, so you have to be careful that they are appropriate.

What are your strengths?

It takes a great deal of self-awareness to realize your strengths. Your strengths will define your capabilities. Articulate how your strengths may help you achieve your goals. It is not enough to mention your strengths – mention as well how you apply them in your day-to-day existence.

What are your weaknesses?

People are scared of being vulnerable even when they don't have to be. Accepting your weaknesses doesn't mean that you're broken beyond repair. It actually means that you're a strong person. A self-aware person will know their weaknesses. But don't drop your list of weaknesses as if it were a badge of honor. At least acknowledge that you're trying to turn your weaknesses into strengths.

What are your religious beliefs?

This question is not purposely for labeling the person's religious affiliation but for understanding their outlook on human existence. A person who is religious will tend to believe that there's a divine creator behind all life, whereas an atheist will tend to align with theories that defy the existence of a creator. Religious beliefs are critical because they inform a person's way of expressing themselves.

Do you have friends?

It might seem like a weird question, but it is actually crucial. Living without friends is not the best kind of life. It may indicate an inability to connect with other people and create meaningful relationships, which is not a great place to be in. If you have no friends, at least admit that you're looking for them; otherwise, refrain from declaring that you have no friends and are not interested anyway.

What is your most defining moment in life?

Various people have different experiences that they consider to have had the most impact on their lives. You want to pick an experience that really altered the course of your life. Perhaps you had not been a "serious person" before, but this experience forced you to start taking life seriously. It helps if your defining moment has a happy ending.

What are your vices?

Each person has their own vices, but whether they have the guts to openly admit to them is another story. Admitting to having vices makes you appear more human. You may reserve the discretion of going into specifics, but it is enough to mention that you engage in practices that are not necessarily productive.

How do you celebrate your victories?

When you achieve your goals, there's obviously tremendous joy, but is there a method to your celebration? Some people jump into an airplane and travel away to a foreign country, and others just want to meet their real or perceived enemies and crow with delight. Whatever the case for you may be, always bear in mind that your method of celebration also says a lot about your character.

Conclusion

This is an extremely vast subject, but the way that I have tackled it in this book is intentional. Emotional Intelligence is something you need to measure for yourself and it is only by being aware of your emotions and reading them in different circumstances that you can really get a handle on why you respond in a set way to given circumstance. When you know that, you are less likely to allow emotions to take over and will exercise your emotional intelligence to be able to control negative feelings toward yourself and toward others.

Emotional intelligence helps you to be able to face different circumstances and be able to look beyond the obvious. You will also find that as you meditate on a daily basis, your intuition will truly become honed. There is a very good reason to want to do this as well. Over the course of your life, you have been programmed by everything that happened in your life. If you watch TV, you get programmed into believing that certain products add to your lifestyle. If you watch too much TV of a mindless nature, you tend to become mindless and this exercise once a day will help you to come back into the real world and find the reality of life is actually much simpler than you may imagine.

Being able to read people because of your emotional intelligence also helps them. You will be able to diffuse bad situations and not fall into the trap of letting the emotions take over when there is always some sense of logic behind why everything happens. By analyzing and keeping notes of your emotional responses, you learn to harness the power of emotional intelligence, so that the next time a situation of that nature presents itself, you are ready and able to cope with it.

People say that emotions are there to protect us, although I would say that they are much more than that. They can also destroy us if we let them. However, when you are the driver in your life, rather than allowing your emotions to be just that, you start to see how to use your emotions to help you rather than to work against you. You will understand people better and have a wider perspective on life. You will be able to help people more because your open minded approach means that you have more solutions than most people. You will also find that you get to recognize those emotions that are helping you to grow as a human being and those which can lead to your destruction.

In this day and age, it's even more important that you harness what emotional intelligence you have since more and more people these days are suffering from the effects of stress and it's becoming worse, rather than better. Your emotional intelligence is what brings you back into this moment in time and allows you to see things from a more neutral perspective. You tend to be forward thinking and also know how to respond to people's weaknesses which strengthen you are an individual. You will also be able to recognize the signs of your own emotions trying to take control and will be able to stem them until you have found suitable solutions to your problems. Everyone is born with emotional intelligence. It is only life that takes it away. The way that you were brought up and the circumstances that surround your life play a huge role in how you manage to handle your emotions. When you investigate and start to understand the triggers that make you weaker, you are able to stem emotional overload and become stronger.

I wish you well in your journey and would suggest you read the book several times and implement the suggestions made within its pages if you want to increase your emotional intelligence and start to enjoy your life to the fullest.

P.S.

Just a small note, would you be able to share what you have picked up so far and a skill or tip you have learnt from this book on amazon.

I would truly appreciate your kind sharing.

Thank You!

Manipulation
Learn To Spot And Avoid
Manipulation As An Empath

Improve Your Emotional Intelligence In Work And Life

Jacob Greene

Manipulation
Learn To Spot And Avoid Manipulation

© Copyright 2018 by Jacob Greene - All rights reserved.

The content contained within this book may not be reproduced, duplicated or transmitted without direct written permission from the author or the publisher.

Under no circumstances will any blame or legal responsibility be held against the publisher, or author, for any damages, reparation, or monetary loss due to the information contained within this book. Either directly or indirectly.

Legal Notice:

This book is copyright protected. This book is only for personal use. You cannot amend, distribute, sell, use, quote or paraphrase any part, or the content within this book, without the consent of the author or publisher.

Disclaimer Notice:

Please note the information contained within this document is for educational and entertainment purposes only. All effort has been executed to present accurate, up to date, and reliable, complete information. No warranties of any kind are declared or implied. Readers acknowledge that the author is not engaging in the rendering of legal, financial, medical or professional advice. The content within this book has been derived from various sources. Please consult a licensed professional before attempting any techniques outlined in this book.

By reading this document, the reader agrees that under no circumstances are is the author responsible for any losses, direct or indirect, which are incurred as a result of the use of information contained within this document, including, but not limited to, —errors, omissions, or inaccuracies.

Introduction

Do you find yourself talking and sharing way too much with certain people? If yes, then you might be getting attacked by manipulators in your life. Manipulators have the ability to make you share your emotional strengths and weaknesses. They have their tactics, which doesn't allow you to protect your emotional side.

People surrounded with manipulators often struggle to find self-confidence. If you don't know how manipulation works, manipulators can shake your life completely. You feel as if you are in debt of them. They control your life, your emotions, and your actions. People who face manipulation feel betrayed and confused in life. Manipulators have the capability to twist realities and make you see what they want; hence, your ability to understand your environment gets corrupted. You start making wrong decisions that ruin your life, but benefit your manipulator. It is a state of psychological and emotional slavery, which you need to break as soon as possible.

What Problems Do You Face At Work And In General Life?

Manipulation is different than social influence. Every person tries to understand other people in order to make stronger relationships; however, manipulators don't think that way. They observe and control people to exploit them. You are nothing but a tool for them. You end up serving a purpose for a manipulator without even knowing it.

- Your self-esteem is attacked by people at your workplace.
- People use your caring nature and then leave you alone.
- You are losing confidence in people because of a few in your life.
- You feel trapped in your family and feel exploited by family members.
- You never say "no" to a certain person in your life.
- You are facing other people's problems and not able to cope.
- Your workplace has become a negative environment for you.
- You feel violated mentally, emotionally and physically.

All these problems and more are possible if you are not ready to tackle manipulators. Not knowing about manipulators makes you vulnerable. Also, you have to understand your emotions, passions, psychology, and habits. A healthy life is the one that is free from manipulation.

What Will This Book Do For You?

When manipulators are out there trying to learn and use you, it is important that you understand their methods. There are many types of manipulations and different kinds of manipulators out there. They all use different methods and target different emotions or psychological state of people. This book will allow you to understand how manipulation works. You will learn to spot manipulative tactics and methods to avoid manipulation.

This book explains how manipulators work in a workplace, in a relationship or in other life settings people indulge in, generally. You will learn how to have conversations with a manipulator and how to not fall for their lies and deceptions.

Apart from knowing how manipulation works, you will find solutions to all the problems mentioned above. This book will also allow you to understand your own emotional, psychological and mental state and remove all vulnerabilities.

Emotional and social awareness is extremely important if you want to live a psychologically healthy life. You can have deep, hidden emotional issues affecting your habits today. This book has a comprehensive approach to how to deal with manipulation and improve your social and self-awareness. You will learn to manage your emotions and open up to the right people. Becoming a self-confident person and dealing with your emotional issues is the way to find true happiness.

With complete self-awareness and social awareness, you hold the steering wheel of your own life; hence, no manipulator can find any room to control your actions.

Let's begin the most important journey of your life!

Chapter 1:
What Is Manipulation?

Manipulation is using people's emotions and behavioral traits deliberately to obtain what is desired. Manipulators use their ability to understand others and get what they want by using trickery, misdirection, persuasion, charm, and coaxing.

In the mind of a manipulator, he or she thinks, "I have the ability to change people's behavior and let them give me what I want." Skilled manipulators can even come out of a situation when they get caught trying to use other people to their advantage.

A manipulator has a tendency to create a certain level of strain in a situation. They use multiple techniques to mold their personality according to their goals. A manipulator can make you feel on top of the world, or the worst person on this planet. It all depends on how that manipulator wants you to act.

Manipulation, as a concept, involves two parties. One is the manipulator and the other is manipulated. While manipulators are extremely aware of their surroundings, some personalities tend to ignore that. People, who are emotionally vulnerable or don't have a clear mindset, tend to get manipulated.

Generally speaking, everyone manipulates without knowing. Lying or hiding the complete story are a few common ways of manipulation; however, manipulators live these tactics as the way of their lives. They use various tactics as their tools to fool you into doing what they want.

That's why you need to understand all types of manipulation and more importantly, learn how to address it positively in different aspects of your life.

Different Types of Manipulation

If you aren't aware enough, manipulators can use many techniques to control you. They change their approach depending on the victim's personality so they first observe you and learn your core personality traits. At the core, you can be a loving person, a lonely person, naïve or too confident.

With personality observation, manipulators create their tactic to attack you. Here are different types of manipulation that you need to become aware of:

1. Hiding the complete story
You can notice this in your office, parties and other conversations taking place around you. There are people who hide certain portions of stories in order to create a diversion. The listener of the story gets to know what the manipulator wants him to know.

What if a colleague in your office tells you how others are bitching about you! It is possible that you are getting half of the side of the story, but if you are unaware of manipulation, this half story can trigger emotions like anger and hatred, and you end up doing something that you regret.

When a manipulator uses a half story, they don't lie. They just avoid telling certain portions so that you see a picture of their creation. The tactic behind this method is to stay on the safe side. If exposed, the manipulator can simply say that he or she has explained nothing but the truth and in doing so, you risk facing humiliation due to your wrong actions.

2. Lying

Generally, people lie when they are scared or want to get out of an unwanted situation, but a manipulator's lie is different. Their lies always have a purpose or an end goal. In fact, they don't even have to plan before lying. They can plan their next lie while having a conversation with you.

Depending on what they want, manipulators can choose different lies to make you their victim. It is a blend of thrill and excitement they feel while trying to play your personality.

3. Love and charm

Narcissistic manipulators use love and charm to control you. This behavior is majorly visible in love relationships between partners. You get hooked and think that your partner loves you the most. They charm and create an illusion of a perfect relationship. These people always want something from you.

When love has built the foundation, the manipulator uses that to control you. They can ask for things, money or just play with your emotions. The goals depend on the personality of the manipulator. Some people have the disorder to love and then hurt their partners. The roots of this behavior lead back to their own previous experiences.

To spot the manipulation of love, you need to notice who is making decisions in your relationship:

- Do you feel afraid of your partner when making a personal choice?
- Has it become your habit to get your partner's approval on everything?
- Are you doing things that you wouldn't do otherwise?

These questions can help you decipher love manipulation in your daily life.

4. Changing behavior frequently

This is different than changing personality traits according to a victim. A manipulator, many times, may showcase a behavioral change towards the same person again and again. Now, you can think of all those people who seem different every time you meet them. This behavior is common in love relationships, and boss and employee relationships as well.

The manipulator wants you to stay malleable and out of balance so, one minute he or she can look happy, and swiftly become angry for no valid reason. However, they make you think that their behavioral switch has a legitimate reason. Your boss can start shouting angrily just for a single typo in your report. Similarly, a manipulative partner can come home with a different mood every day.

We, as humans, understand other people's personalities before socializing. You feel more comfortable around a person who you know well, instead of a stranger, but manipulators use their mood swings to keep you scared and afraid of them. You feel unaware of their personalities and try to please them.

5. Denying accusations

A manipulator can deny things very impressively. If you accuse them of something, they confidently present a believable story. The confidence, combined with an impressive story, makes you believe them.

Denying accusations is the simplest form of manipulation. In fact, this is the first tactic that manipulators use in their early ages. A kid with manipulative tendencies usually denies things with confidence and makes stories to justify their case.

6. Punishments

Punishment is a disciplinary action to control other people's behavior. This is also a manipulation technique that gives control to a manipulator. Physical violence, shouting, and nagging are the visible techniques of manipulation.

Apart from that, you can also get emotionally punished with the silence of a person or mental abuse. A manipulator can attack your emotional vulnerabilities to make you feel bad. They keep on doing it until you start behaving exactly the way they want. Such manipulation is seen in marriages a lot. One partner uses physical and mental abuse to control the other. Also, you can notice these manipulation symptoms in a parent-kid relationship. A manipulative kid can use the silent treatment to control his or her mother.

7. Blaming for overreaction

Is there a person who makes you feel bad about yourself?! That person can be a manipulator.

Using the blame game allows a manipulator to put you on the faulty side of every conversation. If you point out their actions, they blame you for overreacting. They say that you are reacting way too much for a very small thing. This way they become the victim and you end up feeling bad about your own actions.

8. Victim targeting

You are the victim, but the accuser makes you defend yourself in front of others. This way, the manipulator masks his or her own wrongdoings by shifting the focus towards you. The manipulator does it all in front of you, but you feel out of control of the situation.

9. Playing a victim

Have you ever helped people whom you never liked as a person? Then it is possible that you were used with this manipulation technique.

Manipulators play victim from time to time to gain compassion and sympathy. Their end goal is always to use you in some way; however, not every victim is a manipulator. Some are genuinely hurt and require your support, but manipulators can use your helping nature to get what they want.

10. Too much positive attention

The corporate world is filled with such manipulators nowadays. People use expensive presents, give money, and praise to lure you towards them. Excessive charm and too much attention are used for people who seek approval and like getting praised. Manipulators judge personalities and give too much attention to satisfy your emotional needs.

Positive attention works if you are emotionally vulnerable. For instance, if you mention "society" before taking every action, it tells a manipulator about your approval-seeking nature. Your high-class dressing sense and money-focused behavior also give signals to manipulators. They start giving you the royal treatment and manipulate in the process.

11. Diversions

Shifting situations and conversations are also manipulation techniques. You feel you know what's going on, but suddenly a person changes the whole picture. If that happens in your life frequently, then there is a manipulator around you. He or she wants you to stay confused, while they get to twist situations in their favor.

When in a group conversation, a manipulator plays the role of a narrator. If a conversation goes against his or her plan, they immediately shift the topic to something else. These manipulators become the kings and queens of office politics.

12. Isolation

Manipulation is difficult when you are consulting your family and friends on the same topic; hence, a manipulator tries everything to isolate you from other people. This doesn't have to be a literal isolation. The manipulator can tell you to keep things a secret from everyone. Once you agree to that, he or she can twist your behavior easily.

Covert and Overt Types of Manipulation

Covert and overt are two major categories of manipulation.

Covert manipulation combines all the invisible techniques of manipulation. You can't see the psychological attacks of an abuser until it's done. This type of manipulation is intentional, and the abuser prepares to harm you in a psychological way.

You think that all the wrong things are happening accidentally, but the abuser knows what you feel. The extreme covert manipulators are known as psychopaths and narcissists. They follow a systematic emotional attack to break your confidence and control your realities, and you end up as their puppet without knowing that at all.

In covert manipulation, the abuser shows you a twisted reality. This misguided reality brainwashes you and ruins your ability to make correct decisions; then, the abuser guides as he or she pleases.

Overt manipulation includes all those techniques, which the victim can experience and notice, so the physical, verbal and sexual abuses come into this category. It is a situation where you have a higher tendency of knowing that you are being manipulated, but some folks may still end up not knowing what to do about it.

Both overt and covert manipulations deserve to be on your watch list that is for sure, and we will find ways to deal with them later on!

The Different Types of Manipulators

According to the manipulation techniques, you can come across the following kinds of manipulators:

1. The Expert

"I am better than you at everything."

This person wants to stay on top of every situation. These manipulators are driven by their desire to attain a strong social dominance over others. Their personalities include a high ego, which they blend with their ability to locate vulnerable people. These people like to keep people who lack self-confidence, which serves their ego.

Using insults and put-downs, these manipulators exploit the vulnerability of their victims. They are narcissistic, but hide their arrogance with fake politeness. At the core, these manipulators have self-doubts and shame. Manipulation becomes their technique to hide their own vulnerability.

2. The Perpetual Victim

"People hurt me and use me all the time."

In every scenario, you find these manipulators showcasing themselves as victims. Even if the situation has nothing to do with them, they find a way to become the victim. If you cut your fingers by mistake, this manipulator starts getting a headache and blames you for that.

By becoming a victim, these manipulators cause fights and arguments around them. You might argue with others for this person, and they stay behind the scenes and, after every argument or fight, this person will behave as a victim again. This gives power to emotionally control others and gain their sympathy at the same time.

These manipulators seek more attention from their surroundings. You can see them feeling angry and emotionally distressed. They blame their shortcomings on others' hatred for them. They use "ethics" as their manipulation card so many times and project paranoia about everything.

3. Strong Dependents

"Please follow my lead to save me from my life."

These manipulators are strong and weak at the same time. They present themselves as a powerless creature, but they are very much in control from the inside. They like to depend on someone else for their needs. In order to gain that control, they show as if they are weak and unable to live on their own. Giving compliments is the secret weapon they use to obtain control over victims.

The moment you judge them as inferior and try to help, they gain control over you. One by one, all their responsibilities become yours, and if you try to avoid them, they make you feel as if you are letting them down like how others have.

4. The Angry Beast

"How dare you ask me that, it is not my fault at all!"

These manipulators won't let you blame them for anything. They keep people away by using anger as their guard. Teenagers usually showcase these tendencies for a while; however, they aren't aware of their behavior. On the other hand, a manipulator deliberately shows anger.

In many relationships, one partner shows anger if asked about stealing behavior, increasing credit card bills, or cheating. No matter how politely you ask, their reply is always over the top. They constantly avoid confrontation and play the blame game with their partner. For example, a manipulator can blame the partner for his/her affair saying, "I had an affair because you weren't spending enough time with me." A strong denial is their key to keep doing what they want to do so they can scream or physically abuse you if confronted strongly.

5. The Wrong Well-wisher
"I am the only friend you have in this world. Others want to eat you alive."

Lying, hiding the complete story and other manipulation techniques are valuable tools for these manipulators. They want to isolate you from family and friends by feeding lies in your mind. At the same time, they present themselves as your only well-wisher who is on your side no matter what. Alliance creation is the way they live their lives. Their friendly nature doesn't allow you to figure out their true intentions. They gradually create a strong bond with their victim, keeping their nasty intentions hidden. Then, the series of rumors begin and the manipulator becomes the source of information for the victim. They hurt emotionally with their lies and trigger hatred and anger in their victim's mind.

Friends, parents or colleagues, anyone can be this manipulator in your life. For instance, between two close girlfriends, one can start spreading rumors about another's character, just because she has a crush on her friend's boyfriend.

6. The Truth Twister
"Sorry, I think I have misinterpreted what you told me."

Using half-truths, exaggerations, and lies, these manipulators gain control over victims. They smartly alter the victim's words and turn them into reputation-harming rumors. When exposed, they simply deny and apologize by saying, "I misunderstood your words." These people want to feel superior in their group, even if they don't deserve it. Their friendly nature allows them to blend and bond with people to exploit their vulnerable sides. Gaining personal information is the first step they make, and then they create a misinterpreted story around that information. They have the capacity to justify their actions and play victim if confronted.

7. The Stubborn Deniers
"You are bad and I am good. Period."

Filled with a vast amount of ego, these manipulators deny their own behavior and actions. They usually don't understand their own flaws and project those flaws in others. For example, such a manipulator can say, "You are a racist person," even when they have racist tendencies. They see their faults and think that the world has those faults. These manipulators blame their victims and even try to include other people in their blame game. Their stubborn nature doesn't let them realize their own flaws. They actually believe that their actions and beliefs are always right.

For example, such a manipulator will point out the laziness of their victim, when he is the lazy one. In his mind, he will create justifications for his own laziness.

8. The Charming Flirt
"I am gorgeous, so give me what I want."

Attracting people and controlling them, that is how these manipulators operate. Their attractive looks become their weapon. Superficial in nature, these people feel more attractive than they actually are. They have to be the favorite person in every person's life; however, they only care about their needs and desires. Flirtatious nature and sexual triggers help these manipulators lure their victims. They want you to react to their flirtatious behavior in a positive way. These manipulators love creating tension among family members and friends.

These manipulators never stop looking for new partners. They connect with current partners strongly, but keep looking for new potential partners. They don't believe in traditional relationship structures of society. In fact, when friendships and families break, it empowers these manipulators. They want to twist people's relationships and live life like a grand drama show.

9. The Intimidator
"If I get mad, it won't be good for you!"

These manipulators get what they want by using intimidation. They bully others and demand things. They want to become the answer to "what," "why," "when" and "how" for their victims. Anything you do or say, it has to be according to their preference. These manipulators mostly use their physical features to bully others. In fact, many don't mind using physical abuse to intimidate their victims.

But the intimidation is not limited to physically strong people. Many manipulators can showcase their intelligence as an intimidating weapon. If you disagree on something, they act surprised and showcase the evidence of their superiority over you. Their belief lies in forcing their thoughts and shape situations according to themselves. For these manipulators, other people are nothing but tools, which they can use whenever desired. If they can't, their aggression is always there to make people do what they want.

10. The Adaptable Manipulator
"I observe people before I pick my manipulation tools."

These manipulators are probably the most dangerous ones. They have mastery over all the above-mentioned manipulations. They can adapt and change their behavior according to the personality of his or her victims. They combine multiple techniques together to create a perfect mix of manipulation blend that you can't escape. Even if they fail once, they don't stop. They learn and try new things to gain control over the victims. If a person resists manipulation, these manipulators feel thrilled. They search for strong personalities and carefully test their skills of manipulation.

How Manipulation is Started and its Roots

Since the beginning of human society, we have been seeking approval of others. We are asked to be nice to others and always think about the good of others. This behavior creates a certain level of vulnerability in people's personalities. A constant search for approval makes us a perfect victim for manipulators.

The roots of manipulation go deep in our nature to seek approval. The moment you give too much importance to another's point of view about your personality, your mind becomes vulnerable. You start collecting judgments about yourself and create self-hatred in your mind. These things are happening in your mind, even if you don't realize it because "seeking approval" is the basic reason why you feel stressed about everything in your life. One bad outfit choice becomes a matter of embarrassment for you. One bad picture of yours on social media scares you to death. Similarly, there are hundreds of scenarios when you overreact, when you shouldn't.

Social media platforms are a perfect example of how people are hungry for attention. Others' approval has become extremely important for us so if we don't get at least 500 likes on our picture, we aren't beautiful.

When living a life of self-doubt, one day someone appears and explains how amazing you are. This person can be your lover, your boss, or your friend as well. Now, you have finally found the approval you have been looking for since your childhood so you do everything to please that person. That is how a manipulator gains power over your personality.

Reasons Why People Seek Approval from Others

There are five major reasons why people seek approval from others:

1. Low confidence and self-esteem

Low confidence is majorly the result of a bad childhood. Regular criticism from parents, teachers and other elders create a case of self-doubt in a child's mind. This child grows with low confidence and suffers from a lack of self-esteem. All those childhood criticisms become a voice in this person's mind so the person keeps attacking his own abilities in his mind.

To conquer that constant voice of self-loathing, the person seeks approval from others. Such a person seeks approval from friends, family members, a spouse and professional colleagues. To obtain that, these people easily get manipulated and do things to fulfill other people's wishes. A father-son relationship can have this equation, where the father manipulates his son to get married. This is a personal decision for an individual, but a person with low esteem can allow his father to manipulate just to seek the family's approval.

2. Low life achievements

There are two kinds of achievements that a person can gain. One type satisfies the inner-self, while other achievements only satisfy the outer world. If a person is unhappy with his own life achievements, he or she turns towards others for approval. These people want others to tell them how great their life is. This tendency also subjects to getting manipulated.

3. Reduced personal performance

Some people work harder when their performance gets reduced; however, some people try to fill that space with false praise. People suffering from reduced performance in life, like to talk about their old achievements. They tell stories to others and self-praise. Plus, they desire praise from others as well. This sends clear signs of vulnerability to manipulators.

4. No personal fulfillment

People don't feel fulfilled with what they have. They want to present themselves as bigger than they actually are. Their achievements seem low to them, but they want people to approve that they are big in terms of career, beauty, financial state and other things.

Such people seek approval to justify their ego and attain fulfillment in life. This nature makes them a victim of manipulation too many times in their lives.

5. Too much stress

Stress can also be a reason for seeking approval. When life seems out of control, people want someone else to tell them that everything is going to be fine. Even if it is not true, they accept it as truth because their mind wants to get rid of the increased stress.

Most people argue that they are not vulnerable and they do not seek approval from others; however, most of us are trying to get recognized and making ourselves vulnerable in the process.

When you seek approval, manipulators come out to make you comfortable. They present themselves as a perfect solution to all your emotional and life issues. Approval seekers allow manipulators to paint an altered picture in which life has no dark colors. In return, you give your control over to that manipulator.

If you are not aware of your own emotional state, someone is going to take advantage of that. In fact, you should also listen to what others are saying and why they are saying that. Of course, manipulators do that too, but you are just trying to save yourself, instead of using others.

Understanding yourself and other people's behavior is the key to live without being manipulated. This takes us to our next chapter where you will learn how to understand your own psychology.

Chapter 2:
Why We Want To Know More About Ourselves

An examination of your inner-self:

Since childhood, Jennifer learned from her parents that expressing emotions is important. People love you more when they understand you better and, if a person is too rigid to express his or her emotions, it leads to loneliness.

This was the psychological conditioning that Jennifer went through all her childhood, but, as she grew up, her personality started becoming too vulnerable towards her surroundings.

Jennifer is a skilled content creator in an advertising company now, but her lack of confidence doesn't allow her to get recognition. This lack of confidence is not in her skill; instead, she shows emotional vulnerability where it is not required. She tends to apologize too much, even for small things. She worries whether people like her or not. In fact, she asks her colleagues if they like her. These behavioral traits are leading people away from her, which is completely opposite of what her parents told her.

A certain level of emotional vulnerability is good in relationships, but too much leaves you open for manipulation. Jennifer has lost many promotions to others and has faced bad relationship experiences in her 26 years of life.

Emotional vulnerability majorly comes from our psychological conditioning from childhood; however, some current scenarios can also trigger emotional vulnerability from time to time. It is your responsibility to notice that state.

Signs That Say You Are Emotionally Vulnerable

1. You fall in love too easily

Someone smiles at your joke and you create a love story in your mind. Some stranger opens a door for you and you begin your journey of love with that person. Simple acts of kindness and general affection makes you fall in love with a person.

You might be thinking that it is too much, "I don't fall in love so easily," but think about all those times when simple things made you fall for a person.

Love is a connection you feel after a long period of emotional bonding; however, emotionally, vulnerable people get triggered by simple acts. If this happens to you too often, then you should sit and think about your emotional state.

Such vulnerability usually occurs when you have just gone through a rough break-up. Your heart looks for a rebound to revive its state of happiness; however, a wrong partner selection does nothing but hurt you more. You can find a stranger attractive in a single glance, but don't let your heart get emotionally attached without a strong bonding.

2. You don't have any emotional shareholder

Think of your mind as a company, and emotions as shares of that company. If you give that share to everyone, it reduces the strength of your company but, at the same time, handling all those shares alone can become difficult.

When emotions stay collected in your mind and you don't share them, it creates emotional vulnerability. Your problems become the driving force in your life as they guide you. With that comes the need for social approval from everyone.

If you don't share your problems with anyone, that would be a red alert sign. You aren't opening up, even when others share their problems. Of course, you need to stay away from manipulators, but find at least one person who is genuine and ready to listen. Even talking about your problems with the right person can resolve the issue, but make sure you choose a genuine person to share with and not a manipulator.

3. You do everything to hold people in your life

Even if others treat you bad, you want them to stay around you. For that, you do everything that they ask and everything that you might think they would like. This process exhausts you emotionally, but still, you don't find the strength to let people go.

Every relationship in your life is worth the fight if it is a good relationship, but when you allow people to treat you bad and use you in every possible way it shows your emotional vulnerability. This emotional state is not usually in your control. You stay aware that the other person doesn't deserve your attention, but you feel helpless.

4. You're always the first one to say "sorry"

If 10 people make a mistake, you come out first to apologize, even when you are not one of those ten people. You apologize after every third statement and feel sorry for very small things.

Low self-esteem and self-doubt meet an approval-seeking behavior in this kind of vulnerability. You don't feel that you deserve anything, and you apologize to stay on the good books of people around you. Even a stranger's point of view matters to you. If a stranger's bike hits your car, you come out to apologize first without even expecting an apology from the other person.

5. You're suspicious that people don't like you

Self-doubt can make you doubt other people's affection towards you. You start questioning the affection of a friend who has been with you since childhood. You not only think like this, but also vocalize your thoughts many times.

In your office, family gatherings and normal meetings, you keep throwing a question around, "I don't know if he/she really likes me." This gives a chance to a manipulator to confirm your suspicions and become your sole friend.

Liking yourself is the most important affection you need. If you feel satisfied with your inner-self, other people will like you automatically. In fact, seeking approval can create issues in your relationships. People who actually like you might feel offended because you question their affection again and again.

Just do good, be good, and forget about whether people like you or not!

6. Every relationship break gives you the same amount of pain

Whether a crush doesn't reply to your text, or your partner cheats on you, both are the same in terms of pain for you. No matter how strong or new a relationship is, you feel crushed when someone hurts. Even if a professional colleague doesn't return your call, you feel disrespected and denied.

These extreme emotions make you vulnerable. Any manipulator can satisfy your emotions and get control over your personality. A manipulator can feed lies and easily make you isolated from other relationships.

7. Loved ones decide how you feel today

Your moods are not in your control. You feel happy only if your loved ones feel happy. If they feel sad, your mood becomes gloomy for the whole day. Of course, it shows your love for people around you, but the sudden switch of mood also means that you are vulnerable and easily manipulated by other people's emotions. If a manipulator enters your life as a partner, a boss or a loved one, you will easily give away your emotional control to them.

8. You cry alone

The whole day goes fine, you go out with your friends, have fun, smile, laugh, and come back home, and then a glass falls and you start crying. A sad song has the capacity to switch your happy mood to a gloomy emotion, and then you cry as if the world has fallen apart.

This state of mind is extremely critical because you aren't aware of this vulnerability. You live as two personalities, and the sorrowful personality comes out only when you are alone, and it is so intense that you have no control over it so you start looking for someone who can control your heart for you. That is what leads to manipulation in some cases. If you are lucky, you get an angel or a prince charming with a bright heart. If not so lucky, you end up giving your emotional control to a devil in disguise.

There is no shame in accepting your vulnerability. In fact, it empowers you as a person and allows you to become a better version of yourself. You don't just think extremely about "love and hate." Your mind finds a grey area where some people and relationships can exist. You trust yourself and love your own personality. Other people's judgments become a second priority. This is the first step towards diminishing your approval- seeking behavior.

Difference between being "Nice" and being "Manipulated"

Aren't we always advised to be nice to others? Should we stop being nice if people are out there to manipulate our niceness?

NO. That's not right; however, there is a difference between being nice and being manipulated.

Some people CHOOSE to be nice, while others are nice inherently. A person who chooses to be nice has control over his or her niceness. He or she can be nice to the genuine people only and save themselves from being manipulated.

On the other hand, people, who are inherently nice, become vulnerable in front of a manipulator. They don't have control over their nice behavior, which leads to manipulation many times. Just because you don't say no to work, you get more work than other people in your office. The boss is always on your head with unimaginable deadlines.

It all leads back to the conditioning that you gained from your parents and school. Our teachers and parents forget to tell us about the "choice of being nice," and that skipped chapter creates vulnerability in our lives.

Let's consider a scenario:

One day, Victor went shopping for groceries from the supermarket. There was a long line in front of the checkout. Victor was behind three people and a little girl was behind him.

When Victor reached the counter, he allowed the little girl to buy her candies before him. The girl bought and left but, just after that, a woman, with three children, crosses Victor saying, "I am in a hurry, please."

Now, Victor has two choices. He can allow that lady to cut him and buy her items first, or stop her.

If Victor is inherently nice, he would let the lady buy first, but that would allow others to cut him in the line too. However, if Victor is someone who chooses to be nice, he will notice that this lady has seen him as a potential victim because of the earlier scenario with the little girl.

We all come across thousands of scenarios like this when our visible niceness makes us a potential victim for manipulators. You can choose not to allow those people to use your niceness to their advantage.

Reasons Why "Being Too Nice" is a Wrong Choice

1. You come across as a weak personality

"Oh! You're a nice guy, you won't say no." People assume that you would do everything they ask in advance. This is the biggest hazard of being too nice to others. Whenever there is a problem, people burden you with that problem without even asking whether you need that problem or not. Your responsibilities are yours, and others' responsibilities are yours as well.

You say "yes" to help a person twice, and he will hand over the responsibility the third time with complete confidence that you are available at his or her service. People stop caring about your personal responsibilities, your time, and even your emotional state. They think you are weak because you never say no to anyone, and that leads to manipulation and exploitation of your niceness.

2. Some wrong people get attracted to you

Be too nice and get ready for "not so nice" people in your life. This is the harsh reality of real life. Even people, who hide their whiny, angry and bad sides, force all those emotions towards a nice person. In a way, your niceness allows the bad side of others to come out and attack you.

People, who are too nice, find themselves around manipulators very often. People start demanding things from you, instead of requesting. They control your moves and shift your actions as they please. This happens anywhere you go. Unlike manipulation, niceness becomes visible easily. Your family, your partner, your colleagues and even strangers give you a hard time.

3. You forget to appreciate yourself

You have an appointment with your doctor, but your boss wants you to manage a meeting for him.

Or, you want to relax this weekend, but your friend has asked you to fix his bike.

Others become a priority when you are too nice. You don't know how to say no because he is your boss, or she is your friend. But guess what? You have been with yourself since the day you were born, but nice people forget that and give their life to others.

Forgetting yourself in an act of niceness makes you a perfect victim of manipulation. People think of you whenever they need something, and forget the moment you do that thing for them. This leaves you hurt, but mostly your niceness doesn't allow you to learn anything from bad experiences.

4. People stop taking you seriously

When you say nothing but "yes" to everything, your point of view becomes useless to others. You are never disappointed at anything, so your children or colleagues don't ask for your opinion on anything. You never push back; hence, your own projects are completed with your juniors' inputs. You lose your perspective on things, or at least don't find the right way to express those perspectives.

There is no nice way to say that something is wrong; hence, people with too much niceness fail to create an impact on their surroundings, whether it is their household or workspace.

5. People think you are fake

Too much niceness makes your personality suspicious to others. People think that you are faking and your real side is not so nice. This creates a sense of distrust, which leads people away. That is why nice people don't get promotions or find a leading spot in projects. People in your life stop trusting you with important information. They think you are going to use them in some way, while you are the one being manipulated constantly.

Manipulators around you can trigger rumors about your niceness. They can turn your niceness into an evil thing and take advantage of that. As people feel strangely about your niceness, convincing them is never difficult that you are faking it all.

6. You are unable to give tough love

People who are too nice never thrive in a leading position. As a father, a team leader or a boss, such people feel unable to perform.

You can't be nice to your people all the time. Sometimes, they need tough love to grow and become better, but a nice person doesn't know how to project that tough love. Pushing your staff to complete a project, or asking your kid to work harder on his skills, requires a little roughness. It should be a perfect balance of niceness, logic and toughness that motivates people. Without this combination, you can't act as a leader.

Saying, "Please, sit down son, it might make you angry" won't work at all. Your son would know that you expect him to get angry when you talk. Also, you can't talk in circles and try to find a nice way to say the honest thing. Sometimes, ripping off the bandage is the right way to make others realize that you exist. Even if the ripping might take off a little skin with it.

Why Do Nice People Feel Angry So Often?

The thought behind being nice is that you receive happiness in return, but that happiness doesn't come to you very often. If you are nice enough to let manipulators control you, it results in anger and regret.

Nice people feel happy during an act of kindness but then they realize that they were being manipulated. The end feeling is anger towards the manipulator, as well as oneself. This only happens when your niceness is blinded by the tactics of manipulators.

Your goal should be to be nice without falling into the trap of a manipulator. Only then, you can stay happy and avoid anger.

Manipulators love when they see certain traits in a person. They carefully choose their targets who are vulnerable and too nice.

Everyone has doubts, fears, wishes, gratitude, hopes, love and other feelings, but the vulnerable personalities are the ones that don't know about their own emotional and psychological conditions. Manipulators observe that and try to manipulate their victims.

You don't have to become an unsympathetic or senseless person to avoid manipulation; simply understand your inner-self before a manipulator does.

Here are 10 traits that manipulators love to exploit:

1. Fear of "looking like a loser"

If you have a strong fear of looking like a loser, manipulators would love to exploit this fear sometimes for an advantage, but many times just for fun. Manipulators love to play with insecurity in order to satisfy their own ego. They want to feel powerful and find exploitation exciting. Remember all those situations when your friends provoked you to do something you didn't want to do. You face such manipulators in school, college and at a professional level as well. Even some family members can exploit your fear and insecurities to have fun.

Whenever you feel scared of looking like a loser, stop and think. First of all, think about whether you actually want to do that thing or not. If yes, then think about whether you want to do it right there and then. We all give ourselves some adventurous tasks in life, but everything has a right place and a right time. You shouldn't just have your first drink because your friends are provoking you. Even if you want to do it, decide a safe time and choose a safe environment to do it. Never take a risk just because someone else wants you to. Confidently say no, and tell them when you would do that thing. Expect them to understand if they are friends as manipulators are there to just provoke you.

2. Feeling of guilt

Guilt is probably the most favorite trait that a manipulator wants to see in a target. If you are suffering from guilt, you tend to do every possible thing to get rid of that feeling. Manipulators impose guilt on their vulnerable targets to play with their emotions. Once you accept that you are guilty of something, they use that guilt to make you do things for them. This happens even when you haven't done anything wrong. You see, some people have a tendency to feel guilty about everything. They are ready to apologize for everything, as mentioned earlier. This trait attracts and draws a manipulator toward you.

When feeling guilty, question your guilt before acting. Are you guilty enough to feel that bad? Even if it is true, you can apologize with all your heart, but don't follow instructions of another person who might be controlling your guilt. If a person points out why you should be feeling guiltier, he or she is not there to help you. Manipulators highlight the extreme consequences of your actions and constantly tell you to feel guilty. You can't predict another's emotional reaction to your actions. You can just try to be as good as possible so don't be too hard on yourself and stay away from people who impose guilt on you for no reason.

3. Fear of "rejection"

When you hear your parents say, "I will love you as long as you get good grades," it creates a fear of rejection in your mind. You grow up with that same feeling and feel the pressure of performing every single second to gain acceptance from people around you. A teacher, a friend or others around us can induce the feeling of rejection in us, and then manipulators appear in the form of a partner, a boss or a friend to exploit this fear. A manipulative lover can ask a lot of things in return for staying in a relationship with you. This exploitation can be related to money, emotions or other elements.

You are not on this planet to provide your endless service to others. Your life is your first priority and I am not saying that in a selfish way and others come after that. You need to fulfill yourself on an emotional level before giving something to others, and if people around you are trying to gain something in return of their affection, they don't deserve you. An emotional attachment has to be selfless and mutual. It is not a business exchange and, if it is, then you have to get out of those relationships. Love needs nothing but love in return, so don't let anyone make you feel rejected, because no one can.

4. Sense of responsibility

We all have some responsibilities in our lives. Most people understand their responsibilities and fulfill them casually; however, there are people who are driven by their sense of being responsible. They feel a duty towards their family, friends, company, society, roads, shops, dogs and so on. Everything is their responsibility to fulfill. A manipulator sees such people as an opportunity. Close relatives, friends, and colleagues use such people to get what they want. Such people are the most vulnerable to manipulation. Anyone can play the "duty card" and manipulate such people successfully.

Completing your duties are important, but those duties should be yours. If others are creating duties and putting a burden on your shoulder, you need to evaluate your behavior. Turning down your close friend or boss can seem difficult; so you need to ensure that you don't go overboard and harm yourself in the process. Find a balance and prioritize which responsibilities are necessary. Don't just say yes to a transfer because your boss wants you to do so. Think about your personal growth and future plans first. Similarly, it is not your responsibility to pay for your partner's expensive shopping lists. Find a middle ground of responsibilities.

5. Pity and kindness

Do you have compassion and kindness? Some manipulative fellows are out there to use your emotions to their advantage. These manipulators exaggerate their situations to gain your attention. Usually, their conditions are as normal as others, but they ensure that you look at them with pity. These fellows are in your family and in your friend circle as well. You can even find such people in your office. The moment you show pity towards them, they don't miss to ask for what they need from you, and you end up helping someone who doesn't require your compassion.

You need to learn to control your kindness as well. Use kind words instead of helping a manipulator. If you sense that the person is trying to impose something on you, reply with a compliment, "You are talented enough to come out of this crisis." This way, you will stop manipulators from exploiting your kindness.

6. Gratitude

A manipulator plans strategically to use your gratitude for their benefit. A manipulative friend will help you with 500 bucks and ask for 10,000 bucks as help. If you say, "I am short on money these days," he would remind you about the 500 bucks he gave you without even thinking twice. You can't say that it was only 500 bucks. To that, he would question your friendship. Some manipulators consciously create such complicated environments to ask for a big help by reminding you about their small act of kindness. Also, there are people who do this without knowing.

If there wasn't a previous contract, you are not obliged to return the favor. You can help as much as convenient for you, but don't react to the unfair manipulation and let someone use you because of their old favor. Politely counter people who remind you about their favors and explain that you are ready to offer as much help as convenient.

7. Shame

People feel ashamed when their actions don't match the fundamentals of life and society. If publically exploited, the feeling of shame is easily manipulated. For instance, if you question before donating money to a charity, the manipulators can induce the feeling of shame by saying, "You should feel ashamed of your heartlessness." Any person would try to avoid this feeling; hence, you end up being manipulated and used in the process of saving yourself from shameful feelings.

When you make a mistake, it induces the feeling of shame. You can apologize for that and move on, but the wrong situation occurs when someone is constantly trying to induce shame in you. If some other person has certain expectations that you can't meet, it is not shameful at all. If you let it affect you, manipulators will get complete control over your actions. This can lead to some bad scenarios that leave you angry and regretful.

8. Feeling of loneliness

Humans require socialization, but one should also find contentment when they are alone as well. Some people constantly fear that they will end up alone. This feeling attracts manipulators in your life. They know you would do everything for them to keep them so they start by creating a strong bond and finding an important place in your life. Then, the manipulation begins. It is common between a husband and wife, where one partner says, "No one would want you if I leave you." This statement is a constant reminder that a manipulator gives you so that you stay afraid of loneliness.

To avoid such situations, you have to have faith in yourself. Love yourself before loving others and give respect to your own personality. If you can successfully do that, no manipulator would dare scare you.

Chapter 3:
Doing This One Thing Can Literally Save Your Life!

Travelers, writers, and artists talk intellectually about life and people. How do they do that?

A person who spends a lot of time in isolation becomes self-aware, and that self-awareness allows that person to understand how other people think, behave and react.

However, you don't have to isolate yourself in order to become self-aware. Taking correct steps in your daily life can allow you to explore your inner-self conveniently.

Why Do You Need To Become Self-Aware?

Forget about manipulators for a while, self-awareness is meaningful no matter whether you have manipulators in your life or not. A comprehensive understanding of your own personality helps you point out your weaknesses and strengths. You keep stirring your thoughts and emotions and modify your beliefs in the process.

In life, all our actions are motivated by our inner personality and beliefs. Knowing the reasons behind every action can allow you to assess before making any decision. That is what leads to success and personal contentment in life.

Self-awareness also makes you capable of learning other people's perceptions. You can detect the reasons behind their actions and words and decide your actions carefully. It all can seem like a formula, but, with practice, it becomes your lifestyle. Knowing others' perception is not like what manipulators do. You are not trying to use people's emotions to your advantage. In fact, you are able to assess others' emotions and try to help them with no bad intentions. That is the difference between a manipulator and a self-aware person.

The irony is that everyone thinks they have achieved self-awareness completely. If you ask any person, he or she will accept that they know their behavior completely, but self-awareness is not just about knowing your behavior. It is about knowing why you are behaving that way and what beliefs are motivating you to behave that way. A self-aware person knows his or her wrong beliefs and tries to diminish them in a gradual process. A self-aware person knows which emotions are harming his or her life. That is how one can begin to change and find one's best version.

The process of developing self-awareness helps you understand new and better interpretations of personal thoughts. You find out that your mental state was creating your thoughts and developing emotions. You develop enhanced emotional intelligence and stop allowing emotions to control your actions. This control over emotions saves you from handing over the control to a manipulator; however, it is important to remember that self-awareness is a gradual process. You can't think that one day of practice is enough to achieve mastery over your emotions. You have to pick emotions one-by-one and understand how strongly they define your personality. Some people are driven by love, while the sense of responsibility motivates others. All these factors require an in-depth assessment.

Every emotion, thought or behavior leads to a pre-decided path. You have to know which emotions or thoughts will lead you in a wrong direction. For instance, if you know that your sense of gratitude will make you vulnerable to manipulation, you can work to save yourself from the false flattery.

You can become immune to manipulation only by knowing your inner-self. The person living inside you requires a master. Either you can become that master, or a manipulator will appear in your life to take that place. Self-awareness is the course that you need to master your inner-self. Plus, you can focus your mental and emotional energy towards things that lead to a better future. You start reacting to things that actually matter, instead of getting affected by everything and everyone around you.

And finally, all your efforts help you love and believe in yourself. You know that you can win anything in your life just by focusing your inner energy towards it. This improves self-confidence and self-respect in a person, which is exactly what you need to avoid manipulation.

Top 10 Ways to Increase Self-Awareness

First of all, you should accept that there is no one-time formula to become self-aware. You can't take one pill and become aware of all your emotions, thoughts and motivations. It is a continuous exercise. The more vulnerable you are, the deeper you have to dig in order to find issues and resolve. People, who are vulnerable emotionally, usually hide some dark experiences deep in their mind. The way you were raised and the experiences you have received until now, all decide the work you need to do in order to become self-aware.

If you do it regularly, a self-aware lifestyle becomes automatic.

Here are 10 valuable steps that will help you exercise and make self-awareness your lifestyle:

1. Evaluate your motivations

Our motivations allow us to set our goals and work towards it to achieve that goal; however, you don't reach every goal that you feel motivated about.

It is time that you understand your motivations and how they drive your life. First, in a diary, write down two goals that you decided and achieved in the past. These goals should be dearest to you. Only then, you would become able to evaluate them properly. For each goal achieved, ask the following questions to yourself:

- Why did you want to achieve that goal?
- Which reasons helped you reach that goal?
- How easy or difficult was the work for you to reach that goal?
- Why do you still remember that goal?

Write down answers to these questions for both the goals you have achieved in your life. After that, you can move to two goals that you HAVEN'T REACHED yet and feel disappointed about. For each failure, ask the following questions to yourself:

- Why did you choose that goal?
- What reasons were out of your control that stopped you from achieving that goal?
- Were there some things you could do to control the situations better?
- How easy or difficult was the work when you were trying?
- What are the things you missed in life, giving your time to that goal?
- Why do you feel disappointed and how much?

After answering these questions, you can compare your achievements and failures. Try to find similarities in your motivations, and also, look at the differences between motivations. This way, you will know why you won sometimes and failed in a few things in your life.

Remember, these goals are not limited to career or education. You can include monetary, fitness, personal, love and other life goals and evaluate your motivations. This evaluation will help you understand why a relationship didn't work and your mistakes that led to the destruction of a relationship.

2. Become the only friend you need

It is good to have friends in life. A beautiful friendship nourishes our mental state and allows us to grow as a person, but you can't keep waiting for a genuine friend to appear one day and sort all your emotional problems. Instead, you should become your own friend and attain a bonding with your inner-self.

To do that, you need to start by noticing how much time you spend with yourself. Spending time with yourself means that you sit alone and stir your thoughts and have a conversation in your own head. It might seem a little crazy, but thought-stirring is an important task to understand your mind.

Make a list of independent decisions. In life, you make thousands of decisions including the big ones and the small ones, and most people get affected by others' thought process while making decisions. Of course, people's suggestions help us choose the right things in life, but if all your decisions are based on what others say, then it is a bad sign.

There should be a few decisions that you make on your own.

To test yourself, you should make a list including all those decisions that you have made independently. If you want to start small, list all the small or big decisions you have made this week on your own.

If the number of independent decisions is low, then you need to work towards it and become more self-dependent.

Make a list of things you do alone: Listening to music, exercise, reading, writing, or any other activity; doing things alone is not about physical loneliness. You should be able to do things and enjoy them even if no other person is taking part in it. In fact, you should deliberately create such scenarios in order to spend time with your inner-self. Making this list will allow you to know how independent you are. If you only go out if your friends say yes, then you need to make some changes. Why not go out for a walk or a long drive alone? These activities will get you closer to your inner-self.

Give yourself 30 minutes every day: Give at least 15 minutes when no thought from the outer world can enter your mind. Don't even listen to music, those are also outer thoughts. You need things that allow you to manufacturer and stir thoughts in your mind. You can go for a nature walk near your place, meditate, or do something creative alone. Every day, you hear millions of things and it all keeps you outside of your mind but, when you are alone, outer thoughts start fading away slowly and you meet the true thoughts of your inner-self. That is what you need to achieve every day.

3. Write problems your inner-self has with the outer world

All your problems in life begin when your inner-self is not in sync with the outer world. You can also say that your surrounding can bury your inner-self, while you pretend on the outside to be a happy person. It is important to find and evaluate those problems.

When you said "yes," instead of "no": In our everyday life, we tend to say "yes" to people, even when we desire to say "no." This is how the problems begin. Your inner-self knows when you should say "no," but your sense of fear, responsibility, affection, pity and other things don't allow you that so you end up doing things that you really don't want to do. Now, you need to make a list of such situations and audit your problems. Start with the previous week and write all the situations when you said "yes." See if you really wanted to say that or if it was imposed on you. Also, figure out which emotions led you to say "yes" forcefully.

Outer elements that you don't like: There are places, media, activities, and people in everyone's life. Some elements excite us and offer pleasure, while others make us feel negative, exhausted or bored. Make a list of all those elements and start eliminating them from your life one-by-one.

Elimination of negative elements is not about going away from them. If you can, it's awesome! However, you can't go away from a negative office environment or leave a close person in your life. The idea of elimination is to not allow those people, activities or places to harm your inner-self. You can stop indulging your mind in the conversations you don't like. Make those elements a formality in your life without letting them impact you emotionally.

Set some boundaries: Decide a limit for all the negative things that you can handle. A boundary is a comfortable limit to which your inner-self can manage negative things without feeling disturbed. If your outer world crosses that boundary, immediate elimination is the only choice.

4. Talk to your emotions

In the realm of emotions, words are not the communication model, but your emotions talk to you. It is your own cognitive awareness that decides how well you understand them.

Differentiating emotions: The first step towards talking to your emotions is to identify them. This might seem easy when you are differentiating emotions such as "happiness" and "sadness." However, it becomes difficult for people to differentiate whether they are feeling "sad" or "overwhelmed."

Studies suggest that naming your emotions can help in understanding them so, instead of saying "I am scared," you can say "Mr. Scary has entered my brain." This would allow you to see emotions as a third-person and manage them effectively.

Understanding the language of your emotions: Every emotion tries to send a message. It is your self-awareness that allows you to decipher that message correctly.

So, what does sadness say to you?
Is it, "You are feeling the loss of something?"
Or, "This is what's extremely important to you!"
Similarly, what does fear tell you?
"You are a scaredy cat."
Or, "You need to concentrate while doing this."

Becoming an observer is what you need in order to talk to your emotions. Observe how emotions affect your body. Do you get all sweaty when afraid?! How does your heartbeat change with emotions? Observing the impact of emotions will allow you to dictate them.

5. Pay close attention to FEAR

Fear stops you from feeling positive, and any action caused due to fear never ends up right; however, "fear" as an emotion is not negative. It actually tells you to focus and concentrate when working, but people who aren't self-aware, misinterpret and lose control due to fear.

The emotion "fear" includes every thought that comes to your mind due to outer scenarios. Sometimes, fear is imposed by others as well so it is your responsibility to not let your inner-voice get corrupted.

To do so, you need to understand the pattern of fear. Every individual reacts with a sense of fear towards different things. Someone can feel afraid to argue with his or her partner due to the "fear of rejection." Another person can do everything asked due to the "fear of shame."

You can understand your fear better by answering these questions:

- What negative thoughts come to your mind every day?
- Which situations do you hate the most and want to avoid in your everyday life?
- What activities, things, places or people help you calm down?

These questions will allow you to understand the elements that trigger fear in your life. You will also understand the elements that help you remove that sense of fear. With that, you can try cultivating similar habits and qualities in yourself to calm yourself down on your own.

Practice affirmations: In this case, affirmations are the sentences that you say out loud to fight your fears.

For example:
If you feel afraid of something that hasn't happened yet: "I live in the NOW; the time is 'Right NOW'."
If you are afraid or worried of the result despite of your hard work:

"Practice today and enjoy success tomorrow. Success is inevitable because I am working in the present."

Similarly, you can create your own affirmations to make fear a motivational emotion. You can't get rid of fear, but these things will make fear a positive emotion.

6. Find a pattern in your behavior

You might not realize it, but your inner-self is following a pattern of behavior. Things that you learned as a child and the experiences you received growing up are still directing your present activities, perceptions and thoughts.

However, the human brain has the ability to evolve. The genetics aren't everything. Your brain uses new experiences to change your behavior regularly, but those evolutions have a certain limit depending on your core conditioning. If you can understand your behavioral patterns, it will give you the control over your thought and perception evolution.

To do that:

List your childhood lessons: Your parents, teachers and friends teach you a lot about life, relationships, work, ethics and success. Some teachings become our core ideas that drive us the whole life. You need to write all those lessons from your childhood, which you still remember. It doesn't matter whether you still follow them or not. Just include every lesson that you learned as a child.

Separate lessons that helped you: In a new list, you can include all those childhood lessons that you still follow. For instance, you still think that success is defined by a person's inner satisfaction and his ability to protect his or her loved ones. Similarly, you will find many other lessons from childhood that still influence you in a positive way and allow you to shape your present and future.

Separate lessons didn't help you: Make another list with all the childhood lessons that didn't help you at all. They were memorable growing up, but you constantly encountered contradictory situations in life. For example, your mother told you to be nice to let other people be nice to you; however, bullies were still bullying you in school. You followed the teaching of niceness as a grown-up, but people kept using you to gain advantage. These are the lessons you need to work on. You have to refine your core conditioning according to the scenarios and people you encounter in your life.

It is difficult as a parent to teach every variation of every lesson to a child. The same problem was faced by your parents when you were a kid; hence, it is time that you modify your childhood lessons and prepare yourself for the world you live in.

7. Make time your personal asset

You can't become self-aware if you don't own your time. Some people run their own time, while others run with time.

When you start owning your time, you automatically realize that most of the activities in you are worth nothing. You have been doing things just to please others. You can keep doing it, but knowing would make you self-aware, for example, whether you are going out for a dinner because YOU WANT to, or it is just one of the activities that you are obliged to fulfill as a social animal. Noticing these things will allow you to balance how much you want to indulge your inner-self for that particular time period.

Find that HIGH time of the day: Every person feels at his or her peak of mental awareness once during a day. Some people feel self-aware in the morning, while others find their inner-self at night. You need to decide that time for yourself. Actually, you need to find that time for yourself, and then make sure that you choose something that you actually want to do during this time. If you like meditation, choose your HIGH time to do it. This way, you will gain the ownership of your time.

Balance your emotional involvement: Make a list of activities you regularly indulge in without actually wanting to, and then make a habit of controlling your emotional involvement during these times. This way, your inner-self will stay protected from the negative elements of the outer world.

8. Observe your mood swings

Mood swings are a cycle of emotions created by the storage of emotions you already have in mind. Even if you go into isolation, you will still experience rage, sorrow, pain, happiness, frustration and so on. These emotions feel random at a single glance, but they all are triggered by each other. For instance, you can feel happy while thinking about an old relationship, which leads to nostalgia, and then, nostalgia can lead to the sadness of not having that person in your life now.

When you live and interact in society, these mood swings occur frequently. You can feel sad for a few hours and become happy just because your crush said "hello" to you, or your boss praised you for the work you did.

The idea of self-awareness is to observe these changes. This way, you can handle negative moods such as frustration, being overwhelmed or sadness.

Whenever you experience a strong emotion, try connecting the dots. Observe elements and thoughts that have led to the current emotional state you are in. Regular practice will create an autopilot in your mind and you will know why you are feeling a certain way within seconds.

9. Recognize stimuli for recurring emotions

Some patterns of life keep bothering you emotionally which means that you react to the similar things in the same way. They happen again and again. For instance, you can fight on the same topic with your partner and feel a combination of emotions such as sadness, anger, gloominess, and fear.

There is a way you can control these situations better:
When….(stimulus)……….happens, I feel…….(emotions)……
In the place of "stimulus" and "emotions," you can fill the triggers and the reactions you feel. This practice is for negative things that happen regularly and you react the same way.

For example, you can write:
"When my partner laughs at me, I feel angry."

This activity will help you recognize your behavior that wasn't visible to you earlier.

10. Cultivate openness of thoughts

There are two kinds of thought exchanges you indulge in life.

The first exchange is when you pass your own thought to someone else. Passing a judgment such as, "How useless you are?" or, "What is wrong with you?" The thought from your mind reaches others. Now, such thought transfer doesn't just affect the receiver, you also get a thrill of superiority in your mind. A false sense of pride comes in your mind, which stops you from finding your inner-self.

The second type of exchange is when you receive other people's thoughts. Thoughts coming from the outside can make you feel offended, hurt, angry, happy, sad, bitter, jealous, and many other things. This second type also breaks the connection between you and your inner-self. That is how a manipulator gets a hold of your actions.

So, the idea is to cultivate a sense of openness in your thoughts. Don't let negative things hurt you too much, or allow good thoughts to take you on top of the moon. Try to stay as grounded as possible. Some folks achieve that through the daily practice of meditation. It helps to clear the mind, and give stunning clarity to your own thoughts and emotions.

How to Become Socially Aware

When you are self-aware, your social awareness improves automatically; however, you can still apply a few habits to enhance your social awareness:

1. Convey that you're listening

Do you really listen to people or just pretend to be listening? Good listeners actually hear and understand how the other person is feeling; however, you should also convey that you are listening. Sending an indirect proof of your interest in the conversation can enhance your social popularity.

How can you do that?
Repeat the person's statement before replying. You don't have to repeat every sentence that the other person says. Use this once or twice in a conversation to convey your interest in the conversation.

2. Evaluate the voice tone in an ongoing conversation

People can say the same sentence with many different emotions. One can say, "You are the best employee." However, the thought behind this can only be visible by the voice tone of that person. The statement can have a sense of pride or happiness, or it can have sarcasm in it. The same words can mean different things depending on the tone of the person's voice so focus on the tone before you believe someone.

3. Understand minor facial expressions

Facial expressions and body postures send indirect cues about the person's intentions. Even if the person is trying to control his or her voice tone, the facial expressions give it away. You just need to pay attention to those cues.

For example, if you ask your partner to discuss something, and he or she replies, "Yes dear, I am here to talk," but he or she hasn't looked at you and not even moved towards you, this says that your partner is not actually interested in listening to you.

Social awareness is a combination of social sensitivity, social communication, and social insight. With practice, you cultivate the skill to comprehend social situations at a fast pace. This helps in gathering social insights and using those insights when communicating with people. The same awareness allows you to detect when a manipulator tries to overpower you with his or her tactics. Now you have all the tools to become emotionally and socially intelligent. Make sure you practice them with determination until they become a part of your personality.

Chapter 4:
Workplace Manipulation and What You Can Do About It

You imagine a perfect office where people come singing happy songs and work together. Good guys spread their goodness with bright clothes on their body and a big smile on their face. Even the bad fellows of the office are visible due to their scary clothing and devil-like make-up.

Well, in a real-world office, nothing of this sort happens. You can act like a hero coming out of a Disney movie, but your co-workers won't act as open as you thought. There aren't any visible signs to acknowledge the bad guys in a real office.

You get welcomed with lots of smiles. Some of those smiling faces become your friends. You chat with them, they listen to you, in fact, "They get you." Your jokes are funny to them and you share your personal and professional insecurities with those people. However, you may find out in future that they were the ones digging holes in your way.

These people are dangerous in your professional life because they don't just do things for an ultimate goal. It is what they love. Ruining your life in the office gives them pleasure. At every step, you will find these people manipulate the scenarios and turn the spotlight of success towards themselves. They are not afraid to take risks and try everything to control your emotions and actions. If you surround yourself with such co-workers, they can even make you feel worthless.

So, if these manipulators are in every real-world office, how can we save ourselves from them? Is it inevitable for us to get into the trap of a sociopath and lose our dignity, self-esteem, and righteousness?

Let's try to find out how workplace manipulation works, and which techniques are used frequently:

Types of Workplace Manipulation

1. Boosting hope and confidence

"I have never seen such a smart professional like you. I will MAKE YOU the best employee here."

This is the very first manipulation that you go through when joining an office. Your team leader, your boss and other seniors try to include you in their groups. They want you to look up to them, so they can exploit your abilities to their advantage. You do a simple task like searching something on the internet and you are showered with compliments as if you are the Mark Zuckerberg of that office.

After the confidence boosting compliments, you receive messages from some godfathers of that office. Your talent is a tool for them to build their own career, so they give you hope of becoming better if you work under them and listen to what they say. Actually, these people either don't have enough talent or procrastinate too much, so their goal is always to use you to complete their own work.

When Sam joined his first PR company, his first day at the office went like this:

Team leader: "Well, Sam, I think you have the potential to go big here. This company has the scope of growth which is perfect for a qualified person like you."
Sam: "I hope so sir! I am looking forward to not just work, but learn from my work as well. Becoming better is my ultimate goal."
Team leader: "If that's your goal, you have found the right person. I am a hard taskmaster, but I promise you, if you work hard and do as I say, you will learn a lot."
Sam: "I am ready for any task you give me sir! I am all yours."
And, for the next 6 months, Sam worked on his team leader's projects. All this time, the team leader used to come to the office late and leave early. Even in the office, the team leader spent time gossiping and fooling around. The project got completed on time though as Sam was working hard and using his skills, but all the appreciation went to the team leader because Sam was new and not involved in the "office politics."

2. Flaw projection

"These mistakes have never been made in the history of mankind. How could you do such a thing?"

Manipulators hide their unproductivity or inefficiencies with flaw projection. They shift the blame somehow towards you so that their flaws stay hidden.

"This project is ruined because I believed in you and gave you complete control."

"I have made mistakes in the project because this project wasn't even for me in the first place. You don't have managing skills."

This blame game is very common in workplaces where unproductive people are trying to hide their worthlessness. The idea is to twist realities so that the manipulator shields his own faults by bringing the victim in the negative spotlight. All this time you try to figure out how it all became your fault, while the other person shifts the dirt from his shoulder to your shoulder.

3. Destroying your confidence

"You are doing great, but great isn't good enough."

A manipulator wants to keep hitting you and shaking your ground, but if you reach close to your expectations, it can make you confident so they also pull you down from time to time to destroy your confidence.

No matter how good you are, or how logical you sound, your thoughts and deeds will never get appreciated. Even if they do, the appreciation will come with a flaw.

You handle your home and work here as well. Wow, impressive!
But, isn't it easier for single people to manage work and home?
You live alone, right?
Oh! You have parents living with you.
Aren't you too old to live with your parents?
A married life builds character and teaches responsibility.
You shouldn't get married; otherwise, you will lose your professional focus.

These are the kind of conversations you can experience with a manipulator. They can define your whole personality by your marital status. Your hard work, qualifications, and success won't matter. This is the devilish power a manipulator can have over you.

4. Hurtful jokes and cruel sarcasm

"You took 5 hours to complete this evaluation. A blind child can do it better in half the time you spent."

Hurtful jokes and cruel sarcasm come your way when you are not suspecting them. In fact, you expect praise or at least someone to notice your effort; however, a manipulator uses such opportunities to look cleverer than you and make you look like a fool.

Generally, manipulators pass sarcastic comments when other people are present. Others laugh which validates the statement of the manipulator and ruins your moment of shining. Manipulators do it deliberately, while some people have a sarcastic nature, which they unconsciously use to destroy your ability to work in the office.

Have you prepared the presentation I asked this morning?
Oh! You have. Then, what are you waiting for, Christmas? Mail that presentation to my ID.
Have you ever sent an email to anyone? CC boss, boss' wife, Boss' servant, and Boss' dog. In fact, CC this whole office in the mail.

When such sarcastic comments are thrown your way, working gets difficult. You feel negative the moment you enter your office and that negative feeling doesn't allow you to stay productive or give your best while working.

5. Playing victim

"This whole office is against me. You are my only hope."

These are generally your team members and co-workers who play this card. You feel for these people because you actually see that they are being treated badly. Somehow, you are always around when these people are crying about their hard work not being paid. You know their problems and understand why they have not been able to complete the work. You pity them so much that you offer your service to help them out.

"My grandmother is in hospital. My parents are there, but my granny wants to see me only. Can you please finish this presentation for me, but don't send it to the boss, email it to me."

Guess what? You have fallen for this and now it is 7 in the evening and you are still in the office working. Plus, this hard work will not pay you anything. You would be lucky to get a thank you publicly. A *"thank you"* message will reach your mobile phone's inbox. That's it!

6. Covert threats

"You don't know what I am capable of in this office."

Covert threats start with small things, such as a harsh comment on your dressing sense, but, if you ignore it, these covert threats become more serious with time. You start hearing statements that start with "How dare you...," or, "Don't you listen..." and other cruel and threatening ways. Manipulators use their strong words and tone of voice to intimidate. Your boss and seniors can have this habit. They don't know how to respectfully treat juniors. Their behavior is polite when they are around their seniors but, with you, they behave like a dictator.

Threats begin in two major conditions. One is when you stay grounded and unaffected by all other methods of manipulation; then the manipulators decide to use language and other indirect ways to threaten you. They can threaten your job and even attack your whole career, but, generally, they attack your personal sensitivities.
Another condition is when you allow them to make threats. Not pointing out their harsh tone of voice is the biggest mistake an employee makes because, after a while, they use the same harsh voice tone every time you interact with them.

For instance, if you say, "Sir! Ms. Martha is calling you."
He might shout, "DON'T YOU HAVE ANY PATIENCE TO WAIT UNTIL I COMPLETE THIS WORK?"

And remember, no matter how hard you try to be perfect for them; these people will find something to shout about and threaten you with. In the process of trying to become better, you end up giving your emotional control over to these manipulating beasts.

7. Alternating your reality

"It is nothing but your imagination."

Making you question yourself is classic way manipulators try in an office. If you aren't confident about the things you see, feel or hear, you start depending on the manipulator to make decisions. A co-worker, a senior and even a junior can have this manipulative control over you. Anything that you say is turned into an imaginary reality of your own. This technique affects your personality, professional expertise and even your reputation in the office.

So what if I presented your project? I have done everything you asked. It is your own insecurity.

You might have already experienced many instances where people tried questioning your own realities. Make sure it doesn't happen anymore.

8. Irrelevant blaming

"If you do not give me this promotion, you're sexist."

For a manipulator, every office day is a mission in which he or she wants to conquer others and overpower them. Whether it is a simple conversation or a meeting, manipulators keep trying sabotaging your image, and irrelevant blaming is one of the many weapons they use. This technique is used to take an interaction to a whole new dimension.

For instance, if you are not ready to promote a female employee, you immediately become a feminist for this manipulator. The idea is to hit your sensitive side hard enough so you diverge from the actual motive of a conversation. The frustration hits and you start guarding yourself instead of presenting actual facts relevant to the conversation.

Stay in such an environment for long and you will lose your self-confidence. Your image will be twisted and your thoughts will become less important with time.

6 Different Kinds of Workplace Manipulators and How to Deal With Them

Manipulators make you doubt your senses and even ignore them. According to the manipulation technique used, there are 6 major types of workplace manipulators:

1. The drama creators

A drama creator has an over-the-top answer for everything you say. Such people in your office use exaggerations to manipulate your emotions. If you question such a manager about his bad performance in a project, the answer would be, "I have given my blood for this company all these years, and now you have the audacity to question my judgment." During all this, you think how to counter his "blood" argument. This leads to a retreat and you try to stay away from the person; hence, the manipulator gets away with anything he or she wants to do.

These drama creators are also there when you are not even trying to interrupt their way. If you ask such a manipulative boss, "I have a vacation plan with my family next week." The answer can be, "Yes! This company needs to work around your plans."

How to deal: To deal with such drama creators, you need factual intelligence. Always follow and present facts whenever talking to these people.

For example:
If your boss says, "This company doesn't work according to your personal plans."
You can say, "When joining, I was given the right to have vacations if I apply in advance."

Don't apologize if you are not on the wrong side of the conversation. This will allow the manipulator to cave you further. Any time a manipulator tries to exaggerate a situation, bring them back to the normal scenario with factual arguments.

For instance:
"You don't trust my 10 years of experience in this company."
You can reply:
"I do trust information that surrounds this project right now."

Do not engage by confirming the manipulator's hard work for the company. It might be true that the person has given many years to that company, but it is not relevant if he or she is not able to perform in a particular position.
Apart from this one scenario, you can get exposed to various drama creators in everyday work. Notice the signs and bring the dramatist to the factual level of conversation.

2. The distorter

These are probably the most common yet dangerous manipulators you might find in your workplace. They do not use emotions like drama creators. Distorted facts are their weapon of destruction. They gain information from all directions and become completely aware of everything going around. Then, they start leaking information and facts in a controlled manner to ensure you perceive what they want.
In a nutshell, the distorters are out there to mislead you by altering the reality you see. Mispresenting a scenario allows these manipulators to control your actions and decisions.

A colleague can tell you, *"I heard how our team leader was talking to the boss about you. I don't think he likes you."*
Or, a junior can tell you, *"Have you been going to a shrink? They don't say, but people are questioning your capabilities in this office. I think you should do something about it."*

Similarly, there are many situations when these manipulators merge their toxic thought with a fact, to destroy your ability to think correctly.

How many times have you delayed your business decisions because a subordinate promised you a big deal? A few distorted pieces of information felt as if the sales team is about to gain a big deal so you decided to wait for six months and allowed this time for the sales head. In the end, it was nothing but a tactic to overcome the shortfall in sales.

How to deal: A distorter gains comprehensive information and then distorts it so, to save yourself; you need to gain comprehensive information as well. Stop following what people say and conduct research on your own. Whether it is something work related or something related to your reputation in the office. Always be on top of everything. Verify facts before taking any action.
If a person gives you information even when you don't ask, find the real intentions. That person can be your well-wisher or a manipulator who just wants to persuade and use you. An intense inquiry is the only way to save yourself from such manipulators. Using multiple sources will help you find

the loopholes in the manipulator's information, and then you can figure out who is the distorter in your workplace.

3. The attention diverter

This manipulator has the capability to shift an ongoing conversation according to his or her priorities. If a topic threatens to shine his or her faults, the manipulator smoothly changes the topic. These people are skilled in making irrelevant things seem relevant.

"I found some mistakes in the budget report you sent last week."
To this, a diverter can say, *"Man! The whole country is finding mistakes in the budget these days. Anyway, I'll get back to you."*

If you respond to their conversation diverting statements, these people can easily get out of any situation. As a result, you can face failure in your job and end up with bad consequences.

The attention diverter also knows about you. These people read your emotions and habits, so they learn how to divert your attention to other scenarios. They would know if you feel conscious about your reputation in the workplace or how seriously you handle your duties. They can use your personality traits or insecurities to their advantage.

How to deal: Your insecurities are your own and your emotions stay with you. However, it is up to you how much you allow other people to see those habits and emotions. Whenever you find someone trying to divert your attention, call out. Insist and force the conversation to stay relevant and talk about the real problems at hand.

You need to learn to concentrate whenever your mind feels insecure in a conversation. The diverter shouldn't get the chance to take your mind away from the actual topic.

For example, you can say:
"Don't change the topic. I want to finish this issue first."

You can use a mild tone or a harsh one when saying this, depending on the situation. Some manipulators require a minor sign to understand that you are not ready to be manipulated; however, others might require a strong repel from you in order back down.

4. The defamer

A person who is ready to put his or her faults on others comes under this category. A defamer merges the capability of diversion and distortion to manipulate the blame towards others. Such a manipulator can even try to not understand something or deliberately confuse two things as one. With that, they put the blame on others in a subtle way.

A defamer, when asked about the faulty strategy, can say, "I followed the format and guidelines given to me." They present such a vague argument that you can't comprehend the blame game. They use their acquisitions as general information so your focus shifts towards other people who come under a cycle of a decision.

Every office and every activity goes from one hand to the other so defamers don't need to put much effort in to defame others.

"All my customer service related decisions depend on the instructions he/she gives me."

"I send emails straight to her, so it is her responsibility to inform me about the required changes in the work patterns."

These statements are commonly used by defamers who either don't understand their job or don't want to do it properly.

How to deal: You need patience and problem-solving skills. You have to learn to analyze the chain of command and find the right culprit. Also, start noticing whether a person is genuinely not able to reason or is just pretending. You need to break from the deception and avoid the blame without getting affected by lies or wrong facts or hurting others.

You can say:

"If they are at fault, you are too."

Convey that the blame game won't work with you at all, and if someone tries to defame your work or reputation, call them out. Let them know that you have complete control over your work. Confidence and straight-forward conversations are the best techniques to stop such manipulators.

5. The bully

Such a manipulator has an aggressive response to any question you ask, especially if you question their work. When discussing work methods and strategies, you see such manipulators shouting the most. Ask them about their shortcomings and you see aggressive actions.

When asked about the negative sales, a bullying manager might stand up and shout, "Look at the numbers before saying anything." This is just one scenario, but you can see such behavior in many cases. Even if you are polite when asking the question, a bully always responds in a harsh manner. Their goal is to ensure that you leave them alone and don't ask the same thing again. They want to intimidate you and catch you by surprise.

How to deal: You should always stand firm in front of aggressive reactions. Don't let a bully bluff you with their harsh behavior. Keep yourself calm and present a non-nonsense argument to prove your point. The manipulator will keep giving aggressive reactions for a while, but you have to stay direct and don't allow them to affect you.

Aggression in a workplace is conquerable if you remind yourself about the sense of duty. A bully feels strongly about his or her reputation so, if you say, "This is not the way to behave in a professional environment," or, "You are acting completely opposite from our work culture," then these things would allow you to overpower the manipulator's manipulation.

Bullies usually attack their juniors in a workplace. If you come across a similar situation, say, "I will not respond until you talk to me with respect." Steal the option of being aggressive from a bully. This way, they won't get control over your sensitivities.

6. The criticizer

Criticism's impact on a person depends on the scenario. Sometimes, criticism can induce growth and allow a professional to grow, but those criticisms aren't too direct. On the other hand, there are manipulators who use criticism to control your actions and behavior. The goal of a criticizer is not to improve your skills. In fact, he or she wants you to stay bad at your job so that they can keep criticizing you. These criticizers can attack you, even if you are good at your job. These people find something to make you feel inferior and reduce your self-esteem.

Using contempt, labels, and judgments, a criticizer questions your character and personality. They are usually very direct. "Criticism improves your performance." The manipulator hides behind this perception and says anything he or she wants to say.
As a result, such a manipulator makes you feel under-confident and ashamed.

How to deal: A manipulator will always have something to criticize you. It is your job to understand people in your office who are always ready to criticize you one way or the other. These people will come around you to criticize you. If you finish your report on time, they criticize you for the quality of work and say that you are too hasty and unfocused. It is always something or the other for them.

So, you need to stop taking them seriously, and then tell them, "I will accept this same criticism if you say it politely." Don't let them disrespect you. Also, allow relevant criticism only. Don't let manipulators talk about your personal habits or personal life in a criticizing manner. Remind them that they don't have any authority over your life.

All types of manipulators share one thing. They all stand in front of your inner-self and the outer world. They create false realities and play with your perceptions. You get fooled only if your inner-self is not in sync with you. Understand your emotional strengths and weaknesses. You need to train your mind and learn to own your emotions. With that, you can avoid getting manipulated by such manipulators.

Leaving your job is not a solution. All the above-mentioned manipulators are out there in every work environment. You will have to face them everywhere. In fact, it becomes difficult to understand manipulators in a new environment; hence, you should trust yourself and focus on getting stronger in terms of emotions and perceptions. Know how your inner-self works and hold the steering wheel in your hands. Don't allow another person to drive you crazy and let you act according to his or her ideas.

CHAPTER 5

Chapter 5:
Manipulation in Relationships and How to Avoid It

The first year of the relationship was like a dream come true for Teresa. Matt was everything she had ever dreamed of. They went for holidays together, and Matt even attended thanksgiving with Teresa's parents but, after that one year of a perfect relationship, things started to get a little difficult. Matt began to literally command Teresa for things. He asked for money, used her place for parties and stopped giving her attention. Every time Teresa refused for something, Matt fought and gave her the silent treatment for days. As Teresa wanted those old lovely days back, she tried everything possible to keep Matt happy.

It took another 2 years of a messy relationship for Teresa to realize one morning that she was under the control of Matt.

Manipulation in a relationship is a great issue for people, and it doesn't only happen in a partner relationship. A family member or a friend can also twist and control your emotions. These masters of manipulation ruin your ability to think, act and feel at your own will. You experience what they want you to experience and you act under their influence. You live in a false hope of achieving a perfect relationship with that person; hence, it takes a long time to realize that you are being manipulated.

To save you from such manipulations, you will find three separate evaluations of relationships here:

- Partner or love relationship
- Family relationship
- Friend's relationship

Let's begin with the first one!

Partner or Love Relationship Manipulation – How It Works and Things You Can Do

Manipulation is defined mostly as a deliberate action taken by people; however, in love relationships, people tend to manipulate each other unintentionally and intentionally as well. No matter what, manipulation in a partner relationship is always toxic for your mind and life.

Here are all the signs of a manipulative partner:

1. The territory advantage

Are you living your life or your partner's? A love relationship is about sharing your life, but manipulative partners tend to bring you into their life and disconnect you with your own life before the relationship.

Think about:
Do you live in your partner's apartment?
How many times do you go out to your favorite spots?
If your partner's friends are yours, then does your partner meet your friends too?

Taking you in their own surroundings allows manipulators to control you. As you don't understand that surrounding, you decide according to your partner's will.

For example, if you go to your partner's favorite restaurant, you would say, "You come here often, so pick what we should order." Such simple things slowly condition you to hand over your emotional and personality buttons to your partner.

How to save yourself: In the beginning, you don't know whether your partner is a manipulator or just shy to share your life, but you need to test him/her. Make your relationship a 50-50 exchange. Share elements of your partner's life, but also encourage him or her to do things which you like. Clarify that you are committed only if the relationship is equal and healthy.
For instance, if your partner asks to go to a restaurant, say, "Ok, we can go, but next week I will pick the restaurant and you can't say no or cancel the night." Follow a similar attitude of equality in all parts of your relationship.

2. Playing your sensitivities

How many times have you done something because your partner said, "I know you're kind enough to understand?"

Let's consider a scenario:
Suppose your partner wants to shop for a new designer dress or a bike, but he or she is short on money. The right way of asking for money would be requesting you and assuring that you will get the money back. If you explain the financial problems, a genuine partner would understand, but a manipulator won't care about your problems. They would try to twist your affection with something like, "Don't you love me enough to give me some money?" or, "What is more important, money or me? Let's clear this out today." This is a combination of love and force, to play your sensitivity and affection.

How to save yourself: First of all, allow your mind to feel that not following your partner's desires doesn't make you a bad or insensitive person.

Then, you should think of a balanced decision and come up with a reasonable alternative. For the given situation above, you can say, *"My love for you and my money are two different things. You know I would help you if it was possible right now."*
Replying this way, you would ensure that your sensitivities aren't clouding your decisions in a relationship.

3. Dramatic blackmailing

Blackmailing is the most common reason why a relationship turns unhealthy. You start hearing things like, "I will do something to myself if you don't come right now," or, you can hear, "I can't live a single day without you."

Blackmailing comprises a variety of manipulative tactics such as shame, guilt, and fear as well. A manipulative partner can deliberately get hurt and say, "Why weren't you there to save me?" You feel guilty and ashamed of your ignorance. All your attention goes to your partner and the relationship becomes your whole life.

Such a relationship does nothing but ruin your life. You become responsible towards your partner too much, which doesn't allow you to follow your own dreams or lifestyle.

How to save yourself: Such manipulators begin with simple blackmailing to condition your mind. If you promote the initial behavior, it can lead to extreme levels of blackmailing.

If you are already facing dramatic blackmailing, don't get scared. Instead, counter the person with a logical reply like, "If you try anything to harm yourself, I will call the police. We can go to a psychiatrist, but don't expect me to deal with this behavior." It might seem a cruel thing to say, but that's the only way to handle a dramatic manipulator.

4. Self-victimization

No matter how wrong your partner is, you are the one apologizing every single time. Does this happen to you whenever you fight with your partner?

If your partner doesn't apologize ever for anything, it's a sign. Such people always make you the culprit and become a victim on their own.
You are arguing, "How could you take my money without asking me?" But the answer will be, "You are shouting just for a few bucks. Why do you always find a way to hurt my feelings and ruin my day?"
So, the mistake of your partner vanishes and the topic moves to your reaction. You are the one who hurt and broke your partner's heart so it is your responsibility to apologize and you end up saying, "I am so sorry baby, I didn't mean to hurt you like that."

How to save yourself: Remember one thing! Apologize only after self-evaluating your mistake. Your partner can make you feel ashamed with self-victimization. You need to carefully assess those situations and don't let the bluff work on you.

If your partner complains about your raised voice or hurtful blames, politely reply, "I apologize for the way I reacted, but you should apologize too. What you have done is wrong on so many levels." Your partner might try to melt you with tears. Stay there to show your compassion without diverting from your point.

5. Toxic jokes

Manipulative partners criticize, hurt and then say, "I am just kidding. Stop making such a big scene." You feel like you are overreacting to something that means nothing, but that "fun" loving nature of your partner can be a manipulation. Public criticism is usually a way to get control over your behavior. Your partner can say, "Look how she dances," so you don't dance with anyone at that party. You can't react; otherwise, you will be ruining the party for everyone. Such manipulators don't stop from raising their voice if you reply anything.

The same manipulation technique is used privately as well. A manipulative partner learns your insecurities and then attacks them in private to win an argument or control your actions.

"Hello? Is it you or your mom talking? I have read those childhood things you have written in your diary."

How to save yourself: Taking a stand for yourself is a necessity. No matter how funny a comment is and who is making that comment, you should call it out. Stay humble, but make sure that the partner knows you don't appreciate such jokes.

You can say, *"Please don't make a comment like this ever. I don't find it funny at all."*
Call your partner out, *"Are you trying to make me feel bad?"*
"Then, stop saying such hurtful things."

If you shut the person immediately, they won't crack such toxic jokes in future. Or even if they still do, then you know where you stand with them and that makes it clearer on how to handle them.

6. Using society to sell you an idea
We all try to feel a part of a society. The society includes everyone you know outside your blood relations. Your partner can use society as a reference to convince you for something. Social obligations are one of the biggest responsibilities that people feel in their life. So, when your partner says, "Our friends go out for vacation at least twice every year," you think and feel obligated to do the same.

Similarly, your partner can say, "Every wife in our neighborhood has more than 10 designer dresses. You can give me at least 2." Such an argument makes two designer dresses seem logical. After all, others have more than 10 you know! Such manipulation is not always deliberate, but you should have the knowledge to notice it.

How to save yourself: Your partner is using references of others to convince you for things you won't allow otherwise. First of all, evaluate how many times you let such manipulation happen in your daily life. If it is once or twice in a long time, then there is no need to worry about it, but, if it happens very often, then it highlights two things: One is that your partner is trying to manipulate you in order to get things done, and the second is that you are vulnerable towards social obligations.

In order to save yourself, you need to modify how you see society. Control your inner-self and don't allow society to become a huge part of your decision-making process. With that, you will become capable of saying "no" to your partner on such obligations.

7. Neutralizing wrong behavior by giving untrue reasons

Alternative story creation is what this manipulation is all about. Your partner gets caught for doing something wrong, but, instead of apologizing, he or she might create a new story of lies in which those actions are justified. The story would be so believable that you would end up praising your partner for an intelligent action.

For instance, if your partner is caught cheating, he or she might say:
"You are not there anymore! Your work has become everything for you. I know you do it for us, but I am a human, and I desire attention."
"I hope you understand...."
"That was the only way possible..."
"Circumstances made me do it...."

That is how a partner tries to justify his or her behavior.
Even if you don't praise them, they try at least neutralizing their wrong behavior with distorted reasons. They create a reality in which circumstances made him or her do those wrong things.

How to save yourself: Your partner is either using lies or distorting the scenarios so you need to break the barrier of lies first. For that, you need to ask questions. Don't let one action justify another. You can say:

"If I was doing something wrong, you could have talked to me. Why didn't you?"
"Why didn't you explain things to me?"
"This, right here, is your entire fault. Don't try to put the blame on me."
"Why didn't you ask for my opinion on this? How am I supposed to understand this wrong behavior now?"

It is like a light interrogation, which cops do on culprits. If you question long enough, liars start spitting the truth because they can't keep up the same story format.

8. Passive aggression
Your partner agrees to something first but then the silence begins. An upset facial expression stays on all the time until you do as your partner desires. This is how passive aggression feels like.

Such manipulators stop talking or talk only a little to convey that they are upset. To avoid this, you end up agreeing with your partner. However, your partner would say, "You are doing this on your own. I have given my permission to you." The idea is to convince you without asking for it. A manipulative partner knows how much you love him/her but still, they don't want to seem demanding. Their passive aggression allows them to fight the fight.

Suppose your partner asked you to move in to live together. You discussed it and explained that you don't feel ready to move in at that stage. Your partner says, "It's completely fine," and things move on. However, suddenly, your calls are being ignored, and your partner is not available to meet. Even when you are together, your partner doesn't seem interested in being with you. It goes on until you propose the idea of moving in together on your own.

Just imagine, your partner didn't say a word directly, but convinced you to do what he/she wanted. That is how this manipulation tactic works.

How to save yourself: A partner, who constantly does this to you, doesn't deserve your love so control your heart first. Then, you can counter with something like, *"I am disappointed with your childish behavior. I know what you are trying to do and it won't work at all."*
Make your partner realize that your love doesn't make you a weak person. Stand up with compassion and confidence.
"I will be there for you always, but you have to respect my decisions if you really love me."

9. Active aggression

This manipulation is easily visible if it happens. You can see the aggression in their actions, voice, and expressions.

For instance, your partner asks you to make breakfast, but you say, "I don't feel like it." In return, you face an aggressive voice saying, "Don't ruin my day or I don't know what I'll do with you." So, you go and prepare the breakfast in order to avoid any fight. This motivates the manipulator to attack you with aggressive behavior more often. Whenever you aren't ready to do something or agree, your partner uses aggression to force those things on you.

This means behavior can even lead to something dangerous. Manipulators with narcissistic tendencies start hurting their partners physically if not stopped. Eventually, these things happen for no reason at all, just to showcase power and keep you under control.

How to save yourself: This part is a little tricky. If the manipulator is really aggressive, it would be wise to do as he or she says in the present, but you should find an escape eventually. If your partner hasn't reached the physical level of abuse, you can say "no" and show that you are not afraid of him/her.
The ultimate solution is to get out of such a relationship as quickly as possible. Find an escape and file complaints against physical abuse of any such kind.

Family relationship manipulation - how it works and things you can do

Wouldn't you feel surprised to find out that your loved ones are manipulating you? Manipulation in a partner relationship is common; however, people usually skip the sight of a manipulative father, mother, brother or a sister as well.

The desire to control one another drives family members to manipulate each other with physical, mental, emotional and even sexual abuse. A family member with a manipulative nature and a false sense of pride tries to rule the home like his or her own kingdom. In such a situation, other family members become small instruments for the manipulator, which he or she controls as pleased.

Why is it Hard to Understand Mental Manipulation in the Family?

You grow up in your family surrounded by the thoughts, actions, and behaviors of other members. Staying with them conditions your mind towards their abusive behavior; hence, your mind doesn't even realize that you are being manipulated. For you, it is a normal household scenario that happens every weekend.

This is what doesn't allow people to decipher mental manipulation. Such people realize the mental manipulation after getting out, and stay away from the family for a while.

You don't have to feel threatened. Here are a few signs to help you understand all kinds of family relationship manipulation and things you can do to save yourself:

1. Lying, even if it is not required

To protect ourselves from shame and embarrassment, we tend to lie in many situations to our own family members. Sometimes, you lie just to keep your loved ones away from concerns. All these scenarios are justifiable because they happen once in a long time.

However, a manipulative family member can lie on a daily basis for no reason at all, but they will give you a legitimate reality where they are right to lie. This will happen regularly for small things.

Let's go through a scenario:

When Kate gave money to her younger brother for the electricity bill, she informed him about the last date for paying the bill.

The next day, Kate asked her brother, "Have you paid the bill, Sam?"

To that, he said, "Yes, I have."

But on the last day of paying the bill, all the lights went off.

When Kate inquired again, her brother vaguely replied, "I had something urgent to do, so I used that money. You give me money now and I will get that money back soon."

The problem was that Kate has been dealing with this behavior of her brother for a very long time. He does it again and again. If he wants something from Kate's room, he takes it without asking. In fact, he denies if Kate asks for that thing. Most of the time, Kate finds her lost things in her brother's room only. Now, she usually starts with his room whenever she loses her stuff.

A manipulator lies and then replies vaguely if you question them. They are ready to tell multiple lies over and over again.

How to save yourself: If you are dealing with such a family member, it will require patience. You know the behavior, so stop offering important responsibilities to them. Also, tell them, "I am here to help you no matter what, but that won't happen if you lie to me." Point out their lies in front of other family members and slowly motivate them to lose this habit.

2. The disguised selflessness

Some family members are honorable, while some just imitate as caring individuals. Selflessness can be an act of a manipulator in your family. Statements like, "Have I done anything for myself in this family?" are heard from such manipulators. The difference between real selfless people and disguising manipulators is that the latter one reminds you about his or her selflessness very often. The moment they see you getting free from their clutches, they say, "All I did was for you, and this is how you pay me!" Comments like this attack your guilt and sensitivities and you end up giving your control to that person.

How to save yourself: First of all, you need to realize that people who praise their selflessness are not selfless at all, and such a manipulator can be very close to you, which is why protection becomes difficult. But you can say, "I admire everything that you have done for me and this family, but I am old enough to make my own decisions now."

3. Intimidation and physical abuse

Sometimes, family relationships get ugly with straightforward threats and physical abuse. An intimating father, mother or a sibling can turn your life into hell. These manipulators don't believe in indirect methods of manipulation. They create fear with actual physical abuse, threats and intimidating actions.

How to save yourself: Just like an abusive partner, you need to find a way out from the life of an abusive family member. Find any way to escape without making them realize that you are trying to leave them. After getting a safe environment, you should file a complaint against such a family member.

4. Shaming

Family members know about our weaknesses and protect them, but a manipulative family member would use those weaknesses of yours to bully and make you feel ashamed. Shaming to blackmail or just to get control over you is common. The manipulator wants you to act according to his or her instructions.

How to save yourself: It is all about building your own self-esteem. These manipulators work your insecurities so, if you conquer them, the manipulator will have nothing to play with. Remind yourself that everyone has one of the other weaknesses. In fact, learn to flaunt your weaknesses on your own. This way, you will own your personality truly. That's what real confidence is.

Friendship Manipulation - How It Works And Things You Can Do?

Do you feel as if you are the one always giving something to a friend? You agree whenever that friend asks you to go out, but that person is always busy when you need him/her. If so, then there is a chance you are dealing with a manipulative friend.

A one-sided friendship is another form of manipulation you can come across. Some friends find it amusing to control people and use them as their puppets. Such manipulations can begin at the school level and go on for life.

If you make a narcissistic person your best friend, things are bound to go south for you.

Here are how manipulative friends work:

1. They constantly try to control you

A manipulative friend wants you to follow his or her ideas. Whenever you are around that person, you feel like you are being controlled. Such a friend chooses places to hang out alone and you are supposed to follow them. They can even try to control your dressing style, your personal decisions, and other relationships as well. Such a manipulative friend acts like a guide in your life, but, actually, they are just enjoying your vulnerability.

How to save yourself: Find a pattern of a manipulative friend. Look how many times your friend questions your judgment and tries to force his or her point of view. If you see clear signs of being controlled, stand up for yourself. You should say, "I am capable of making my own decisions."

2. They ignore you

Having a conversation with a manipulative friend has no meaning. A manipulative friend doesn't really care about you so, if the conversation is not interesting to them, they won't listen. For instance, you had a bad day at work and you are now sharing that experience with your friend. A manipulative friend would look away, keep using his or her phone, or interrupt you in the middle of the conversation and change the topic.

How to save yourself: Realize that your friend has no concern for what happens in your life. Evaluate this behavior and call them out, "I am talking to you. Please focus or let me know if you are not interested." This will not allow them to take you for granted.

3. They always need a favor

You help your friend once because of the relationship but then, the behavior gets repeated again and again. The manipulative friend tests your extent of kindness by asking for little favors at first. They can ask, "Can you give me your car for 30 minutes?" or, "Do you have an extra dress for me? I have nothing good to wear." Eventually, these little favors increase to larger scales, for example, "Please lend me 10,000 bucks, and I will pay you next month." If you motivate such behavior, such a manipulative friend will keep using you.

How to save yourself: Learn to say "No." Whenever you are asked for a favor, you should think, "What was the last time I helped this person?" and, "How much this favor is going to cost me?" If you find the situation not comfortable for you, politely refuse to help with a legitimate reason, such as, "This is not the right time for me to help you."

4. They use emotional defense

Just like a partner, a manipulative friend can also use emotions to play you for a fool. If you confront, they tend to act in a defensive way, and their defense involves an emotional attack. They can blame you for hurting them emotionally.

How to save yourself: Whenever you find yourself in an emotional attack, stay calm. The manipulator would try to resist the conversation, so, you should say, "We need to talk about this whether you like it or not." They can try to make you feel guilty, so you should read such signs too. Don't feel sorry for the person just because he or she wants you to. Make sure the conversation stays on topic.

5. They tend to bully a lot

Best friends make fun of each other, but a manipulator doesn't take jokes, as he/she just wants to make fun of you. A manipulator would bully you more in front of others. They have a need to present themselves superior to you in every scenario. This is their inner-complexities and insecurities that motivate them to behave this way.

How to save yourself: Sit your friend down and explain things clearly, "I don't know whether you do it deliberately, or without knowing, but I am not going to take your jokes anymore." Become firm and take a stand for yourself. If your friend still doesn't back down, it is time to put an end to that friendship.

6. They are nowhere to be found when you need them

These friends appear in your life once in a while only. Whenever they do, they desire something from you. After you fulfill their desire, they vanish without giving you any clue. You try to call and get in touch, but they are always busy, and their social media profiles are always filled with pictures of places where he/she goes to hang out with other friends.

How to save yourself: These people are not your friend at all. You just need to stop giving them any attention immediately.

A manipulative friend attacks the same emotional vulnerabilities as your partner and family members so it all comes down to taking care of yourself. You should learn self-love and give priority to yourself. Make every relationship a 50-50 give and take exchange. This way, you will earn the respect you deserve and the satisfaction of being in a healthy relationship.

Don't ignore the signs. Your intuitions tell you everything about a bad relationship. Act on those signs and find true people to have relationships with.

Chapter 6:
Get Into Their Heads. Know Thyself and Also Know These Manipulators

Don't you think how a person could deliberately try to control other people? We all are taught to believe in the goodness of people, but then the reality brings us to the ground with manipulators who can easily become the master of our inner-self with their deceptions.

A manipulator sees the world in a different way. In fact, it would not be wrong to say that manipulators understand life and people better than an ordinary person does. However, they use this ability to con and deceive people to get what they want.

In the mind of a manipulator, the whole world is a big board game of chess. They see you as an expendable tool. On the outside, they will give you care, love and protection, but this protection and affection are only there because you are useful to them.

Believe or not, a manipulator begins his or her observations by learning their own insecurities. They decipher their own emotional problems and evaluate the reasons behind it. This gives them the insight over how emotions affect our actions. With that insight, they observe other people on a daily basis. Your facial expressions, your reactions towards things, and your words help them learn about you. Things that you say and things that you don't, it all gives some insight to a skilled manipulator.

Using your emotional state and personality characteristics, a manipulator molds his or her personality accordingly. They can act like a very different person in front of two different people. For you, they are fun loving and outgoing, but, for some other person, they can be a victim of unfortunate incidents. They love creating stories and building a character that aligns with their victims so, if they feel something, you feel that same emotion too. It happens due to the strong bond a manipulator forms with the victim. This bond can include intimidation, love, authority, victimization, guilt, friendship, kindness and other emotions. This way, manipulators control your thoughts and make you see reality as they desire.

They Enjoy Tricking People

A con artist likes fooling people into giving him/her money or other things. For manipulators, manipulation is an art which they enjoy. They feel rewarded when you do as they say, or think exactly how they want you to. If a manipulator wants you to feel scared, he or she will use shame, bullying, lying and other tricks to make you feel that way. When you do, it would give the manipulator a rush they crave.

Manipulators score themselves whenever they win or lose. They have their own justifications for their actions.

"If you are so open, the world will use you at every step. Why not me?"
"I am using my talents to win what I want, and having some fun in the way as well! Everyone does that."
"Everyone is trying to manipulate each other. I am just good at it."

Their justifications are good enough reasons for them to manipulate people and don't care about them. These justifications further enhance the pleasure of control and tricking people. Manipulators define their lives around their ability to make others do things for them.

They Do Everything to Win

Every move, every word and every action of a manipulator is well-calculated. They might not always win, but their intentions are towards the victory every single time. Manipulators want every single person around them to submit control. Whether it is a love relationship or a corporate colleague, the goal is to find vulnerabilities in people and use them to manipulate. In fact, they can even use your personality strengths against you. For instance, if a person tries to be happy instead of all the bad things happening around, a manipulator can paint an altered happy picture of life to get the submission.
The techniques depend on the purpose of manipulating the victims. A manipulator can be charming or a big bully, depending on what he or she wants from you. That's the reason how some partners become a completely different person at different phases of a relationship. They seem charming at first because they want the other person to fall in love. As the relationship goes on, they desire control over the actions of their partner; hence, the blackmailing, silent treatments and intimidation begin.
A manipulator has more than one mask and he/she will try each one of them to win.

They Have Sharp Communication Skills

Communication skill is the biggest weapon used by a manipulator. Victims don't even realize when words impact their subconscious and conscious mind.

A good communicator is not always a manipulator, but a manipulator is always a good communicator. Their communication skills include:

- Their command over words.
- Their ability to say vague statements as facts.
- Their confidence when arguing or lying.
- Their ability to use sarcasm and irony.

If you come to confront a manipulator about a disrespectful statement, the manipulator can make that statement feel like a compliment to you. Similarly, they can wrap their hurtful statements in a compliment.
"Wow! You have read Gautama Buddha. I thought you were a dumb girl, but you're not!"

They use language to shake the ground of their victims and comfort them whenever required. They can say the best things about you in one second, and turn them into insults in another. It is all to grab your reactions on different scenarios, which allows them to read you better.

All in all, their insults hurt and their compliments melt your heart. That's how communication allows a manipulator to get out of any situation and create different scenarios.

They Look for the Scope of Vulnerability

In the mind of a manipulator, every person is vulnerable. Just the extent of vulnerability differs from person to person. Less vulnerable people are difficult to manipulate, while high vulnerability makes a person an easy target. Many manipulators like to assess and attack less vulnerable people just to enjoy the game; however, they do it in only safe scenarios. Otherwise, their goal is to pick the most vulnerable and twist their emotions to get what they wish for.

So, for example, a person with a few friends would be a better target than a person with many friends. Similarly, manipulators judge the scope of vulnerability in terms of self-esteem, confidence level, career, happiness, desires, and hopes. If they get to choose, the most vulnerable personality will get attacked in a group of options.

They don't stop if they come across a firm-minded person. Their idea is that every person has hopes, no matter how happy or confident he or she is so they attack those hopes as vulnerabilities. The manipulator can lose as well, but a loss is a big pain and the manipulator tries again and again to ensure his/her victory.

They Fool Their Own Mind As Well

In order to lie with confidence and keep up their character, manipulators create stories. They work on those stories in detail and make them believable in their own mind as well. Even when they are lying, one part of their brain treats those lies as truths. That's how they flawlessly remember their stories and tell the same lie for years and years without changing a single detail. They think about every potential question against their story and prepare an answer for that. If someone tries to question them, they immediately present an answer. Eventually, those lies become a truth for the manipulator as well.

"Where did you spend your weekend?"
"Ah! In a great beachside resort with my girlfriend. It was magical."
"But you said you had some personal thing to take care of?"
"Yeah man! That personal thing was my lovely girlfriend's birthday. She has recently lost her father, so I wanted to give her a much-needed vacation."

After such a conversation, don't be surprised to find out that the guy doesn't even have a girlfriend. He wanted a vacation, so he took it, and then he wanted his colleagues to think of him as a caring family man, so he created the girlfriend and a whole story around that. Now, this girlfriend would get gifts and restaurant dates whenever this manipulator wants to ditch the office and go out.

10 Common Characteristics All Manipulators Possess

Every manipulator holds some personality traits he or she uses to control people, situations, and actions.

1. Self-protection

Manipulative people are driven by the idea of self-protection. To protect themselves, they can engage others because they can. Some manipulators don't know they have skills. It is only the sense of self-protection that drives them to manipulate people without knowing.

You can consider self-protection as a motive and manipulation as a technique. For every bad thing a manipulator does, self-protection becomes the legitimate reason, "I did it to protect myself from the world." As a result, abusers, controllers, and other manipulators don't question their actions ever. It is ultimately about their feelings, their motives, and their desires. Other people's emotions are just a way to get what a manipulator wants.

The instinct of self-protection is in every human being, but not every one of us possesses the skills of manipulation. The strong desire of protecting self-motives meets a manipulative mind to create a dangerous, manipulative personality. Such people truly believe in their actions, which is why manipulators are so fluent in rationalizing their bad actions. They can present an amazing reason for something that is completely out of line.

For a girl who manipulates her partner to gain power over his life, it is just self-protection. She would say something like this, "You don't know how difficult it is for a woman to live in this world. I did what I had to for survival." She will explain her life in a story where she has been a victim of this cruel world, and that the cruelty of the world makes her actions completely legitimate and right.

Similarly, manipulators use the weaknesses of society and people to play them. The characteristic of self-protection gives manipulators the confidence over their choices.

2. No regards for personal space

Manipulators, who don't know they are manipulators, lack the understanding of personal identity. On the other hand, manipulators who deliberately manipulate don't care about people's personal space. A manipulator attacks emotionally, physically, spiritually and psychologically as well. Sometimes they attack just one aspect of personal identity or, sometimes, they can also attack all aspects.

If the manipulation is forceful, the victim feels different stages of exhaustion. Abusers, intimidators and other direct manipulators demean the personal space and weaken their victims.

On the other hand, a subtle manipulation hurts at the end. The manipulator attacks the victim like a silent parasite and starts corrupting his or her psychology; however, the person doesn't realize that he/she is being manipulated. The realization period occurs after the manipulator leaves the personal space, which leaves people in a rage, feel regret, and other hurtful feelings.

Personal space of people is the working ground for manipulators. They can only hurt their victims by learning personal space and its elements. That is why every manipulator holds the ability to read people's personal identity. They observe the physical, mental, and emotional capabilities of people before manipulating them.

If you ask a manipulator about the personal space of people, they would say, "It is personal only if you live in isolation. People showcase their identities with their words and actions. So, how is that a personal identity?" A manipulator believes in accessing every door possible to learn about their victims because, if the door is accessible, one has the right to open it and go inside. That's how they feel entering into a victim's psychology to observe.

3. Self-confidence

A manipulative person is always confident about his or her actions and thoughts; however, they tend to show or hide their confidence as they please. It allows them to avoid taking responsibilities. They like other people to take responsibilities. This way, a manipulator can easily turn the blame to another person for his/her own actions. They work behind the scenes, but come out as a confident person if it benefits them. If taking responsibility suits their purpose, manipulators come forward to satisfy their own needs.

Whether they show their confidence or not, manipulators leave no room for their victim's survival. When playing a victim, a manipulator hides his or her confidence to make the character believable. On the other hand, a manipulator shows maximum levels of confidence when using intimidation, sarcasm or other methods of manipulation.

You can hear the same person say two different things on different days:

"I have no clue how to handle my money. Can we open a joint account?"
"I decide how I spend my money, what to shop for, where to go and what to wear. Don't try to control me."

The confidence level changes according to the scenario and motives of a manipulator, but that only happens on the outside. On the inside, that person has always been confident about his or her abilities so, in a way, self-confidence is not a trait. Instead, the ability to show or hide confidence is the true trait a manipulator holds.

4. Motivator

Manipulators have the ability to motivate people towards something. Their power over communication skills allows them to convey what a victim wants to hear. Manipulators understand a person's sensibilities and sensitivities. This way, they learn about how caring, kind, practical, or emotional a person is. Using this observation, manipulators start motivating the side they want to attack. For instance, if a person is insecure about his or her looks, a manipulator would praise their facial features.

"You have a desirable smile and your caring nature makes that smile more beautiful for me."

If they know the insecurities of a person, they praise in a subtle way with specific compliments so, instead of saying, "You are beautiful," they say, "Your eyes talk your beauty," plus they would combine this compliment with the person's kindness or caring nature. This way, the victim tends to buy those lies.

Similarly, a manipulator can motivate bad feelings in a person if he or she wants to. If a victim is feeling sad, a manipulator can motivate that sadness to fulfill a purpose. The same goes for fear, hope, anger, jealousy and other feelings that a person can struggle with.

The ability to motivate feelings is common in all types of manipulators. They use this characteristic to create a relationship and strengthen the bond with their victims.

5. Practical empathy
Empathy is the ability to understand other people's feelings and share those feelings, but a manipulator doesn't feel general empathy. Manipulators have a practical sense of empathy, which means they understand people's feelings without sharing them. A manipulator is like a robot looking at a happy or sad person. The feelings are visible to them, but they practically observe those feelings to fulfill their purpose.

If you talk to a manipulator about relationships in general, they usually tend to divide relationships into needs, wants and other practical aspects. They will tell you logical reasons why two people are in love with each other. If two celebrities marry each other, a manipulator would say how one celebrity is trying to climb up the ladder and the other is just trying to get over an old relationship. Manipulative people see the dynamics in relationships such as intrigue, jealousy, rivalry, affection, attraction, hope, and need. They use these dynamics to play multiple people together and ruin the harmony between these people. They can encourage or discourage you to love someone or hate someone. It all depends on what means you fulfill, in their big plan.

6. Hidden insecurities
Behind all that confidence and charm hides an insecure person in a manipulator. Their ability to observe feelings allows them to understand their own insecurities as well; however, just like their self-confidence, they can hide their insecurities as well. Every time you see a manipulator victimizing himself, there is a certain level of truth in that. They use their insecurities as well to mold into a character and fool people.

Sometimes, the insecurity drives manipulators towards vulnerable people. They want to gain attention and feel superior but, that would be possible only if they can find a person more vulnerable than them, so the search for vulnerable victims begins and people end up getting hurt in the process.

The insecure personality traits of a manipulator give him or her the obsessiveness towards their goals. In a relationship, an insecure, manipulative person tends to find reasons to blame the partner to hear apologies. Manipulators want their victims to follow their lead. Some manipulators desire praise, and some desire control over the victim. Also, the motives can change from victim to victim as well.

7. Multiple personalities
Manipulators are like chameleons. They have a tendency to change themselves depending on the situation they are in, or the person they want to persuade. Multiple personality traits live inside every person; however, not everyone deliberately hides or showcases those personalities to gain something but manipulators do that. They mold themselves to create a disguised persona in front of a victim so, if a manipulator wants you to feel scared, you will never see him or her laughing or talking to you in a light manner. It is a constant character play they perform. You think your boss or partner is very serious and scary, but the same person behaves completely different in other situations.

The ability to change personalities make manipulators extremely dangerous. In relationships, we tend to create a picture of our partners or friends, but what if that picture is all wrong? You see a perfect partner in front of you, while he or she is cheating on you and getting away with it.

When changing personalities, manipulators work on three aspects - behavior, opinions and feelings. They choose to behave in a certain way in front of certain people. They blend righteousness in their behavior to build trust in people. Manipulators can shake their victims with multiple behaviors on random days. A manipulative wife can choose to switch her mood often to keep her husband under control.

Manipulators can debate for or against at the same time. They present opinions in a vague manner so that no-one can hold them accountable for anything. Switching sides and opinions allows them to say exactly what a victim desires. If two different victims are talking to the manipulator at the same time, he or she can easily get out of the situation with a vague opinion, such as, "You both are saying some logical and intelligent things. We should keep an open mind to gain the best of both worlds."

In terms of feelings, manipulators can be ruthless. They have the ability to observe how a person is feeling. They use this skill to change their persona and convey their feelings accordingly. This means that if the victim has done something bad today and feeling remorse, a manipulator will use that remorse by acting like a victim. In remorse, a person desires to do something good, so manipulators use that to make victims do what they want.

8. Indirect communication

Although manipulators are great communicators, they like to use other people to convey what they desire. They will present themselves as if they are a straightforward person who talks what he thinks; however, they like to plant seeds in the mind of people. You won't even realize when a manipulator is making you his or her messenger. They fool you into thinking that their ideas are your ideas so, when you do it, the blame is on you, "Nobody put a gun to your head buddy! You came on your own."

They design their conversations in terms of questions and constantly ask whether you agree or don't. This way, they can always stay out of sight and get you to do exactly the way they want.

"Dude! Someone needs to do something about Damon. He is talking bad things about us everywhere in this office."
"What, really? I can't take it anymore. He will face me directly this time."

That's how a conversation happens with a manipulator. He or she plants a seed conveying the hidden message. The manipulator wants you to do his or her dirty work without even taking any part in it. After you act for them, they simply say you did it on your own; 'I just shared my feelings because I was concerned.'

Using other people as a messenger allows manipulators to hide themselves and get out of every situation. They create a scenario and look at everything from the outside. Nobody even suspects that it was them triggering each one of them and, even if people find out, manipulators hold other people accountable for their actions. In any scenario, they ensure their victory.

9. Jealousy

A manipulator won't admit it, but jealousy is a big part of their mindset. For many manipulators, it is the driving force that motivates them to play people's vulnerabilities. The feeling of jealousy comes from almost everything because manipulators desire to feel superior to everyone so a manipulator can feel jealous of his or her own parents, siblings, spouses and friends. The jealousy stays on until, and unless, they get control over that person. Holding a person's emotions and actions in hand, manipulators feel more powerful and better than the other person.

A manipulator can feel jealous of someone's money, so he or she can target the loneliness of that person. Similarly, a manipulator can feel jealous of someone's look, so he or she tries to sabotage that person's relationship. Anything good in your life, whether it is physical or emotional, can make a manipulator jealous and they can choose to destroy that good feeling with their tactics.

A manipulator may also simply exist in your life to exploit your resources. They enter your life to enjoy the good things you have. They do feel jealous of you, but the idea is to make you share what you have. If you have a great start-up, they will present themselves as a valuable partner without even actually doing anything for your business. Similarly, if you are a successful independent person, a manipulator would decide to lure you into a relationship to share your life.

They just want what you have - a feeling, a physical item, a lifestyle or even your emotional control.

10. Self-centered

All characteristics come down to this one idea. Manipulators are self-centered. They do not understand or care about other people's thoughts, life, emotions or mental state. They only care about what they need. If people get hurt physically, emotionally or psychologically, it is all collateral. People are expendable if it fulfills some righteous purpose for a manipulator. That is how a manipulator sees the world. No matter how caring, logical and charming they sound, they don't mean a single word. It is all a formulated combination of words, emotions, and expressions to manipulate people and situations.

A manipulator can be surrounded by hundreds of people who love him/her and feel like a lone wolf in his mind, and this lone wolf is cold-hearted and ready to hunt no matter who or what comes in the way. Every situation is an opportunity to obtain something. If people are going through bad situations, manipulators find something to gain from it. They actually feel good and excited inside if bad things happen to other people because, in this way, they can use those vulnerable people.

The life of a manipulator is in his or her mind. They keep on plotting something in their mind. It is all a game to them, which is why they don't feel exhausted. Their personalities are rigid inside but they act all moral from the outside. This act of morality allows them to target other people's vulnerability and sense of morality too.

Now you know how to spot them, it gives you a better line of defense against such manipulative folk. Though it may seem harsh, but the line know an enemy and treat them as such resonates strongly here. You know how to identify manipulators; the next segment will equip you with the tools to deal with them.

Chapter 7:
Self-Defense Class 101

In nature, manipulative behavior is deceptive, sneaky and devious. Victims might feel a sense of uneasiness in some cases, but recognizing a manipulative situation seems difficult. Manipulators tend to alter victims' reality which makes them feel crazy but, while you are thinking it is all just your imagination, the manipulator is playing you.

Manipulators start learning and cultivating manipulative dysfunctional methods as children. Either they learn from the manipulative people around, or cultivate manipulative behavior to handle an authoritative parent. Twisting emotions and changing personality become the only way for them to get out of their miserable childhood but, eventually, the manipulation becomes a part of their personality and begins playing innocent people who are vulnerable.

Although there are hundreds of variations to every manipulative tactic, you can get an idea by going through the major ways of manipulation. Knowing how someone can try to manipulate you will allow you to immediately get yourself out of those situations.

Here is every manipulative situation with conversation examples that you can come across:

Using Group Affiliation to Borrow Strength

A manipulator can attack your morality, or gain superiority, by using group affiliation during communication:

1. "As women, we desire/don't desire this from men."
The power of a group is strong enough to put pressure on an individual. The group doesn't even have to be present physically. A manipulator can use a false sense of group affiliation to manipulate you. A manipulative woman can use sentences like this to shut you down.

For example:

- **If you are trying to show mistakes in a project to a female employee**

A manipulative woman can try something like this, "Why are you being disrespectful? As women, all we ask is basic respect."
To this, most people back down, lower their voice and even stop the conversation. The idea is to divert the conversation by building a sense of guilt and shame in your heart.
To find a way out of this, you need to firmly stand your ground and choose words wisely.

You can say, "I am not disrespecting you, dear! I am talking to you exactly the way I would talk to any other male or female employee. As your senior, I have the right to point out your mistakes, and you should listen and learn from them."

2. "People, older than you, know better, so listen to me..."

These types of interactions happen when a manipulator is scared of your skills. If you have better skills or knowledge of something, an older manipulative person would cover his or her fear with arrogance.

Knowledgeable people pose threats to manipulators. To win arguments, or to shift the focus away from you, a manipulator tries to use his or her age as some sort of superiority. "I am better than you because I came to this planet before." That's what they are trying to convey. Sometimes, this technique is used to win control over your actions, or some elders try to hit your morality and respectful behavior with such conversations.

The age card is played in various scenarios, such as:

- **When a manipulative father wants his son to join the family business and stay under control**

Son: "I think I'm going to join the environment care center in our town."
Father: "Why? We have our own seafood supply chain. Join our company. You will find me there to help you as I have been always."
Son: "I guess I'm ready to face the world now, dad!"
Father: "You see this white beard on my face?! I know this world better than you because I have been here longer. People don't waste time when they listen to their elders. You will be ready when I say you are."

Manipulative fathers try to keep their children near them. They have their personal agendas to fulfill.

To save yourself in a situation like this, say, "Dad! People become what they are because of the experiences they receive in life. I also want to become as experienced and wise as you are, but with my own wins and losses."

- **When your knowledge shines in a meeting in front of your older boss**

You: "I think this AI should be our next step to get a competitive edge in the market. We don't have to begin right away. Just a little research in this direction would help our business."
A manipulative boss: "Well, I hear you, but people older than you have been managing this business for years so don't mind if I decide to not act right away on a young man's suggestion. In fact, I think AI is nothing but a stupid trend that would vanish away in a few years."
In such situations, you need to respond very politely. Don't let them convey that you are arrogant.

In a humble way, you can say, "I am not as old and experienced as you are, but I do have some skills that impressed you to hire me in the first place. I am just fulfilling the responsibility I was hired for. The ultimate decision is always yours. Just remember that it is my idea."

- **When your senior manipulates you to work overtime**

You: "I have enough work for today. I will pick the rest of the work tomorrow."
Manipulative senior: "Buddy! I never act like your senior here, but you shouldn't forget that seniors know how things work. I have reached this position with hard work, just like other seniors you see in this office. I have done more overtime than you can even imagine. Believe me, today's hard work will help you tomorrow."
By using the seniority, the manipulator tries to build hope in your mind. Reluctantly, you decide to work overtime, and the cycle of overtimes starts from that day on.

To save yourself, you need to make your own decisions. Analyze whether you want to work late or not. Don't let your senior decide when and why you should work overtime against your will.

You can respond with something like this:
"Sir, I do understand the importance of hard work and I am following all my responsibilities here, but there is a life outside where I have more important responsibilities so I do have to prioritize. I am choosing other priorities today."

Generalizing Your Personality or Habits

A manipulator can try to label you to bring your value down:

1. "You are so stubborn"
Every time you want to stand your ground, manipulators shake you by saying that you are stubborn. They want to sell you their idea so, if you don't seem to buy their manipulation, they play the stubborn card. They confuse you into thinking that you aren't open to new ideas.
Friends, family members, lovers, or any manipulative person in your life can trick you like this. If you don't agree with what they say, you are a stubborn person.

If you observe closely, you will find manipulators using this tactic very often:

- **When a manipulative wife wants to move to the city where her parents live**

"My parents have found a great property for us there. We can start a new life. It will be an exciting start for us."
But husband says, *"Are you kidding? I have my friends, my job, and my family here."*

This forces to a situation something like this, *"Oh! You are such a stubborn guy. Move with the flow, my dad has a great post ready for you in his office."*

The wife desires her husband to move to her territory. This way, she will get better control of her husband. In fact, she can also control his career through her father.

Similar manipulative tactics are common in a girlfriend-boyfriend relationship and a parent-son or parent-daughter relationship as well.

To save yourself, you need to realize when you are being generalized. Anytime someone generalizes your decisions as a stubborn personality, shut them down.

"My decisions are driven by my own personal reasons. Don't generalize my decisions. I won't respond to those false accusations."

- **When you buy a car more expensive than your budget**

A manipulative salesman can push your buttons with this tactic. Sales professionals are taught tricks to play consumers; however, if a manipulative person becomes a salesman, he or she can make people buy things they don't even want.

You go out to buy an affordable car, but the salesman starts talking about the latest technologies and modern features.

"Sir, I am telling you, this car right here is what you need. People avoid technology due to stubbornness and end up facing consequences. This one is expensive, but it comes with better safety and comfort."

Whether you feel good about that car or not, afterwards, it is a different question. Don't let a salesman push the "stubborn" button and twist your decision. The wise move would be to start avoiding the salesman if he or she calls you stubborn directly or indirectly.

- **When a manipulative friend wants you to try something you don't want to do**

Friends can be really persuasive, especially if they have manipulative skills. A friend can make you try alcohol or make you do other things that you won't do generally, and it all happens due to the "stubborn" card.

"Just do it. We are all doing it. Why do you have to be so stubborn?"

Don't let this imprison you into doing a wrong thing.

"I am not stubborn. I don't want this right now."

If you stay firm with your decision, the manipulative friend will stop those efforts.

Similarly, you will find many situations where people will come and call you stubborn. Don't ignore them completely. Not all of them are trying to manipulate you. Think and evaluate to make sure that all your decisions are yours only, and not forced.

2. "You always create drama..."

A manipulator can accuse you of overreacting to question your actions. This majorly happens if you get close to discovering a manipulator. They try to hide their actions by telling you that you are the one thinking too much and creating a drama over a small thing.

- **When you ask why your partner doesn't spend more time with you**

You: "You promised we will have dinner together this Sunday."

Manipulative partner: "Sorry, I have something important this Sunday."

You: "Why is it so difficult for you to find time for me? I see you spend time with all your friends."
Manipulative partner: "You are creating drama over nothing. I am working hard for our own future and everything is fine in our life. Stop making things up!"
The manipulator wants you to stop questioning.
If your partner accuses you of overreaction, you need to calm down first of all; then, make sure that your partner doesn't change the topic after that.

Say, "Don't try to stop this conversation like this. Give me valid reasons why things are going this way."

Also, you can include, *"Maybe I am overreacting, but it is because these things are important to me. Give me a legit answer for your behavior."*

- **When a colleague tries to steal your limelight**

You: "Why did you present that idea to the boss? I shared it with you in confidence."
Manipulative colleague: "Oh! Sorry man! I thought you were pitching that idea to me so I took the initiative of moving that idea forward."
You: "Are you kidding me? I clearly remember telling you not to say anything to anyone. I was waiting for the right time."

Manipulative colleague: "You were waiting for the right time! This is not a theatre man, it is a professional environment. I saw a moment and I pitched the idea. Stop creating drama over a small thing. Go tell the boss it was your idea if you want to."
You: "Not me. You should confess in front of the boss that it was my idea."

Manipulative colleague: "Such a drama every single time. What is wrong with you man? Calm down."
Manipulations like this leave you with a loss of many opportunities of growth in your career, and manipulative people get the promotions, which you deserve.

To save yourself, you need to learn to keep secrets. Do not share your ideas with a colleague just because he or she is friendly, talks to you, or brings gifts for you. A manipulator can disguise you into liking him or her and then get information from you. Secrets that don't harm anyone are not bad at all so there is nothing wrong with keeping your ideas to yourself, until you are ready to present it to the right authorities.

3. **"Why do you have to be the most negative person in the room?"**

The accusation of a being a negative person is embarrassing for everyone. No-one wants to be perceived as a negative personality but, sometimes, our concerns are presented as negativity, which doesn't allow us to convey our point. Manipulators do this to make our points of view worthless and make their ideas look positive.

- **If you stop fellow professionals from making a wrong business decision**

"I don't think we should move ahead with this plan. There are many variables associated with this. Things can easily go south."
Manipulators: *"Don't listen to this guy. He is always the most negative person in the room. Business is about risks and rewards so move forward with this plan."*

The manipulator tries to label you as a negative person. This way, other people in the room stop focusing on your point of view. Even if you present logical reasons, everything becomes an opinion of a negative and scared person.

To come out of such a situation, you need to present some positive decisions that you made before. Say, "I am not a negative person," and remind yourself of all those times when your decisions have been right. This manipulation affects multiple people, so you need to patiently react to win the trust of all those people.

After presenting your authority, you need to call the manipulator out, *"So, hopefully you now know about my decision-making abilities. I don't want you to call me a negative person ever. Keep your labels away from me."*

You can face similar accusations in your personal relationships as well. A manipulative partner can call you negative because you suspect he/she is cheating on you. In that situation, you should say, *"I am ready to hear your side, but don't accuse me just because I demand some answers."*

Always deal with patience and shut the manipulator's generalizations down. That's how you win over labeling.

Hooking You With Emotions

We all deal with one or many emotions on a daily basis. Emotions like pride, love, affection, guilt, and hope are a few of the major emotions that we all deal with every day. Manipulators can attack these emotions with certain hook lines. They know which statement will impact you exactly the way they want.

Knowing those emotional hooks can help you fight the temptation and charm of falling in the hole dug by manipulators.

1. "You are my savior"
Manipulators can act like a victim to gain sympathy. They call you their savior, which makes you feel like a hero. A little sense of pride is induced in your mind, which allows you to come forward whenever the manipulator is in need. The sympathy can also turn into trust. You don't feel that a person can harm you in any way, so you start sharing things. Eventually, the manipulator gains more control over your life and emotions.

- **When a person knows you have a crush on him/her**

"Every time I find myself alone, you come from somewhere to help me out. I have no money on me right now, so can you clear this bill for me please?"

You are already in 'awe' of that person, so you become ready to do everything to impress. They make you feel as if you are important, but you are nothing but a tool for those manipulative people.

- **When you are trying to impress your seniors in your workplace**

"There is no way I can complete this presentation on time. The work is out of control today. Then, I thought, where is my savior? I know you are the only one responsible enough to share this work I have."

A manipulative senior uses your sense of duty and presents himself as a victim of being a burdened employee. To this, you find yourself helping them every time and even feel good about it.

First of all, remind yourself every day that you don't need to impress anybody in this world. If you are responsible and follow your morals, don't let people turn you into their puppet.

When a person calls you his or her savior, judge the reasons behind it. Then, if you find signs of manipulation, break the conversation immediately with something like, *"I can't be a savior today. In fact, I need a savior right now with my work."* If you can, add some legitimate work that you have to do immediately, and the manipulator would go away.

Manipulators never want to repay favors so, if you ask for it, they tend to leave. You can use this against their self-victimization tactic.

2. "I can share anything with you."

It is a famous tactic that manipulators use on their victims. They share fake emotional feelings so that you open your heart to them. If a manipulator says, "I can share anything with you," he or she tries to condition you to share your emotions and information with them. They want to know which emotions drive you as a person and what feelings you are currently dealing with so they create an emotional bond by saying this statement. Actually, a manipulator never shares his or her emotional state with others. Everything they say is just a fraction of their feelings, combined with fake scenarios.

- **In a new relationship with a manipulative partner**

Manipulator: *"I have never told these things about me to anyone before. You are so easy to talk to. I can share anything with you."*
You: *"Even I feel the same way."*

Have such a conversation two or three times, and you will end up sharing your emotions and other personal ideas that you never share with anyone. The manipulator will give you simple and fake information and call them his or her secrets. With these conversations, a manipulative partner finds your push buttons to control you in future.

To save yourself, you need to understand that if someone is sharing things, you don't have to do the same. Even if that person is your partner, decide the level of secrecy depending on the time you have spent with him/her. Never share your emotional weaknesses in the early stage of a relationship.

- **In a professional relationship**

Manipulators build professional relationships to gain information. They are generally eager to talk and share random information with conviction.

"I heard other teams have prepared their ideas for the project. My team hasn't even started yet, but I am telling this to you only. I know I can share these things with you."
"By the way, what's your plan for the project? Any ideas?"

Similar situations occur and you end up falling for this emotional hook in a professional environment. The solution is the same for this situation as well. You need to learn to keep your secrets yours only and to those you know you can trust. In a professional environment, all information has to be presented in front of the right person at the right moment. Keep this in mind and you will never fall for this manipulative tactic.

3. "Don't you feel any guilt because of that?"
The guilt trip is worse and a manipulator can further induce this feeling to control your actions. Some people are firm in their morality and try everything possible to stay righteous. It is a positive quality, but these are the people most prone to being manipulated with guilt. Manipulators can create scenarios with their dialogues and make you feel responsible for something bad.
Here are a few situations when manipulators can use this tactic on you:

- **An argument with a manipulative partner**

"Whenever we start becoming a perfect couple, you do something to mess things up for both of us. Don't you feel any guilt for your behavior?"

Or, something like this:

"I feel happy away from you and cry when I am with you. That's the effect you have on me. I hope you at least feel guilty."

Manipulative partners stir your emotions with such statements to shut you down. They don't want you to get out of their control so the guilt factor comes into play.

To save yourself, you need to have better control over your emotions. Don't allow your partner's statement to induce guilt in you. Feeling guilty is a positive emotion if you feel it on your own, but don't let other people decide when and why you should feel guilty.

You can reply, *"I am not doing anything deliberately. I still apologize if you are feeling bad, but I am not guilty of anything."*

- **A manipulative relative decides you stir emotions during a family gathering**

"Your parents always treated me with respect and you do not even care to call me even on festivals. You are ruining the reputation your parents built. You should think about it before it's too late."

In such a situation, you can't turn things towards the manipulator. The only way you can win is by not allowing that guilt trip attack your integrity. Respectfully reply:

"I respect my elders and my parents know that."
Family members use such tactics for no reason sometimes. Their goal is to stir things and enjoy people feeling bad. If you start explaining things too much, it would make them happier. In fact, they will further manipulate you into doing things for them so stop the conversation as quickly as possible and don't feel bad because someone has said something.

4. "You are perfect, just change this one thing."

We all hope to become the best version of ourselves. We want to be a better person, a better partner, a better professional and gain other improvements. This hope also becomes a method of manipulation for manipulators. They often come into your life as well-wishers, motivators, teachers and other personalities you look up to. Even your partner can use your hopes to control you.

Manipulators want to control your actions so they give compliments first to make you feel good. Eventually, they start seeding ideas of changes that would make you better. As you become addicted to their approval, you follow through and act exactly the way manipulators want.

Such manipulations occur in families, relationships, and work as well:

- **Your parents ask you to leave your partner because he/she is a bad influence**

Manipulative parents condition their kids with their manipulation. Kids grow up, but the habit of manipulation doesn't go away in parents. They try to control the kid's actions.

Suppose manipulative parents see their son getting freedom from their manipulation because of a new partner in his life. They would say:
"You have a perfect life with us and now things are changing because of this new girl. This change will ruin your life. Just get away from this girl and you will become our perfect child again."

There are parents with manipulative behavior. They don't want their kids to get out of their control, and that can make things ugly for the child, especially if the child has a caring and responsible nature.

If you are going through something like this, realization is the first step towards the solution. Your childhood conditioning might not allow you to see the manipulation coming from your parents;

hence, you need to start thinking and making decisions on your own. Take suggestions from your parents for sure, but don't allow them to make decisions or emotionally blackmail you.
Similarly:

- **A manipulative partner can ask you to change your behavior**

"Why are you again asking about shopping bills? You are a perfect boyfriend. Just stop asking questions that I don't like. I have the right to spend your money as I wish."

Not cute, right, but it happens a lot. Both girls and guys can fall into such manipulative relationship traps.

Breaking such manipulation comes down to how confident you are as a person. Low self-esteem and seeking approval allows manipulators to use this tactic on you. A partner won't behave the same way if you show self-confidence.
"We both have our own identities. My money is my money and I decide whether you get it or if you don't. If that defines my love, you don't love me at all."

You can choose your own words, but make sure that the partner sees your confident side.

- **There is always some lame reason why you are denied promotion**

Unfortunately, workplaces have become a hub to manipulate and use vulnerable people. Your vulnerability is tested by your seniors but, instead of saving you from those vulnerabilities, manipulative people use them to their advantage.

No matter how hardworking you are, your promotion goes to the next person who doesn't even deserve it and you get one silly reason:
"Your work is great. Just listen to your seniors more to learn and prepare for the position you are aspiring to attain in this company."
Less-deserving people will keep getting promotions unless you stand up for yourself. The first step would be to ensure that your work performance is top-notch. Others will try to point out strange and irrelevant mistakes. You have to learn to defend your work. Use facts to describe your professional work and decisions.

Then, stand up for yourself and ask for a promotion. This way, your seniors will understand your importance and won't get to steal away your promotion.

Conclusion

You can bring down everything to one idea - **Learn to understand, control and protect your emotions and psychology.**

Manipulators are out there learning vulnerabilities. To fight them, you need to understand your vulnerabilities and resolve them. The more you understand your inner-self, the stronger personality you attain.
Also, when you come across a manipulative personality, try to walk away as quickly as possible. Use the tips and ideas given in this book to read the signs of a manipulative situation. Face such situations with integrity, and don't let a manipulator enter your emotional and psychological space.

Hopefully, reading about manipulation will help you improve your life, and allow you to fight people who are out there to just use you one way or the other.

Now, I would like to make a small request here.

If you have enjoyed or found even one piece of advice useful in your daily life, would you please share with others by leaving your review on Amazon here.

This will mean loads to me as well as the folks who read it such that they know how you have benefited from this book.
Many thanks once again!

Catch you around and meanwhile don't forget to practice the skills and strategies taught therein so that you can lessen and avoid the impact of manipulation in your life!

The Procrastination Fix

36 Strategies Proven To Cure Laziness And Improve Productivity

Daily Training For Mental Toughness And Self Discipline

Jacob Greene

The Procrastination Fix

Prologue

Jim is a New Yorker who has spent the bulk of his life living downtown New York. He finished college 3 years ago but has struggled to gain admission to college. His SATs have been terribly poor, and one wonders what has really happened. A few years ago, he wasn't exactly like this. A brilliant chap who understood calculus as early as 10, He had the best score in the regional Queen's Project Aptitude test by 12. He was destined for greatness given all the feats he had achieved at such an early age.

When he tried writing entrance examinations, he was never prepared. He always waited till it was almost deadline before making moves to study. Since there were new additions every year, he had to update his collection of books and knowledge. However, he had to wait till last minute before doing so. This wasn't enough time to cover for everything done. He was a chronic procrastinator. He always waited till the last minute before doing anything. This always spelled doom for him.

Do you see any of Jim in any of your friends, family or just perhaps maybe even yourself? I know. It is sometimes tough to acknowledge that we procrastinate and delay things which we ought to have done like eons ago, and it is no mean feat to cope with a colleague or loved one who does that consistently too! So it doesn't matter if you are getting this book for yourself or others, the main thing here is, what you will find in this book would be the tried and tested, proven solutions with which you can use to combat and rid yourself of the most debilitating effects that procrastination brings!

Get ready to be boosting your productivity and bringing about daily doses of self discipline which will see you clear through all those hateful tasks and then some, all without the shadow of procrastination lurking in the background. It shall be banished!

Of course, this whole gamut of productivity and anti procrastination techniques aren't going to be very much useful if anyone who reads it actually Procrastinates on taking definitive action isn't? It becomes a literal situation of all talk and no action which definitely would not serve us well at all. So, it is important for you to know that within the confines of this book, you will be getting two of the most powerful methods with which to halt and stop procrastination perpetually in its tracks. I kid you not. I am so excited about sharing this with you that I am just seriously tempted to write it all down here, but no no, it is not going to be beneficial to you just to hear it like this. These two secrets need to be coupled with some degree of thinking and self reflection to really unleash its usefulness.

I am really delighted and excited that we will be walking this journey of learning and sharing together, and more importantly to be able to bring about positive change in any lives which utilize the valuable knowledge that is contained within this book.

Remember, the purpose of this is to give anyone the tools to fix that procrastination habit and bring about increased productivity to work and life. Daily training and habitual usage of the tips contained therein will definitely aid in creating letting anyone see results much much quicker.

The excellence of life has always been a product of smart and hard work, consistently applied at the right areas, and with the proper guidance. This book will be your proper guidance. You will need to apply it consistently in the right areas. Together, you can achieve all that you want and more!

© Copyright 2018 by Jacob Greene - All rights reserved.

This document is geared towards providing exact and reliable information in regards to the topic and issue covered. The publication is sold with the idea that the publisher is not required to render accounting, officially permitted, or otherwise, qualified services. If advice is necessary, legal or professional, a practiced individual in the profession should be ordered.

From a Declaration of Principles which was accepted and approved by a Committee of the American Bar Association and a Committee of Publishers and Associations.

In no way is it legal to reproduce, duplicate, or transmit any part of this document in either electronic means or in printed format. Recording of this publication is strictly prohibited and any storage of this document is not allowed unless with written permission from the publisher. All rights reserved.

The information provided herein is stated to be truthful and consistent, in that any liability, in terms of inattention or otherwise, by any usage or abuse of any policies, processes, or directions contained within is the solitary and utter responsibility of the recipient reader. Under no circumstances will any legal responsibility or blame be held against the publisher for any reparation, damages, or monetary loss due to the information herein, either directly or indirectly.

Respective authors own all copyrights not held by the publisher.

The information herein is offered for informational purposes solely, and is universal as so. The presentation of the information is without contract or any type of guarantee assurance.

The trademarks that are used are without any consent, and the publication of the trademark is without permission or backing by the trademark owner. All trademarks and brands within this book are for clarifying purposes only and are the owned by the owners themselves, not affiliated with this document.

Chapter 1 :
What Is Procrastination

Never postpone for tomorrow or the day after tomorrow what you can do today; barns are not filled by those who postpone and aimlessly waste time. Work prospers with care; those who postpone battle with ruin.

It is not uncommon to see many people take procrastination for laziness. It is often referred to as an abominable flaw. However, this is a very wrong notion that has to be refuted. Procrastination is the act of postponing the execution of an action or an activity. Such actions are carried out at the last minute or when it is a little too late. More often than not, such executions are below par and unacceptable. Laziness refers to the unwillingness to do work or put efforts in a particular action. There is no inclination to do any activity. This shows that both subjects are quite different. Someone who procrastinates might be inclined to do work but shall postpone the execution to a later date. Often, such a person can engage in frivolous or less important activities instead of concentrating on the task at hand. In the case of Jim, his PS4 console is laden with various games ranging from FIFA 18, Call of Duty: Modern Warfare, Modern Combat 5, Grand Theft Auto V to Assassins Creed. He invites his friends over on a daily basis, and they play multiplayer mode, or he connects to the Internet to play against other internet users. If he doesn't want to play games, he is glued to his laptop to keep himself up to date with Madam Secretary, Suits, House of Cards and the like.

This example shows that procrastination is intentional, pre-planned and not accidental. It can become a habit that might not be realized on time until it has gone so deep it can't be stopped in an instant. Also, if someone undertakes a project and is unable to complete the project due to the undue and needless postponement, this is procrastination.

What is procrastination?

Giving a holistic view, Procrastination is gotten from a Latin origin *procrastinus* which is a past participle of *procrastinare*, which when broken, means a *pro* (forward) and *crastinus* (from tomorrow). When putting together, the word procrastination is given a full picture, and clear direction is fully provided.

Procrastination is the act of engaging in actually less pressing tasks instead of the more pressing ones or carrying out trivial tasks in place of the more important tasks. That moment you find yourself trying very hard to do the required thing at the moment that you should or would like to do, procrastination has set indefinitely. Having said so, procrastination is also engaging in the more pleasurable things than engaging in, the less pleasurable activities, and postponing and putting off waiting tasks to another chosen time. To classify a particular behavior as procrastination oriented, certain attributes are present in such behavior. They are unproductive, time wasting, unnecessary and delaying.

Constantly, procrastination is voluntarily delaying a planned course of action despite expecting the worst of doing the wrong thing that moment. Therefore when you see yourself taking on trivial tasks with a long history of putting things off instead of performing the meaningful tasks, you have started procrastinating. Notably, it is safe to say that procrastination is the bridge between intention and taken action.

How Procrastination Can Hurt You in Business and Relationships

Procrastination showing its weight can go ahead to affect an individual negatively in business and relationships by acting as a barrier from living life to the fullest. More recent research studies have gone to show that people regret more for the things they haven't done than the things they have done. The feelings of regret more often tend to stay with people much longer. The result of procrastination is a result of wasting time that could be invested into something much more meaningful or a task that requires that it attention or completion. When the enemy in the form of procrastination is conquered, you will be able to achieve more, while in so doing your business and relationship life will be improved; thus enjoying the potential that they both have to offer. Having said so, it is also important for you to know that your self-confidence is also a crucial part of your success in both your relationship and business life.

It is even more important for those in leadership as procrastination may influence employees and colleagues to feel that you are delaying progress. Another mistake we make is not recognizing the procrastination habit and its complexities; we do not consider it a habit and believe we are just doing it for now because we have a lot on our plate. It encroaches on other aspects of our lives that we even postpone the minutest of tasks because we believe there will always be time. You need to take action on a task — even when you're not in the mood to do it. Naturally, you will not always be in the mood to perform tasks or responsibilities, but the ability to motivate ourselves into doing them is the difference between a lazy procrastinator and a hardworking person. Properly plan your life in such a way that you won't be heavily reliant on your to-do list. Quickly complete daily tasks using a simple time-management technique. It is quite easy to cultivate the habit of procrastination, but it takes a more disciplined and determined effort to say no to procrastinating. You just need to cultivate the same habits used by several successful people such as Eric Schmidt (Executive Chairman, Alphabet Inc.), Steve Jobs (CEO and co-founder of Apple Inc.), Jeffrey Bezos (founder, chairman, and CEO of Amazon), Brett David (29-year-old CEO of Prestige Imports Motor Group Miami) and adapt them as part of your routine. While these successful people also experience identical fears and limitations as you, they have been able to take consistent action due to personal training and discipline. To quit procrastinating has to do with training the mind to always stick to its plans, to undertake its due tasks at their set time, to say no to anxiety caused by stress, fear and a sense of incompetence. Identify the important things in your life, so you won't have any qualms ignoring everything else. Decline pointless tasks without upsetting your friends, loved ones or boss. In our daily lives, we will receive invaluable tasks which may be compulsory or not and tasks which are the direct opposite of invaluable - cheap; it boils down to you to decide which is pointless and which is important to accept as a task. This reduces the amount of stress you will go through as a result of tasks and gives you ample time to do them before their appointed time is up.

WHAT DO PEOPLE PROCRASTINATE ABOUT?

There is nothing in life that cannot be procrastinated really. People procrastinate about going for a medical check-up while they are fit even though they are meant to undergo such process once in three months. When they fall sick, they do not have any choice than to seek the medical attention they ought to have sought as a preventive means. In the case of Jim, he procrastinates about his education. He does not do the required study when necessary. He waits till the 'dying minute' before he acts. He never covers the number of books he ought to.

The most obvious areas that are affected by procrastination include but not limited to study, work, etc. while the less obvious are health, food, exercise, relationships, etc. The fact is any project we want to undertake or any task we want to be pursued can be affected by procrastination. Individuals set certain goals, aims or objectives that need to be met or achieved. Such can be viable sources of procrastination. Everyone procrastinates in different measures. Some can keep on top of a situation while others wallow in the procrastination pool.

At one point in our lives, we are required to assess what facets of our lives suffer from procrastination. We need to create a chart and think about the moments we have procrastinated. What were they related to? What were the tasks? What were the deadlines? Did we meet them? Those are questions that shall provide answers to our various problems. Information gathering is quite important to ascertain specific problems.

What is this book going to teach you and how it is going to be structured?

Types Of Procrastinators

- *The Perfectionist:* **People who belong to this category are disturbed by the thought of not meeting expectations. They think of every possible outcome, and they think that they might be a massive flop. They strive so hard but do not meet up to standard. Sometimes, they do not even start because they have decided the outcome themselves. An illustration is given of a soccer player who is signed by one of the world's biggest clubs (e.g., Manchester United) from a relatively low club like Hellas Verona. He is placed on the bench and on Matchday 1, he watches Paul Pogba dazzle in the midfield making somber runs and doing flicks and tricks that help the team secure a massive 3 points win. Pogba is the player's rival and having watched him that day; he thinks he cannot measure up to him. Therefore, he strives so hard to gain his manager's confidence in the training ground. Unfortunately, he has the weight of the world on him, and he thinks he is not performing up to expectations. He is shorn of confidence by his thoughts and gives up too easily.**

- *The Dreamer:* **A lot of people suffer from this kind of procrastination. Many people are so great at planning actions in their head. They envision an almost flawless execution of plans. They think of the potential hindrances or stumbling blocks that can come their way. They think of ways to counter such occurrences. However, the greatest hindrance they face is doing the actual work. They feel stressed sitting down to go through a task for a given time especially if it is a mental one. They tend to postpone taking actions till the 'convenient' time. Writing could be seen as one such activity. Thinking about putting pen to paper and letting those** linguistic phrases pour out in easy verses will appear much easier to do in the head than when actually doing it for such folks.

- *The Worrier:* **Many people tend to worry about the negative parts of undertaking a project. They are pessimists who are based on 'what ifs.' They query the feasibility of a task. They think there is a chance it might not be successful neglecting the chance of being successful. They shy away from making decisions and do not like to delve into untested waters.**

- *The Crisis Maker:* **Those who belong to this category practically act when it is the last minute. This is the category Jim belongs to. They do not act until the 11th hour. Their favorite phrase is "We work best under pressure." They like to wait until the deadline is approaching before they make any move.**

- *The Defier:* **These kinds of people are always defiant. They are aware of certain deadlines but do not care a hoot about it. Living up to expectations is not their primary concern. They just want to live life as it comes without having to worry about goals or objectives. They shy away from taking responsibilities for whatever situation they find themselves and the kind of choices they make.**

- *The Overdoer:* **These people load themselves with too much responsibility and more often than not, they fail to complete various tasks assigned to them. They lack the initiative to say no to certain requests. They have too much on their plate, and they cannot 'consume' all. They never have sufficient time to complete the various tasks at hand. On top of that, they like to make people happy thereby neglecting their emotional state.**

This Book Will Teach You How People Develop Procrastination

"Procrastination is the thief of time." It is usually developed when people fear or dread, or have anxiety about, the important task awaiting them. Procrastination is an automatic, negative, problem habit of needlessly postponing and delaying a timely and relevant activity until another day or time. It always involves a negative emotion that ranges from a whisper of affect to panic. The process always includes a diversionary activity. It practically always involves procrastination thinking, such as "I'll fix the problem later." This complex, automatic, problem habit typically coexists with other negative states, such as anxiety, depression, impulse control challenges, organizational challenges, distractibility, substance abuse, self-doubts, perfectionism, indecisiveness, and other. When procrastination co-occurs with other conditions, it is a complex form of procrastination. To eliminate this negative feeling, people procrastinate preferring to play a video game or check Pinterest. That brings about a better feeling temporarily, but unfortunately, reality stares at them in the end. Procrastinating involves waiting and delaying, avoiding and languishing over tasks and responsibilities. It is a self-defeating behavior and can have lasting effects on our lives. Procrastinators waste tremendous amounts of time. The pleasure principle has a vital role to play in procrastination; one may desire to evade negative emotions and to defer stressful tasks. As the time limit for the task you procrastinate draws closer, the stress starts getting to you, and you may eventually procrastinate more to avoid this stress. Procrastination is not a decisive action; it is not a one-time decision but a continuous decision to put aside important tasks and responsibilities because of feelings of anxiety, incapability, fear and mostly the envisioned stress we think it'll bring. It's quite easy to find excuses for not starting or completing a task. We just find the time to eat the tub of ice cream, play that game, but just not do the task that is silently awaiting us.

You need to find a balance between finding a valid reason to procrastinate and finding a creative way to avoid taking action. Most of our feelings of procrastination arise from self-limiting beliefs or a subconscious fear. By taking your time to explore these thoughts, you'll realize it's easy to overcome them and build a mindset that is action-oriented.

Your mind is an incredible machine that enables you to create anything from your imagination. It could, however, limit your ability to get things done if not properly monitored. At times we get stuck with a project not because we lack the desire to do so but because of maladaptive thought patterns that spring up in our heads.

The root cause of why people procrastinate comes from our low self-confidence. When these thoughts are not promptly checked they lead to you making "excuses" for why a task or project can't be completed. However, when these excuses are challenged, you'll realize that most arise as a result of hidden fears or destructive habit patterns.

The first word we utter most times we procrastinate is that "It doesn't matter." People often avoid tasks which seem unimportant. Sometimes it's not time-critical while at times it's an unpleasant task that is unrelated to a long-term goal.

No matter what your thoughts are, there are times when we defer a task because it doesn't seem to be important. Of course, most tasks or responsibilities are placed on a priority scale, and we decide which comes before which and which should be done before which. However, tasks, which we consider minute or too simple, may be postponed even if there is no other task on our plate because we consider it simple. It, however, becomes complicated when there is pressure attached to it as a result of postponing it to the last minute. Making simple decision making a habit will help you overcome the "It doesn't matter" excuse.

You either get busy with completing a task or be bold enough to get rid of it. As you'll learn, one of the effective ways to get rid of procrastination excuses is to make tough life decisions—even if that means getting rid of things that once seemed important. It is either you will do it at that time, or you decide that you will not do it and get it assigned to someone else. But, for tasks which are official, handed to you and are compulsory, the best solution is to do them at their appointed time.

Another way we develop procrastination is when we say "I feel overwhelmed and have too much to do."

We all experience overwhelming moments which seems like our to-do lists never gets exhausted no matter how hard we work. This problem usually affects those who have the "Superman mentality" where they feel responsible personally accomplish tasks on their own. Concentrating on essential projects and delegating or eliminating the rest can remove feelings of being overwhelmed.

Once you understand how to identify the important things you'll realize that it's easy to handle each task single-handedly and consistently accomplish things. Another valid excuse those who procrastinate often give is "I don't have time right now." Sometimes you may be engrossed in a certain project, and it doesn't make sense to commence another one. However, the excuse of having no time often leads to a disgusting procrastination habit where you always defer undertaking important things.

Saying there is not enough time seems to give empty promise of a perfect future when work will be easier, and you will have more time to work.

In some peoples subconscious mind, they just hope that the need to do the task will eventually disappear. By delaying action until that imaginary "someday," there is a high likelihood that you'll never undertake this project. By thinking of this task, what negative thought pops into your head? Find a solution to that thought by countering it with the truth. For instance, thinking "I'll never be able to do this," you might say to yourself, "If others can do it, I can also do same." The task has been thought about, dealt with what's holding you back, and your destructive thinking fixed. Now, break down the big job into a series of little actionable steps, so you focus solely on handling the next little task. Delve into the nitty-gritty for each project, including little details like whom you will talk with, where and when you'll be working, and duration for each step. (This will stop you from getting overwhelmed as each step is actionable).

Nobody is above making procrastination excuses. No matter how successful you have been, you will sometimes experience a reason not to take action on a project. That's why one needs to form habits that specifically prevent the excuses leads to procrastination. Once you know the reason for developing the habit of procrastination, it makes it easy to proceed to the next step. Low self-confidence, low self-esteem and lack of self-compassion are feelings that develop the habit of procrastination. Low self-esteem or confidence will ultimately affect every aspect of your life, even your daily tasks. It hinders the ability to be creative; reduces or even eliminates the conviction that you can surpass difficult tasks and situations. But in the long run procrastinating will begin to affect job performance. The mood and state of mind will also be affected as worry, fear, or stress sets in. Psychologists accept that procrastination is an emotional reaction. One of the three core emotions always drive it. For example, it may be fear that's driving your inability to get the job done thoroughly and on time. Another is anger; maybe because you have to do something you hate or resent? Or may it is sadness because you feel inadequate or not fit to handle the task. Study yourself and try to identify the emotions responsible for why you procrastinate. Fear, anger, and sadness are just pure sensations that get stuck in the bodies. If they're bottled up and not allowed to gain expression, they will build up inside us like a pressure cooker. Privately, do exaggerated shivering to get rid of fear; punch a pillow or throw your fist in the air to release anger; or watch an emotional movie that makes you shed tears to get rid of sadness. It may sound silly, but it works.

What about Procrastination and Depression

There is nothing wrong about postponing completion of a task in order to allocate enough time to do it properly. But, putting things off impulsively is a different story. Procrastination and depression go hand in hand just like obesity and diabetes. Depression is a factor that causes procrastination and the most time comes before it. However, depression can also come after a series of continuous procrastination which may seem to choke you up, leaving you anxious and afraid of their impending due time. The common symptoms such as fatigue and ineptness, make it easy to say, "I'll just postpone this till tomorrow when I feel better." Within a twinkle of the eye that deadline has dawned on us, and we have started panicking. How best can we deal with this panic? Bury your head in the sand like the vulture and hope it goes away! No, that won't do, although one can easily fall into the trap of procrastination and as the panic increases, so does the depression.

The more depressed we become depressed, the more reality we avoid. Procrastination is a form of avoidance thereby one can view it as a coping strategy albeit one that comes with negative effects. We all develop our coping strategy for difficult situations over time, but we may be faced with varying situations to cope with. Procrastination is developed from a lack of experience, inability to manage time effectively, lack of interest, underestimating the difficulty level of the task, pain aversion, and fear of failure. While evading decisions or actions has the potential of offering short-term succor, over time the effects can be psychologically harmful. Other negative, coping strategies include drug abuse, alcohol, and even overworking. Most depressed people find it difficult to be productive. Most work such as paid employment, babysitting and housekeeping is a chore to the depressed. It exhausts us, leaves us feeling worse than before, physically and emotionally worn out, instead of us to be energized and proud of ourselves. Other depressed people seem to work very hard all the time, but, they achieve little a reward for their efforts. Procrastination and depression have a strong connection to each other and inaction can make you feel that your life is falling apart. This feeling makes hope disappears while you have a generally negative view of life. It's a negative cycle, the less action taken to remedy things, the more depressed you become. Various reasons abound why you might experience procrastination, but it yields the same result: a feeling of, helplessness and being unable to find a solution to things. Depression is quite different from feeling sad. While sadness simply means being unhappy for a short time, depression goes beyond that. In depression you don't only feel sad, you also have the feeling of hopelessness in things getting better.

Once this feeling persists, you will find it very difficult to take action, and that's where procrastination sets in. According to doctors definition and explanation of depression and sadness, it observed that depression is an intense feeling of unhappiness that goes on for weeks, months or years in some cases. One damaging effect of depression is that it can negatively impact your day to day activity and the way you feel generally. Procrastination may be an indication of hopelessness and lack of motivation which may also come from your depressive state.

I'm of the view that they are both connected and that inactivity can make you feel that your life is stagnant. This feeling brings about a lack of hope and a generally negative perception of life. There are several reasons why you might experience procrastination, but the result stays the same: a feeling of inability to effect a change and helplessness.

However, it's certain that depression worsens procrastination and when you realize that you are procrastinating, and you refuse to take action at the appropriate time, you feel worse, and your depression worsens. The first question is: "Does depression lead to procrastination or is it the other way round?" No, depression doesn't lead to procrastination, but it can make it worse. However, frequent procrastination without taking action when you know you should lead to depression. There is nothing as motivating as you taking steps towards achieving your goal, but depression or lack of motivation can inhibit you from taking any step, and that will surely, make you feel even more negative. Data was collated from undergraduates with the use of a self-report measure, and an interesting finding was made. As expected, she found a significantly positive correlation between depression and procrastination. This positive correlation shows that the more depressed we are, the more we tend towards procrastination, and vice versa. This is expected because depression comes with the inability to finish tasks. The person tries to shy away from activities that will cause anxiety, distress or discomfort. Ironically, the act of evading the activity doesn't make it leave, so tensions are heightened because of this avoidance. It is like an emotional weakness which corrupts every other aspect of our lives, hindering us from performing simple tasks or daily routines. And since we feel a kind of emotional weakness in performing them, we tend to postpone them till a date when we hope we'll feel better which, is under probability. When you feel depressed, you suffer from a painful down mood. You may withdraw from life, feel a profound sense of loneliness and worthlessness, and believe that life will continue in this way forever. Can you turn this bad situation around? You can if you don't procrastinate. Procrastination goes in two ways here; when in a bad situation we postpone tasks, shifting them to a further date. But, we also do not try to comprehend the reason(s) why we are in that bad situation, or we are depressed so we also postpone that thinking the situation will dissolve all by itself. Sometimes it does, and most times it doesn't. It is either we forgo the unpalatable situations surrounding us and focus on performing our tasks to avoid procrastination, or we try to source out the reason for that unpalatable situation, putting an end to it and moving on to completing our tasks.

In both procrastination and depression, you may avoid taking corrective action. For example, if you feel lethargic, you may believe you don't have the energy to take corrective actions. This pessimism is a catalyst for procrastination. Believe you are helpless to overcome a depressed mood and reconnect with other people, and you've given yourself an excuse to procrastinate. When this secondary procrastination follows depression, you'd better learn to get past this barrier. One easy way to fail is to disbelieve your capability. The inability to overlook temporary weaknesses that will fade out once the task is being performed will hinder you from performing it. It takes a never say die attitude to keep being strong in the face of depressing situations.

To the barest minimum- our phones, it is very evident that a depressed person may not even pick up the phone to entertain or amuse him or herself even if he or she is a phone addict. Depression comes with a general distaste for everything; even the liked and more for the unliked. So when you are depressed, and there are dishes all over the counter, it is not because you are lazy. It is because you don't have the energy to motivate yourself. Telling yourself words like "Never mind move my body off the couch," even if I feel worse by mere seeing the dishes. So the dishes accumulate and the more they do, the worse I feel. You are failing the first step of housekeeping. When you are well, you find it easy to make decisions and keep them in a positive perspective that if I can do this now, I can do it again. When you are depressed, you cannot manage that optimism in such a healthy way, which is bad enough, but even worse is the shame that goes with it. It's the loss of an ability that you depend on, and you are used to having. The notion that what you did before you can't do again is shattered because of the feeling of depression, making you postpone that task that you have performed before.

Depressed people procrastinate a lot. Procrastination means putting off what you "should" do now for a later time. The word "should" may arise from without, as with the student who delays over the assignment, or from within, like you planting your garden. When it comes from without, it's easy to notice the change that procrastination brings. When it comes from within, it becomes difficult to notice that procrastination comes from depression immediately. Procrastinators perception and assumptions about work are so false. They assume that those who are productive are always in a positive and energetic such that they easily jump right to work and quickly do what needs to be done.

Contrary to this belief, motivation comes after action instead of the other way around. When we compel ourselves to face the task at hand, we realize it isn't as bad as we think, and we start to feel good about the progress we are making. Work proceeds the positive frame of mind. Closely related to this mix-up about motivation is the thought that things should come easy. Depressed people believe that those who perform excellently well at work always feel confident and attain their goals easily; because they don't feel this way, they play down their chances of success. But again, most successful people are of the belief that they will experience hard times, frustrations, and setbacks along the way. Knowing this beforehand will not make them get thrown off their game and descend into self-blame whenever they encounter a problem. If we decide to wait until we feel prepared and fired up, we'll spend a lot of our lives waiting for an opportunity that won't come.

On the other hand, procrastination can help protect the self-esteem of the depressed. You can make positive confessions like "I would have done it better if you I been able to do it." Procrastination also results from the depressed person's tendency to be a perfectionist which is a serious problem. Research has it that the harder a depressed person tries to be perfect, the worse his chances of recovery. Striving to achieve perfection with every single little piece of a project exposes us to disappointment and frustration. There is a connection between the way a procrastinator thinks and mild to serious depression in many people. For some, procrastination leads to depression (reactive depression) as a personality trait, while for others, innate depression causes procrastination due to their illness.

Consequently, procrastination can cause depression and depression can lead to procrastination. Depression arises when one is withdrawn from the normal psychological activity. Depressed people perform less interaction with the society than they did when they were thinking and behaving healthily. Depressed people are detached from people because they may find human interaction too stressful and they live in fear of disappointment. If you experience innate depression, you will also experience low motivation. This triggers a chain reaction where one leads to the other. This implies that you procrastinate about making serious life decisions and even feel incompetent and nervous about making decisions. The lack of motivation ensures you to start a task only to stop mid-way. Part of that behavior is looking for several excuses not to make decisions and perform the needed tasks.

Awareness is the first step in overcoming procrastination. It means figuring out your thoughts and habits. If you're going through a moment of depression, this can be challenging, and it may do you much favor to consult a therapist who will help you pull out of depression. It is possible that you've been procrastinating because you face a daunting decision or tasks ahead of you. You need to break these task into small, realistic and achievable goals. Try to avoid situations that encourage easy distractions or that disrupt your positive mindset or productivity. For example, if you need to study try to find an appropriate environment, away from friends and noise. Break off habits that could warrant distraction.

An example might be a teacher listening to great music alongside marking of papers. Instead, the music should be used as a reward for accomplishing the task. Recognize that depression has correctable features. For example, if you believe you are helpless to change, find exceptions to that line of depressive thinking. You can take that corrective action. Depression normally feels debilitating. Nevertheless, you can act, even in small measure, to progressively master techniques to end your depression.

It will show you that Defeating Procrastination starts from an idea

What is an idea? It is the seed of every civilization that has been built. The Mesopotamian civilization became great in their ideas, architectural structures, and code of laws because numerous men within the civilization held ideas. The ancient Pharaohs of Egypt had ideas, and these were the driving force that enables them to embark upon the construction of the great edifices that continue to blow our minds at the present day. An idea was the driving force that enabled movie directors like Stan Lee to begin a revolutionary process within Hollywood. In the same vein, the entire Marvel franchise which includes comics, movies of superheroes like Thor, Captain America, Black Panther, etc. as well as the DC universe which includes the Franchise of Superman, Wonder woman, etc., were all driven by a single idea. The freedom of the United States of America from the rulership of Britain started as an idea that continued to be spread among the founding fathers of the nation such as Jefferson, etc. The turn of the World War 2 in favor of the Allied powers that included France, Britain, Russia and the United States, began as an idea in the mind of seasoned statesmen like Winston Churchill as well as Josef Stalin and Theodore Roosevelt. The fall of the Soviet Union in the 1990s started as an idea in the mind of a revolutionary mind of Mikhail Gorbachev who was the ruling Premier of Russia at the time. The creation of the Eragon franchise by Christopher Paollini, Kingkiller Chronicles by Patrick

Rothfuss, Harry Potter Franchise by JK Rowling, Percy Jackson and the Olympian franchise by Rick Riodan as well as other book franchises all started with singular ideas. The super-fast Boeing passenger and cargo planes began as a result of an idea. Ford, Ferrari, Mercedes and a host of other companies began as a result of nagging ideas. These ideas were held in an esteemed way within the minds of the people who got them, and one binding factor that is noticeable within all of them is that they were careful not to become the ones that procrastinate. This is because they held fast to the

In the business world, the first lesson that you get to learn is that everything you do begins from your mind. Even as the book begins to delve deep into the particular topic of procrastination, you should be able to adopt the open mindset that would enable the lessons within to sink deeply into your subconscious mind. No one on earth can afford to remain like a granite rock that is impervious to any element: rather, we should all strive to have an open mind that would enable us to internalize lessons that we are being taught on a regular basis.

It will show you that Procrastination can be very deadly

Procrastination can lead to one's death as I have seen and heard of people who died from it. "It can be something like noticing a lump in your breast and keeping silent about it and leaving it untreated." An unnecessarily delayed medical visit can definitely lead to something more dangerous.

Ignoring the fact that procrastination exists and not paying attention to its causes can significantly impact one's life in general. Procrastination tends to be a more serious problem when it affects every aspect of one's life. There are countless causes of procrastination one of it is depression which comes with symptoms such as hopelessness, helplessness and a lack of energy. When procrastination becomes full-fledged, it translates into a personality trait, at this stage its called chronic procrastination. At this stage, procrastination has become a habitual self-destructive pattern. It has now become a habit to put tasks off impulsively.

The chronic procrastinator cannot undertake any task on time which will eventually result in serious career struggles, recurring financial problems, and reduced quality of life. Chronic procrastination may lead to disability psychological and dysfunction in several aspects of life and may bring about low self-esteem and a persistent sense of shame.

Many individuals considered as "chronic procrastinators" are in reality suffering from an associated mental health problem like depression or Attention Deficit Disorder (ADD). These individuals often find it difficult to understand why they struggle to "get it together," and can eventually settle for a life of frustration, struggle, and underachievement. Unfortunately, this is caused by their limited knowledge about what procrastination is about. Even amongst mental health professionals, some only view procrastination as a "bad habit." How many of us avoid seeing their doctor or dentist only for us to realize that the delay has brought about more complications? The health implications of depressed procrastination vary, but according to research, it shows that they can lead to higher risk.

It will teach you about the Chronic Procrastination and the Time Management Problem

Procrastination is the act of deferring or delaying a task. It's the avoidance of doing a task that needs to be accomplished at present, more or less postponing a task until its deadline. Procrastination becomes chronic when little things which do not take any effort to do are postponed; it may be regarded as a very high level of laziness. Procrastination can affect any aspect of life such as putting off house cleaning, seeing a dentist for that toothache, submitting a job report or business proposal. Procrastination can cause feelings of guilt, depression, self-doubt, and inadequacy. To procrastinate can hinder productivity. Most times we as human beings tend to postpone our tasks and responsibilities until the last minute, practically because of the notion that there will always be time. We fail to understand that time is a measurement of periods; there is always a specific and limited period for everything. From the time a task or responsibility is given, the duration for that task begins to countdown. We often forget that time doesn't wait for anyone and continue to postpone our responsibilities till they reach their expected time. We, however, make it a habit that we not only do it for one task or responsibility but for several, and in their due time, we have multiple tasks choking us up which we have postponed over and over again.

Most times, when we procrastinate, we end up worse off for it. Whether academically or socially, procrastinating leads to a lot of tasks being on your plate with more than half of the allotted time to be used to do them gone. Everyone procrastinates things until the last minute at some point or the other, but procrastinators are chronically used to avoiding difficult tasks and are always on the lookout for distractions. Some people are of the view that they suddenly become highly productive when they procrastinate! Instead of filling the tax form, they choose to clean the whole house, even though they do hate to clean. While others try to forget about the urgent task by doing something fun instead. While it might seem harmless pushing tasks to one side with the intention of doing it later, it can have negative ripple effects. Procrastination at large shows our perennial struggle with self-control and inability to tell yourself that you need to do what you need to do now! It depends partially on our state of mind, as well as our inability to predict accurately how we'll feel the next day. "I don't feel like it" is prioritized over goals; however, it then sets in motion a downward spiral of negative emotions that prevent future effort. We forgo our goals because of a temporary, unrealized feeling of laziness or weakness that seems to override every other feeling of responsibility. We tend to view our tasks and responsibilities as stressful, no matter how minute they seem to be and ignoring them which is the same as procrastinating just brings more stress on us. It's like a cycle of ignoring our tasks because they look or seem stressful which results in more stress and our bid to continue to ignore this leads us not to realize that the feeling of stress will never end until we complete these tasks.

When we procrastinate the temporary feeling of ease has no foundation and is easily shattered by the feeling that there will come a due time for these tasks. So there is more or less no rest for a person that procrastinates since it'll always be at the back of his/ her mind that there is a task waiting for you which will not go away, is compulsory and has a limited time. The unrelenting feeling of stress leads to fatigue which will eventually lead to both physical and mental exhaustion. Exhaustion will also not allow you to perform in other aspects of your daily life; it will deter you from performing to your full extent in other spheres which will affect your creativity. Procrastination was revealed to be higher on tasks perceived as unpleasant or imposed than on tasks which people believed they lacked the required skills for accomplishing the task. Once a task seems big or greater than we presume we can handle we become anxious. Humans generally tend to shy away from things that make us uncomfortable or move away from our comfort zone. If a task is going to make a person uncomfortable most times, we do everything to avoid it, passing it onto the next person and the next person does the same until he or she has no one to pass it on to. Nevertheless, financial incentives can spur a person not to procrastinate. But, a person who takes on tasks, which he or she is incapable of executing because of the monetary incentive attached to them, will probably procrastinate in the end due to the number of responsibilities he has taken on his plate.

It is evident that a bulk of the world's population delay tasks. However, researches done over the years have indicated that a frightening percentage of people are chronic procrastinators. This category of people does not do tasks frequently. Rather, they tend to delay the execution of tasks.

They are of the opinion that time management cannot be effective due to certain situations. They do not think of time management as the ideal thing to worry about. As long as they can meet deadlines, they do not have to worry about any other thing. They tend to make an excuse for every failure or shortcoming.

Chronic procrastination can be defined as an irrelevant, nonsensical delay or a very important project or task. It also refers to postponing the execution of tasks or projects until the last minute. It is important these delays are done so frequently. This confirms the reason why they are called chronic procrastinators.

Different features characterize chronic procrastinators. They include, but not limited to, low level of self-confidence, social and emotional anxiety.

Various researches conducted has revealed that various people who exhibit chronic procrastination, engage in self-destructive behaviors which include frequent excuse making, non-review of performance, shifting blame on others apart from them. Many have been thought as reasons why people procrastinate, but the chief causative agent is fear of failure has been identified as the principal causative agent. It is not uncommon to hear procrastinators say that they do not have enough time to start or finish given tasks or projects. However, if a non-procrastinator is given the same amount of time to complete a task, he or she shall do so with ample time left.

Chronic procrastinators may say they perform better under pressure, but more often than not that's their way of justifying putting things off. The result of working under pressure can never equal that which is done when you are ease; it far outweighs that which is done when you are choked up with tasks. We have all faced procrastination at one point or another. For as long as we are humans, we have always struggled with delays and procrastinating on issues that concern us. To procrastinate can hinder productivity. Due to the number of tasks postponed, fatigue and stress will set in thinking about their deadline. They act as deterrents to creativity, as a mentally tired person will not look to further stress his brain in ruminating on an issue to bring results. During our moments of productivity when we figure out momentarily on how to stop procrastinating, we feel satisfied and accomplished.

The positive side? Overcoming procrastination is possible and realistic albeit with effort. Most perfectionists are also procrastinators; it is psychologically permissive never to undertake a task than to face the possibility of failing. Putting off a task is not procrastination as long as there are rational reasons for doing so. The rational reasons justify this act, which forms a reasonable excuse to postpone the tasks. Since there is a reasonable excuse that will be proffered there should be no stress in postponing the task. It, however, does not mean the tasks or responsibilities will leave the mind, but they are however put aside for several reasons and obviously for a greater purpose or task.

Chronic procrastination is as a result of feelings that the task seems large, complex, and too overwhelming. When a task is more than the person's ability, or when it is exaggerated in the mind of the person procrastination sets in. It may also be that the task looks tedious and boring and the person feels it may dim his or her creative spark. Not knowing how the task is done makes it difficult to start and some people view it as hard to get motivated until things become urgent and a deadline is close. Negative thoughts and feelings also get in the way of doing the task, which may not serve as reasonable excuses to postpone the task but deter you from performing them. A person that procrastinates must realize they have a problem and find effective ways to overcome procrastination because they are putting their health, family, and job at risk. It becomes a lifestyle when it becomes chronic. Some people don't view chronic procrastinating as a bad thing due to the common belief that they, "work best under pressure." However, the truth is that procrastinating can cause harm to one's life.

Chronic procrastination impacts Relationships. When a procrastinator works in a team, their inability to do the required task assigned to them can delay completion of projects. This will, in turn, affect the relationship the procrastinator has with the other members of the team. This may signal the end to such friendships and cause others to avoid working with the procrastinator on future projects. It is a fallacy to believe that people work better under pressure. Procrastors put unnecessary stress and pressure on themselves, which may cause them to be developmental and physical exertion.

Issues with Self-Regulation - procrastinators tend to develop excessive consumption of alcohol since they are dully stressed with all manner of tasks and responsibilities they are struggling to forget. Alcoholism provides a simple way to forget procrastinated tasks, but its results are very negatively exerting. Increased Health Issues will come the person's way since he or she is under great stress daily. Procrastinators tend to have their immune system compromised which predisposes them to colds and flu. Also, procrastinators have issues with insomnia as the tasks keep lingering in the thoughts hence inability to sleep. Procrastination affects people of all ages. People suffering from this habit don't hurt their academic or careers only, but they also create an unnecessary relationship and health problems.

If you or a close friend is a chronic procrastinator, some steps can be taken to change such behavior.

For a student experiencing chronic procrastination, it can be due to the Fear of Failure – Some people avoid working on school projects due to their fear of failure. They have the feeling that even with their best they will fail, so they get discouraged from doing the work. By abandoning things and not putting all their efforts into a project, the procrastinator is setting themselves up for failure. Another reason is the Fear of Success – This is the opposite of fear of failure, people who perform excellently on a project and achieve great things fear to be unable to repeat that success. They have the mindset that they may not be able to perform as well as, or better than, their previous accomplishment, so they resort to procrastinating. Some people also procrastinate due to the expectations placed on them by family and friends. If someone grows up in the family where the educational and career standard is high, such individual may delay doing class assignments, score less than average, and potentially fail the course, all as an act of rebellion.

Boredom and/or Lack of Motivation – When a subject seems boring to a student, such student might experience procrastination. Such a student finds it difficult to find motivation or inspiration. Such can lead to incomplete or poorly written assignments.

This Book will teach you ways to Stop Procrastination

There are various strategies we can make use of to stop procrastinating. Each concept will be outlined, explained with examples of strategy in action. The first step is to give an instant reward for taking action. If you can find ways to make instant rewards for making long-term choices, procrastination becomes easier to avoid. One great way to bringing future rewards into the present moment is to employ a strategy known as temptation bundling.

6 Tips to Get the Best From This Book

1. Read with an Open Mind

2. Practice daily

3. Have your jotter and pen with you

4. Share it with Friends and Family

5. Make ample Research to add to your knowledge

6. Understand that you have to apply the values inside into forceful action

The process of reading this book will prove to be a difficult task at most times for the reader who has not learned the value of being firm in his character, but it will prove to be an excellent first step for you

QUOTES ABOUT PROCRASTINATION

-------"*Things may come to those who wait, but only the things left by those who hustle.*"– **Abraham Lincoln**

-------"*My advice is never to do tomorrow what you can do today. Procrastination is the thief of time.*"– **Charles Dickens**

-------"*Never put off for tomorrow, what you can do today.*"– **Thomas Jefferson**

--------"*Procrastination is the bad habit of putting off until the day after tomorrow what should have been done the day before yesterday.*"– **Napoleon Hill**

--------"*The really happy people are those who have broken the chains of procrastination, those who find satisfaction in doing the job at hand. They're full of eagerness, zest, productivity. You can be, too.*"7– **Norman Vincent Peale**

--------"*A year from now you may wish you had started today.*"– **Karen Lamb**

--------"*Don't wait. The time will never be just right.*"– **Napoleon Hill**

-------- "*You cannot escape the responsibility of tomorrow by evading it today.*"– **Abraham Lincoln**

---------- "*One of the greatest labor-saving inventions of today is tomorrow.*"– **Vincent T. Foss**

--------"*The two rules of procrastination: 1) Do it today. 2) Tomorrow will be today tomorrow.*"– **Author Unknown**

--------"*What may be done at any time will be done at no time.*"– **Scottish Proverb**

--------"*Tomorrow is often the busiest day of the week.*"– **Spanish Proverb**

--------"*The best way to achieve something is to begin.*"– **Author Unknown**

--------"*I remember that I read somewhere about an organization called Procrastinators Anonymous. It seems they had existed for some years but never had the chance to hold a meeting.*"– **Unknown**

--------"*Procrastination is like masturbation. It feels good at first, but in the end, you realize that you are only screwing yourself.*"– **Author unknown, possibly from Monty Python?**

--------*"How soon not now, becomes never."*– **Martin Luther**

--------*"In delay there lies no plenty."*– **William Shakespeare**

-------*"Anyone can do any amount of work, provided it isn't the work he is supposed to be doing at that moment"*– **Robert Benchley**

-------*"Whatever you want to do, do it now! There are only so many tomorrows."*– **Michael Landon**

Chapter 2 :
Why Do People Procrastinate?

There are numerous reasons why people procrastinate. Most of these reasons always turn out to be valid or unnecessary reasons, but it all depends on whose perspective we see them. Take for example, if as an employee, you are given a task to carry out by your manager, and you decide to procrastinate because you do not have an idea of where to start or end. The reason behind your procrastination, of course, is valid to you at this point, but not to your manager whose job is to get you to perform the task. So the reasons for procrastination are highly dependent on a particular perspective. Although most times, perspectives tend to be a mutual thing, like you just procrastinated because you are just lazy. We will be discussing these reasons with no particular perspective in mind. When reading these reasons why people procrastinate, I want you to hold the torch of examination very close to yourself in order to easily spot out the reasons why you procrastinate. The reason for this is that human beings often make the unconscious effort to spot out challenges within other people without pausing to think that they may constitute part of the problem. As this book will begin to reel out the reasons, I can mentally picture you saying,

Yeah. That is how Mary my co-worker acts

True! Bob, my ex-husband, procrastinated due to these reasons.

Yes! My son does this all the time.

While it may probably be true that those people you just called are chronic offenders due to the reasons listed below, the aim of this chapter is to help you recognize the reasons why YOU, not Mary, Bob, or Dylan, continues to procrastinate because frankly, their reasons for procrastination may have simulated from your inability to make the first move. Like a cow chews its curd after eating, I want you to ruminate deeply on that while we dive into the reasons why we procrastinate.

Lack Of Definition Of Goals And Objectives

Why exactly are you doing that task? What are you going to achieve in doing it?

The lack of definite answers to the questions above is the bedrock of procrastination. Do you have a particular task that you have been procrastinating? Check it, you are either yet to define the goals and objective of that particular task, or you simply have forgotten about the goals and objectives you had set. Defining your goals and objectives means that failure to finish the task will bring about consequences. This makes it a two-way thing; one is such that we procrastinate because we have no idea why we are to do a particular task. The other is such that we haven't considered the consequences of not having to do that task. For example, at one certain point in time, when you realize that you add weight and then decide you will work out every morning for a whole month to shed the weight. In doing this, you will start to diet. The goal of your task will be to lose weight; the objective was to work out every morning by jogging and of course being on a diet. The consequence therefore of not achieving this task for most people is that they would add more weight and will end up being angry.

The Fear Of Failure

Naturally, failing is not the desired result. Procrastinators have the tendency to believe that trying hard and failing is worse than not trying at all. Procrastination, therefore, becomes a way to protect ourselves from the perceived failure that we dread so much. Failure can be either inability to finish a task or not getting expected results.

Usain Bolt will probably never turn up for training if he is so scared of failing.

Barrack Obama wouldn't have become the first black president US if he was scared of losing at the polls and therefore refuse to run for the presidency.

There wouldn't be Facebook today if Mark Zuckerberg was so scared of failing that he didn't take Facebook outside his dormitories

And I probably wouldn't have written this book if I was scared that it will fail.

Most times, the building blocks to our self-esteem are hinged on how much we have either succeeded or failed. Everyone has their particular reason as to why they fear failure. Using myself, for example, the number one reason why I fear failure is the fact that I don't want to disappoint my loved ones. Some people fear failure because of ego; others fear simply because they simply hate failing.

Irrespective of the drive, procrastination tends to be an easy way to avoid tasks that will likely bring us a failure. The fear of failure is a two-way factor. It can either motivate you to get a job done, or it can get you not to get a job done.

The Feeling Of Being Overwhelmed

When there are so many highly prioritized things to do, it leads to the feeling of being overwhelmed, and this can either slow us down, or it will lead us to do something entirely different from what we should have done. For example, the secretary to the manager of a company, who is told to prepare a report for a board meeting, at the same time, being given a task to prepare a contract-bidding document for the manager. Then she closes early so she will pick up her little child from school, and then gets a notification of an unread message from her friend on her WhatsApp, asking her to help her choose between two shoes she hopes to buy. Which task do you think she will do first?

My best bet is that she will do the one that will take lesser time, and it will be to reply to her friend's message. This is because it is easier than the other tasks, even though it is relatively unconnected to the tasks assigned to her office as a secretary, or the duty as a mother. The fact is that when there are too many seemingly important things to do, it becomes difficult to get our priorities right. This, in turn, leads to a poor decision on what to do and hence, procrastination comes to play.

The case of having to stop working into the midnight in order to be able to work out every morning is also a good example of being overwhelmed. I know the whole scenario doesn't look overwhelming, but I needed to stay awake late to get my projects done while doing this; I tend to take a whole lot of junks to keep me from sleeping. And then again, I needed to shed some weight by working out early in the morning, but I can't afford to go late to school. So I have to wake up early. To wake up early, I either have to sleep early or sleep for a shorter period of time; this will either affect my health or my work. Does it look overwhelming now?

Priorities

The part of the human brain that controls thoughts and action functions by protecting itself by tending to take our prioritized actions serious because not having them sorted out will like a threat to its sanity. Procrastination can arise as a result of our inability to prioritize tasks and actions in order of their importance. We unconsciously do things that we have given more importance to while postponing or not even doing the less important ones. The best-selling movies on motivation till date are rooted in the athletic world. This is because athletes are perfect examples of individuals that have their priorities set and ongoing for years. A young athlete that wants to represent his country in the Olympics knows that he has to train more than just any other athlete because he has to be his best. Usain Bolt, the fastest human alive today was once asked what his number one goal is at the starting line and he said it was to finish better than his previous record. He went further to say that the race is not run in the field but before the race; outside the tracks. Here is someone that has set a goal for himself and to achieve it, he has recognized that there are priorities and one of them is to train – before the race. Training cuts across so many disciplines. In the case of Bolt, having to train is the most important task for him. Hanging out with friends all-day or spending his day chatting on social media comes last. Still on the weight shedding experience, when some people finally get over the procrastination of the need to work out and to go on a diet, the next problem they encountered is, having to stop activities that will keep them late into the night, thereby impeding their desire to wake up early. In short, they discovered that staying late awake had a major influence in their intake of junks.

Denial

For procrastination to be identified as procrastination, it has to be with acceptance on the side of the individual. But what happens when we pretend that a particular act of procrastination is not actually what it is? Does it stop it from being procrastination? Well, no. Denial of procrastination itself is one major reason why people procrastinate, and this denial always comes with alternative excuses.

We convince ourselves that we are not procrastinating because we are doing something else. Sometimes we tend to be totally oblivious of the word 'procrastination' while all this is going on. For example, there was a time a friend had a rash skin reaction to a particular body lotion she was using. She knew she had to see a dermatologist immediately, but she kept on postponing her appointment. It didn't seem like procrastination at this time, because she was in actual denial as she gave silly excuses as to why she was yet to see a doctor. The excuses were so invalid that it got to the point that she thought this way, "I haven't slept in a while. I will sleep; after all, I have stopped using the body lotion."

I don't want to go ahead to tell you that it got to the point that she couldn't sleep any longer. When she finally went to see the doctor, she spent more than she would have in the early days of the occurrence.

It could have been worse; many fatal cases of cancer in Third World Countries are blamed on late diagnosis which is hinged on the procrastination of patients. This is to show you that procrastination actually cost lives. You probably aren't doing that particular important task right now, because you have convinced yourself that you are reading a book on procrastination for the first time but it is important we define procrastination again, so you recognize it at every turn.

Procrastination is the avoidance or the action of delaying or postponing a task that needs to be accomplished.

Indecision

Sometimes procrastination can be as a result of indecision. These indecisions range from inability to determine what is important to us, to why a particular action or task should be done, or how it should be done. There is a difference between a student studying for his SAT exam, who simply cannot make a decision to either read his books or go partying with friends, and a student who is yet to do his assignment because he simply hasn't decided on the way he will do the assignment. One is a problem of priorities, which, by the way, can be relative because the student sitting for his SAT exam might actually think that partying is his number one priority. However, the student with the assignment is a typical problem of indecision.

Procrastination also arises at a pivotal point between deciding what to do because of the uncertainty of the outcome, or when there are a whole lot of alternative ways to get the job done.

Are we going to fail? Or succeed?

The unconscious inability to answer this question dampens our morale in finishing tasks. For example, in an attempt to make the maiden edition of the school annual magazine spectacular, the editor in chief – a student - had decided to interview president Donald Trump. She had drafted a letter, sealed it, and it was ready to be mailed. She had also gotten the phone details of the chief of staff to the president while not forgetting to collect the official email address of the office of the president. But for weeks, she couldn't use any of the mediums that were made available for her because she was not sure of the particular one that would be more efficient.

Humans have a tendency to act on the basis of inspiration. Every single action is backed by inspiration, and this inspiration can either be positive or negative. It's interesting to know that even procrastination has its own inspiration. A particular set of psychologists in the United States, with the use of Neuro-linguistic Programming (NLP), have successfully harnessed the concept of procrastination in anger management, this they do by teaching their clients on how to procrastinate anger and depression. But before they can do this, they tend to get the patient inspired and motivated to want to get rid of anger. Here is a perfect example of riding procrastination on the back of inspiration.

The creative industry tends to be a perfect example of where inspiration is a reason why people procrastinate. It is believed that it is impossible for a poet to write a poem, a singer to pen down songs and for a painter to paint without inspiration. Therefore, most people decide to go out and chill with friends or engage in other activities with the excuse that they are seeking inspiration. The fact is that the absence of inspiration, or the belief that nothing can be done without a certain level of inspiration, causes procrastination.

Even with inspiration, the absence of motivation will get you nowhere. It is one thing to sit down with the height of inspiration of what to write and another thing to actually write when you want to write a book. When things get terrible, or when you run out of inspiration, you will definitely need to stay motivated in order to get the task done. A humanitarian once journeyed deep into a town in Thailand. The leaders in the community had been expecting her for over a year and asked her why it took her so much time to come finally. She smiled and told them that it was because of procrastination.

Did you read that? A whole year filled with procrastination!

What happened was that the humanitarian had planned her journey to this town early with her motivation being the desire to help in family planning. Along the line, however, she started considering the living conditions she was going to be subjected to in this town, and the difficulty in adapting to life in a new environment. While she was at this level of considerations, she lost motivation: that was the reason why she arrived a year later.

Downplay Of Tasks/Trivialization

Trivialization, which is the act of making something to appear insignificant, can be likened to denial. The difference, however, is that in trivializing; we actually recognize that we are in deep into procrastination. When presented with two or more tasks, we simply tend to downplay the more important, or the more demanding ones as totally being unimportant. Take the dermatologist, for example, trivializing a potential visit to his office will mean that I am downplaying the importance of seeing the doctor. But denial, on the other hand, means that I actually recognize that seeing a doctor is important, but I am yet to see him.

Trivialization does not just affect the important tasks; it also affects the not so important tasks. The cat you do not feed before leaving the house because it didn't seem important; the task you couldn't do because there was no reward and even the poem you couldn't write because you felt that nobody would read it after all. If at the edge of getting a task done, we trivialize it, there is a likely probability that our initial conclusion will cloud our sense of judgment. For example, as a student, if you are given an assignment that you regarded as not important because you need to hang out with your friends, there is a probability that you will not get back to that assignment.

Lack Of Rewards

Most times the wheels of the motivation to get the job done are filled with rewards that can be gotten from the job. Rewards cut across different definitions. They could be monetary, gratification, satisfaction or a sense of belonging. If faced with tasks that require equal attention, there is a great tendency that we will complete the one with a greater reward before any other one. Let's say you are an architect and you have a task to design three structures for three different clients, the first task will bring you a lot of recognition, and it will be a boost for your career, but the monetary reward is low. The second one has a lot of monetary rewards, but it won't bring you recognition. And the third one will bring you both recognition and a lot of money. It is a common intuitive that you will go after the one with greater reward while relegating other ones to the background. The case of choosing a task with greater rewards is mostly a result of having overwhelming tasks at hand. If a student is given two different assignments, despite the fact that his reward is not in money, he will perform the tasks because of the rewards of mental satisfaction that would come later. Rewards do not, however, justify procrastination, as it is a relative factor. It is a relative factor such that sometimes, when the rewards are too much, it can actually freak the individual out, leading to procrastination too.

Perfectionism

The fear of having to do something and it turns out not to be perfect to put a whole lot of pressure on people. Perfectionism contributes to procrastination. We either aren't doing a particular task because we are waiting for the perfect time to get a perfect output, or simply because we don't want to do it at that point or any other time; this is rampant among people who are perfectionists. Another example of procrastination that arises as a result of perfectionism is performing a task halfway. Some people will refrain from performing a task if there is no possibility of finishing that task. This is because they like finishing what they start. Pete, a fictional character, will rather not start something if he would not be able to finish it. Thus, when he is faced with such tasks, he freaks out.

Distraction

Mankind has never been so exposed to as many distractions as what we are currently experiencing in the 21st century. Social media, news media, movies, mobile phones, music, etc. and all other sources of distraction you can think of, contribute to procrastination. I am sure we can all relate to this. We have all experienced situation where we had to postpone a particular task just because there was a certain WhatsApp or Facebook message we had to reply or a particular trend or Twitter that we simply couldn't ignore. We are in a generation where the smartphone is now the closest companion of man, but enough of the new trend of distraction. The truth is that even before the arrival of these technological advancements, there was a distraction. Distractions like emotional distractions; responsibilities to the society; and the family, extra-curricular activities and many others are perfect examples free from the pendulum of the 21st-century technology.

Studies show that students who tend to be easily distracted are the ones that hardly get their assignment done. Also, most students that get easily distracted are either from a broken home or are experiencing emotional problems. Apart from subjective distractions, other tasks that might seemingly be important at that point in time distract us. For example, a friend while working on a proposal for his company sometimes ago experienced some challenges with a leaky faucet that caused him to be distracted. After they called the local technician to fix the fault, he realized that he had a relatively small amount of time to finish the proposal for the company; he had unconsciously postponed the processes of getting the work done. Distractions!

The Fear Of Success

As strange as it might seem, sometimes we tend to procrastinate because we are scared of the responsibilities that come with success. It is common knowledge that with success comes a bigger expectation. Maybe the only reason why that very talented singer has been postponing his chance to record his first studio song is that he is scared the song will shoot him to spotlight, a life he is not ready to live just yet. There is no contradicting to the fact that you would not belong to the same circle that you once belonged to when you were not successful. Success would mean taking on more responsibilities than you can shoulder. In the case of relationships, it may be that a delay in getting married is caused by the fear of the responsibilities that would come with jumping the broom with your partner.

Rebellion

This is a subtle reason why people procrastinate. It can simply be a tactic to go against some certain rules or standards in an organization, or simply due to external evaluation. Procrastination may be a form of rebelling against people. When a friend was younger, his uncle grounded him for two weeks because he was out late. Three days later, the same uncle gave my friend his shoes to clean for him. On a normal day, my friend would have cleaned the shoes without having a second thought, but being grounded for two weeks meant he was going to miss playing video games with my friends. Because of that, he didn't clean the shoes because he simply wanted to rebel against his uncle. Also, there are cases like a student failing his courses intentionally simply because he didn't like the school he was put in. That student would have postponed the performance of academic tasks like assignment and tests. Employees in companies rebel against management by procrastinating their duties. There have been reports of strikes being held by labor unions of the Hollywood movie industry in order to rebel against the directors that refused to pay what had been agreed upon in their contracts.

Unassertiveness

Being unassertive makes us agree to do things that we don't really want to do. Having to do unreasonable tasks just because we cannot simply say "no" can get us pretty overwhelmed with so much work that our only way out is procrastination? Few years' back, a friend gave his nephew a task to do on the computer with Microsoft Excel, thinking he was familiar with it. The nephew, on the other hand, accepted to do the task, not wanting to say no to his aunt because she had promised to get him a gift once he is done. In the end, she got to know that in the quest to get this particular task done, he spent time learning how to use MS Excel. This affected his school assignments and other house chores to the extent that he started waking up very late because he was mostly doing his research into the night. His inability to say "no" didn't just end up in him procrastinating the task she gave to him, but it also led to the procrastination of other important things that he could have done without stress. Many people tend to fall in this category: "the fear of the unknown" when we simply refuse a task, grips us so much that we accept anything that is thrown our way because we want to win approval.

Reframing

Reframing has to do with leaving a particular task undone until the rush hour; believing that doing the work at an early stage will do harm to the expected output. It is one of the prevalent excuses that aid procrastination. For example, I might have a deadline to get a task done in one day, but due to my past experience and knowing that I tend to work better in the midnight, I will skip working on the task in the afternoon and even in the evening; many people have been in this situation. The strange thing about reframing is that it can form a routine that tends to develop into a habit. For example, being a worker living in a city with so much traffic gridlock, a person may be always getting back to his apartment late. After having his bath, he eats and watches the news update, after which he turns on his computer to work on tasks that need to be worked on. This became a routine, and the person may begin to find it difficult to work immediately after he gets back from work without eating or taking his bath- not even without watching the news update. The most definitive of it all was that such people had conditioned their minds to only work after doing the normal routine. This is harmful because failure to get it done at this unhealthy time will mean they are not going to beat the deadline. Reframing is also common among students who start reading their books days to their exams believing that starting early will lead to them forgetting what they have read during tests and examinations.

Laziness

Laziness comes in different folds. It is generally the quality of the inability to work. The word 'Laziness' over the years have been associated with poverty. Many people are lazy not because they were born lazy, but because they have no sense of direction as to what to do, or simply because they know what they ought to do, but they aren't doing it. Sometimes we procrastinate tasks; just because we do not in any way, have intentions of carrying out these tasks. I believe I can use an example that we can all relate to. Have you ever had to wake up from sleep knowing fully well that you have to get up from the bed in order not to be late for work, but you find yourself still lying on the bed? In some cases, there are times people wake up, and they just cannot believe that it is morning yet. They then convince themselves that they could get some extra bout of sleep for an extra twenty minutes, and go back to sleep. This habit of postponement is not one that is present in the lives of some people and absent in others; rather all successful people encounter this and sometimes fall to the nudge. There are some days that Bill Gates would feel the need to stay back in bed for some hours and allow other people take charge of the daily tasks for the day since he is the richest man on earth. There are days that athletes would feel the need to flunk practice and spend quality time in bed or engaging in other activities.

Lack Of Energy

We need the energy to do work. To finish tasks, we have to be active and productive, and there is nothing that affects the productivity of humans more than anything that affects their energy level. Ill health, poor eating diet, lack of sleep and many others are a major determinant of our energy levels. We tend to function less efficient in moments of our low energy, and the best option that appeals to us becomes procrastination.

In numerous occasions, growing cases of obesity may contribute towards bringing you to the point where you procrastinate on a very frequent basis. Karma , they say, is like a mobile Insurance guy who keeps coming back to visit your door and in this instance, the consumption of too much coke on a daily basis in addition to eating numerous junk foods like pizza, burgers, etc. will eventually contribute towards helping you to procrastinate on a more frequent basis than ever. Perhaps, if you had tried to live a little bit healthier by sticking to veggies and a healthy routine, the procrastination would have been avoided. Sometimes it is actually hard to diagnose these ailments, so it is advised that just maybe, the reason why you procrastinate is hinged on a medical condition that can only be diagnosed by a specialist.

Negativity

Negativity on its own clutters the mind. There is no way we can get a particular task done when we expect the worst output. Sometimes, it is not even the output that causes procrastination but the path taken to get the task done. For example, if as a construction engineer, you are to travel a long distance to get building equipment with a negative mindset, you might end up filing your mind with things like the possibility of an accident, the possibility of getting robbed on your way, the possibility of not getting exactly what you want and even the possibility of you failing as a construction engineer in that particular project. And so in order to avert this negativity, you procrastinate.

Lack Of Patience

Some tasks like writing a movie script, directing a movie or even farming can take so much time in preparation and also, an even longer time for fruition. Some come with so much hardship and difficulty that without patience, we tend to procrastinate or simply not do the job. In those cases, some distinguished screenwriters had to admit this is one of the famous reason as to why they procrastinated in getting a script ready for production. Javed Akhtar, who happens to be a legendary screenwriter in his Tedx talk stated that lack of patience was a potent reason why he had streams of abandoned projects while he continued to move on to newer projects. On some particular occasions, lack of patience can make him abandon a task even after starting since the particular fuelling drive that caused him to begin, seemed to fizzle out. This is very easy to understand unlike Rocket science: just like that time you began an early morning jog and began to enjoy it at the beginning stage. The thrill of feeling the gentle wind hit your face accompanied by the music playing from your headphone may fuel you to keep jogging for more than thirty minutes but when you begin to reach an hour, the real stress sets in. After the thrill comes to the stressful feelings for this task and it is at that point that most runners begin to feel the overwhelming desire to stop to catch their breaths especially if they are engaging in a marathon. This thrill can be found within many homes during the weekends when the father may set out to do the laundry and clean up in the home. In such instances, the father may wake up with so much enthusiasm to get the job done so that in the end, the house would be sparkling clean. But the twist is that just midway into the cleanup, that dad would realize that he had spent more than two hours cleaning and things begin to spiral out of the range of his control. It is at that point that he may begin to feel the need to go out to the park with his dog or go to the pub to catch up with his old friend who tends the bar there. The interesting thing is that he may even begin to think about dumping the job halfway, getting into his car with his family and then zoom off to the cinema to see the latest Avengers film. That is the nature of how the mind works concerning some tasks. I do not believe the mind of anyone can be sufficiently stimulated to begin a task and then finish the task using the same driving force that propelled the start even if the task was a favorite hobby. You may have heard some seasoned bikers go into the tattoo shop with the aim of getting a scary looking tattoo, and then begin to feel the need to leave during the process of getting the tattoo. This particular thing can even be found within couples that choose to engage in a task together. At a point in time, the zeal of continue will come due to lack of patience, and they may feel the need to engage in procrastination.

It Might Be Beyond Procrastination

Do you feel tired when it comes to the period that you wish to engage in a task that may be grueling? Perhaps that task may be skipping due to your need to lose weight or maintain that hourglass figure of yours. Away from procrastination, it is possible that what seems to be procrastination might be a symptom to something serious. Procrastination has previously been linked with hypertension, cardiovascular disease, bipolar disorder, and anxiety issues. Also, procrastination may be the offshoot of that terrible mental ailment called Depression. We all know what it means to be depressed. That period of time when nothing seems to appeal to you and every task becomes a bore. In some cases, such depression may be so crippling because they arise from a feeling of un-fulfillment. Just like in the case of every successful person, they would be faced with those times when they would be filled with feelings of not reaching their potentials: some medical personnel would call this 'Mid-life crisis.' Nevertheless, if you begin to notice that you procrastinate often, a visit to the counselor or psychologist may be good so that you are able to identify the issue and nip it in the bud immediately.

Now, I am not saying to jump up and rush off to a psychologist at just the slightest tinge of feeling down and out. This is more serious than that. A seasoned helping hand who is trained should come in to intervene when you are feeling almost energy-less. The day feels sooo long yet you are loathe to actually do anything. Even thoughts of doing anything feel you with such overpowering weariness that you just want to continue lying down in that couch or stay in bed. When thoughts of mortality creep in, then it is most definitely time to seek professional, medically trained help.

Chapter 3 :
The Meat Of Things
36 Ways PROVEN

36 Proven Ways To Help Anyone Beat Procrastination

Goal Setting And Monitoring

The goal of writing this book on procrastination is to take you to a point where even the thought of procrastination begins to seem repulsive to your thoughts, and that is why it is important to set goals and monitor the progress of such goals. Goals are particular tasks that you have deliberately written down and placed in a strategic point that is easily accessible for you to see. Examples of such goals may be;

I want to be the greatest showman in the circus I am working now

I want to be the greatest vet doctor and the best friend to all pets

I want to become the next President of the United States of America.

I want to be the best Talk-show host that the world has ever seen.

All these are great goals that many people have set over the course of the years, and they have been reached after much perseverance. The key to happy living and avoiding procrastination is setting a goal that is realistic. By realistic, I mean that you should set a goal that has a definite time frame and can be broken down into smaller parts. For example, if you set the goal of becoming the best in your ballet class, the goal can be broken down to little tasks that would help you reach it steadily. Those little tasks must be spelled out in explicit details and placed in strategic places around your home. For example, you can write,

"Ballet lessons by 5."

"Jogging time by 7."

You can easily get a sticker and paste these two on your fridge so you can easily see them and be reminded of their importance. However, you would have to ensure that you follow through with them by being strict with your time consumption.

Goal Monitoring is a task that has been engaged in by the greatest achievers in the world. An achiever like Oprah Winfrey was so dedicated to monitoring the goals that she always engaged in getting feedback from her close circle on her progress in her career as a Talk-show host. While this may seem to be awkward to other people who see her as already successful, the only way to become more successful, for her, is to engage in a constant critique of her performance that would show her progress. This process also enabled her to defeat the negative habit of procrastination.

It is pointless trying to avoid procrastination when you do not have a goal that you are chasing. Generally speaking, everyone either ends up achieving their personal goals or the goals of other people. While this may sound shallow, it remains the truth because you can either employ your efforts to helping yourself become the best or help other people become the best by choosing to remain rooted in your spot. Find your goal today and make sure that they are well spelled out so that you are easily motivated towards chasing them.

Do not Feel Comfortable with Your Level of Success

How much do you think you have achieved? The answer to this would greatly determine how much you procrastinate because people who generally feel comfortable with their status do not feel the need to advance and then begin to procrastinate more.

Let us take the example of an athlete like Mike Tyson. The Boxing profession is one that requires the fighters to give it every shot and attention on their way to the top. Being a boxer who yearned to reach the top, Mike Tyson could never afford to procrastinate about the time for engaging in early morning and evening jogs. Since he needed to build his punching skills, he could not afford to procrastinate about hitting the gym because he needed to engage in intense workout sessions with the punching bag. Also, need to learn the best way to anticipate any opponent he would face in the ring, Tyson never procrastinated when the time to fight other gym fighters and his trainer, arose. Through his lack of procrastination and strict adherence to his regimen, Tyson was able to keep rising through the ranks at even the expense of other fighters who were more talented than him. At a certain stage in his career when he had reached the top and was sufficiently well known after fighting Evander Holyfield, Tyson began to lose focus and then procrastination sets in.

You should never feel comfortable with your level of success because when you do, you will immediately lose focus and an up starter, who keeps taking everything into detail without procrastination, will upstage you. Imagine that you were a pop-singer and you have risen through the ranks from playing at local theme parks to have sold out concerts and winning the Grammy awards. At that point when you have won the Grammys, it would seem that you have reached the pinnacle of your career. Most pop stars would then begin to procrastinate on the time for rehearsals or procrastinate when they need to attend important meetings with their sponsors. This procrastination begins to build up and cause the pop star to fall off the favor list of the fan base, and if there is no source of stimulant, such a pop star may fall back into obscurity. That is the reason why you should always continue to discover better ways to stimulate yourself

One of the excellent ways to avoid feeling too comfortable is when you begin to place value on getting rid of pain and humanitarian challenges in the world. Take the example of Bill Gates who has always been on the list of the richest men in the world. In his case, he has set up companies that would continue to bring income for him and can afford to procrastinate, but he sought out a new challenge that he devotes his time to face now. The challenge he chose and is pumping many funds into is the alleviation of poverty from numerous Third World Countries through the provision of health facilities, portable water, the sound educational structure as well as sustainable energy creation. Through the Bill and Melinda foundation, you can easily see how he uses the new challenge to defeat procrastination.

Understand That Your Talent Will Not Guarantee Your Success

The graveyard is often referred to as the greatest treasure place on earth. The sentiment is echoed across different cultures in the world, and the reason is very clear; it is the resting place of people who never achieved their full potential. People who think that they are talented and that is enough end up becoming the worst procrastinators who do not reach anywhere. Every child is very talented in one aspect of life while some can exhibit numerous talents in many fields.

However, what happens when you think that talent is enough? The answer is that the person begins a downward spiral into procrastination. If you get to watch sports on a regular basis, you may hear the sportscaster make mention of lines like, "here is the new Wayne Gretzky" for those who are hockey enthusiasts. If you were watching the tennis game, you might have heard the sportscaster state that a certain player was the "New Roger Federer" or the "Heir to the throne of Borg and McEnroe." The reason why such sportscasters may have said it is that such players exhibit great gifts that would be able to propel them towards becoming personal greats in the game. However, the bitter truth is that a significant amount of such players often fall off the radar because they believed in their gifts too much and began to make procrastination when it was time for training.

Which talents do you have that has attracted the attention of people? You should be careful with the praise and understand that your gift is not the only ingredient that would make you succeed. You must be able to develop a strict routine of activities that will help you build your talents. Presidents such as George Bush, Barack Obama were not born; rather, they recognized some leadership talents at a little age and began to consciously set down routines that were meant to help them rise through the political ranks until they were eventually elected into the White House,

Let Technology Help

We are in the global age wherein ideas continue to transform into workable projects and ultimately become the new technology that drives our society. There are now technological applications for almost everything, and there are apps that can help you beat your habit of procrastination. Have you ever heard of BZ Reminder? It is an application that can easily be downloaded via Google Playstore and you can begin to use it to overcome procrastination. So how does it work exactly? To begin, you would need to mentally organize yourself through the identification of your goals as well as breaking them down into actionable routine actions.

After you have done that, you then begin by inputting every action that you intend to take at the particular time that you want to take it. There is an option where you get to write down notes, and this will be vital in case you will need that note to remind you of the dire need of the action. After doing this, you then save the actions and the application would begin to issue out prompt reminders to you at every point in time. Other applications that engage in this are Wunderlist, Life Reminders, Remember the Milk and others. Reminders are very vital as they serve as the stimulant that tells you what needs to be done and reminds you to get your butt up.

Other technological advancements that can monitor the level at which you are reaching your goals, help to serve as tools that enable you to ward off procrastination. For example, Samsung Health, which is a pre-installed application on Samsung devices, help the owners to be able to monitor the number of steps that they have taken in a particular day. In most cases, individuals who wish to engage in a weight reduction routine and adopt jogging or power walks, make use of Samsung Health that they can use to create a target for themselves. A beautiful aspect of the application is its alarm feature that informs the user that the daily target has been reached or not. With a reminder like that, it becomes very difficult to procrastinate.

Get To The Root Why Are Procrastinating

Do you know what usually happens when you go to a dentist with a tooth that you desperately want to remove because the pain it is giving you? The dentist would begin the procedure by checking other teeth that are close by before focusing on the tooth that is making you feel dis-comfortable. The same thing applies to other Medical Doctors who tend to ask you questions that may seem to be totally irrelevant to you but hold the most answers for the doctor.

The reason they do this is that they wish to determine the root cause of the sickness because it may spring up another sickness if the present is cured. Just like the way obesity is the root cause of numerous heart related medical challenges, there is a particular root cause that is causing you to engage in so much procrastination.

One of the most devastating root causes is a type of Temperament you have. There are basically four major temperaments that every human being falls into, and they are;

1. Sanguine

2. Phlegmatic

3. Choleric

4. Melancholic.

Every reader of this book must make a conscious effort to discover what their temperament is and then research on the ways they can manage them. The major temperament many chronic procrastinators fall into is Sanguine. The Sanguine is a person that can be the life of the party and may be someone who loves to aspire. However, the major challenge with the Sanguine is that she or he gets easily disinterested in activities and relationships. While a Sanguine guy may initiate a relationship with a lady and seem to be smitten by her, he may begin to show disinterest as the days go by and the same happens vice versa. If a Sanguine was to aspire to become the greatest drama writer after William Shakespeare, she would begin the process of writing with much enthusiasm and would experience true happiness at the beginning stages, however, as the days roll by, and the thrill disappears, while another temperament like Melancholic will retain a staunch focus to complete the work, the Sanguine would shelve the work and move on to the next interesting thing while procrastinating that she would return to work at a later date. Unfortunately, the Sanguine is often filled with too many projects that are screaming for completion, but she is still chasing newer ones. If you recognize that you are a Sanguine, you should begin to engage in extensive research that would enable you to manage your temperament as well as overcome the challenge of procrastination.

Another root cause of Procrastination is fear. Fear is one of the most dangerous killers in the world because it delights in early truncation of projects that have reached halfway. There are many individuals who wished to become wildlife photographers that would be popular enough to work at the National Geographic, but they never ventured further because of fear. In such instances, they may become afraid of the hazards that may come with exploring the Amazon or getting close enough to take pictures of Polar Bears. In some other instances, other people have abandoned their dreams of becoming top Class chefs because they are afraid of the nature of reception that they would receive from people who would taste their meals.

In both cases, fear has made those individuals engage in a series of prolonged procrastination until they eventually drop such goals in pursuit of other. Everyone harbors fear at one point or the other, but the achievers always face their fear head-on since they recognize the need not to procrastinate. Successful business tycoons such as Tony Robbins who has made millions out of the practice of Networking tell that when faced with fears, he does not flinch at all. Rather, he walks up to the individual he intends to pitch to and begins without fear. The reason is that there is absolutely nothing to lose when you try and fail. However, when you do not try at all, you have everything to lose since there is a possibility that you could have overcome. Another excellent way which one can overcome such fear is when you build up a practice of repeating self-affirmative words over time. This has proved to be a very potent confidence booster while it enhances people's belief in their capacity to take on every task. Identify the root cause of your procrastination today and begin to deal with them

Get A Coach

There is absolutely nowhere you can get to in life without the help of others, and there are very limited heights you can reach without a mentor or a coach to guide you. When taking on the task of defeating the enemy called Procrastination, you will surely need all the help you can get.

Who are your mentors? Members of some interviewing boards sometimes ask that question because the answer to such a question can help them form a quick opinion about you and your motivations. To identify your mentor/coach, you must take your time and never choose based on personal sentiments arising from your relationship with the person.

In most cases, many people choose their parents as mentors and end up procrastinating because their coach has not been able to overcome procrastination. Choose a person who is insanely dedicated to their work and has been successful in the career. This means that if you are pursuing the goal of becoming a musical artist in the genre of New Age Music, you can get Enya and Yanni to be your mentors as they would be able to provide you with information on how to conquer procrastination as your career advances. However, on some occasions like the one previously stated, you may choose a mentor that is not easily accessible and that is why you should work toward getting a coach that can be easily accessible.

Boxers wisely choose their coach because their coaches are the ones that come, looking to drag them away from their homes when the fighter begins to procrastinate. In your case, you should always inquire from your coach on the best way to be stimulated enough to overcome procrastination because that is the best way to overcome. While many Top 500 Forbes companies adopt the measure of deadlines to stimulate their employees into completing projects, that kind of stimulation may not work for individual human beings. Ask your coach to teach you the best way to set deadlines for yourself that you will be able to work towards with the same vigor you would adopt if you were at your workplace.

Join Arduous Tasks With Pleasant Ones

One of the easiest ways to get discouraged and begin to adopt the act of procrastination is when you separate easier tasks from the difficult ones. In the course of achieving any goal that you set, there would be the easier ones that would give you an immediate thrill when you finish engaging in them, along with the difficult ones that can be physically and mentally draining. Your goal will be to do the hard tasks immediately after the easier ones so that the thrill can stimulate you enough to tackle it.

Let's assume that you are harboring the intent of writing an important professional exam that will bring you a promotion at your job and you need to take both Statistics and an English exam. Let's imagine that you someone who is totally inclined to the arts but find the statistics course to be mentally challenging and nothing you do seems to be working. Naturally, what happens is that you may begin to passively postpone the period of reading your Statistics books because they frankly bring you no joy while you relish the time spent with your English books. You can overcome your procrastination and get it right by choosing to read your Statistics immediately after you drop your English book. The reason is that it has been scientifically proven that your brain is more excited when you try out enjoyable things and this can enable it to pick the more difficult things immediately while it is still flooded with the feel-good dopamine.

You will have to make the self-conscious decision of writing down the most enjoyable tasks which you have to engage in and the 'most annoying jobs I would rather not face but must be done.' Penning them down in a detailed manner is the first step.

The next would be to pair them together in order to ensure that complimentary tasks go together. If you are into web designing and have to learn how to code using JavaScript and the likes, you will have to fix the time for coding, which a few web developers do not like to do, along with the time for designing on paper. This is because it is thrilling to design how the website would look on paper and the dopamine that is released during that moment can be used to attack difficult tasks such as coding. I have discovered as well that the most people who make the killing gains on the Forex market are those that forecast immediately after making a huge profit. At that point, they are able to shed off some form of restraints of fear and buy the shares while adopting some form of caution as well.

Do Not Try To Overstretch Yourself On Tasks

The simple truth that is being said here is, don't overtask yourself.

Frankly, you are not an automated machine that can perform a billion tasks at a given time. Even automated machines can run into bigger problems when they are taxed to engage in the tasks that they have not been programmed to do, so slow down.

You cannot become everything. That fact is very vital for you to understand today because so many people are stressing themselves over becoming many things and then get to realize that they are failing badly at most of them because they are procrastinating.

Imagine you meet a lady who is training to become a Black Belt holder in Taekwondo, studying to become a ballet dancer, studying to become a financial expert and also trying to become a screenwriter. I know that you may be so much surprised and feel that she is awesome but in reality, she will be struggling with avoiding procrastination since most of the tasks would require her to focus on them.

If she chooses to focus on screenwriting as well as Taekwondo strictly, she would be able to effortlessly manage herself and draw up concrete plans that she can focus on achieving without overstretching herself. Your ultimate goal should not be to acquire as numerous titles as you can in reaching the top but to acquire one and work your butt off to becoming excellent in that field.

Take the case of Steve Jobs, the co-founder of Apple: he could have chosen to take on his tasks by singing with a band, but he did not. Instead, he focused daily on building tasks that were solely within his niche and worked tirelessly at achieving those goals he set. Today, Apple has broken through the One Trillion dollar valuation margin, and it is mainly thanks to one man who chose to stick to one task.

Let us take a scenario that you may be more familiar with. Have you ever seen an Olympic 100 meters race? The thing you notice is that each athlete has a special lane set up for him or her. The white line that separates them mainly defines these tracks, and you notice that when the gun pops, each athlete begins to run within their lane so as to avoid reaching the finish line in another person's lane that attracts disqualification. Usain Bolt won all his titles by sticking to his lane and not crossing into the lane of other contenders like Asafa Powell, Tyson Gay, Justin Gatlin, and the likes. The immediate lesson that you can get is that there are no gains for running in too many directions. Often, such people do not end up reaching the finish line of any of the directions because they would have procrastinated so much.

Don't Beat Yourself Over What You Cannot Change

There are some things that won't change so don't get frustrated by trying to change them. You will have to recognize this fast in order not to engage in tasks that would be extremely frustrating for you and make you engage in the act of procrastination.

The general idea is that you should find a goal that you have a passion for and then begin to engage in it with much vigor. However, during the course of reaching your destination, you will meet with some challenges that you cannot solve and will have to adopt the option of letting them go.

For example, in the course of building your team that will spur you to achieve your goals, you will recognize some team members who are going to slow the group down considerably because of their inefficiency. There are other team members that may be very brilliant but have terrible character traits that they are unwilling to change. In such cases, you will have to let the two sets of employees go so that you can be able to advance speedily towards achieving the group goals. This has to be done so you don't expend much energy trying to change what such group members may be unwilling to change.

Seasoned achievers like Steve Jobs easily recognized this fact and began to apply them at an early stage of their business. They first began to scrutinize the ideology of their would-be employee or team members. When they ascertain that a group member is not on par or is not motivated, they immediately pull the plug on the involvement of such team members in order to keep the team morale high. They did this particular action when it involved their family members because they realized that there was no place for personal sentiments in building a unique brand.

Also, if you are in the practice of trying to salvage a relationship that is going off the rocks and the other party keeps dragging it down with a force of habit, it is time you consider pulling the plug. For example, if you are in a relationship that is perpetually filled with accounts of domestic violence that seems not to have an end, you should try and work it out with the partner and then leave if the partner is not showing promising signs of changing.

The reason you have to leave is that your sanity and esteem are very important and you do not need to continue remaining frustrated as time goes by. Within frustration lies the seed of procrastination as it becomes easy for you to lose focus of the most important part of your goals while you try to change something that will never change.

For every challenge that comes your way, there are a plethora of options that present themselves as potential answers. However, in order to avoid giving room to procrastination, stick to one option and work hard at it until you become excellent at it.

Let us examine Nations as an example, with the Nation of Israel being the case study.

The Zionist movement that comprises of the Jewish people identified a problem that was the fact that the Jews had no homeland, and then began to work towards buying up lands in Palestine progressively. Ever since the Dreyffus affair, most Jews within the areas they lived in Europe experienced intense anti-Semitism riots and disenfranchisement, and all this piled up to the German genocide that was initiated by Adolf Hitler.

Because of the constant persecutions, the richest Jews formed the movement and then proceeded to buy up Palestinian lands where they began to emigrate until they finally gained their independence in 1948. Since that time of their independence, Israel has been actively engaged in one main course of guaranteeing her continued survival that is through the building of their defense ministry through military buildup. Till date, they continue to pump a large number of funds into the acquisition of the latest military technology while also building her missile detection systems so as to avoid any form of external attacks.

Any observer can easily see that Israel could have chosen to stick to diplomacy to achieve her aims, but she chose to adopt the option of the military buildup in order to deter any form of action against them. On the other hand, the Palestinians have a noble cause but have been deterred because they are chasing too many options. While the Palestinian Liberation Organization chases the more peaceful and diplomatic way of getting a Palestinian state through the United Nations, the Hamas has continued to engage in a series of terror attacks against the Israeli and these terror attacks serve to undermine the efforts which the PLO has been engaging in.

The idea that is espoused here is that you should stick to one option and hone it into perfection. Sometimes, this process would take years, but the most successful people have taken years to master their craft. Take a look at Tiger Woods who identified the particular sport he was good in and began to focus on reaching the top. Becoming an excellent golfer is a mastery that takes years to perfect, and that is the exact thing that Tiger Woods did. You do not have the luxury of time to keep exploring option ever because you may discover that none works since you did not give it enough time to explore. Develop a key principle of Patience.

Get Rid Of Distractions Both Digital And Human

There is absolutely no way you can reach the top by taking note of every little thing that happens around you. Athletes like Mo Faran who are engaged in marathon races are always so focused on running that they are not even deterred by natural phenomenon. When racing through the designated route, they do not stop to take selfies with excited fans or stop to engage in other things because distraction brings loss of focus and then ultimately leads to failures. This brings us to the first point that you will have to clear out every mental distraction.

A Formula, One racer like Sebastian Vettel, cannot afford to come into the race with the mindset that he will lose the game and the same thing happens for individuals across all sports except the ones that are scripted like Wrestling.

Other mental cobwebs that you will have to clear out within your mind are factors like low self-esteem which is harboring the thought that you are not good enough to engage in a task: What often happens is that such an individual begins to falter and then falls into a vicious cycle of procrastination that may bring failure at the end.

After you have sufficiently cleared your mental obstacles, the next sets are the physical obstacles starting with technology.

While technology has been a source of blessing to mankind as we have been able to achieve phenomenal feats in the fields of Artificial intelligence, Nanotechnology as well as other technologies that are boosting human relations, it has served to be one of the greatest drawbacks as there are more than enough applications which can derail individuals from achieving their goals.

Let us take, for example, the case of little kids and video games. That is an aspect where parents are still finding very difficult to communicate their desires to the kids. For example, a kid that is playing God of War and is so engrossed in it would not be happy when reminded of the need to eat food. The parents of that kid would even find it greatly difficult to get that kid to perform his school homework, as the kid would keep postponing it. One of the ways that the parent can help that kid is to take away those video games for a while and even though the child would sulk for longer periods of time, the parent would be able to get him to do his homework.

If you are a college student, you would understand the reason why technology provides the greatest source of an obstacle. Social media applications like Facebook, Instagram, YouTube, and Vine preoccupy the attention of many college students who are constantly seeking to connect better with friends or become more popular. Viral challenges have also been the cause of procrastination as social media users are so obsessed with joining in the train without paying attention to their personal career paths. If your career path aligns with the use of social media, you would need to engage in these, but if you are not chasing a career along that part, you will have to drastically cut short your use of the social media in order to focus on reaching your goals. Seasoned winners have understood this fact and ensure that they hire social media managers in order to avoid getting caught up with social media because it will bring about procrastination into the time that should be used for other profitable pursuits.

Another distraction that you need to put away is human distractions. Human beings have generally been wired to seek after companionship at some point in their lives, and even though there is the need to build up a network of friends that would be around you to support you at most times that you are down or celebrate with you, you would need to learn how to be lonely at times. This is because friendships can become the cause for your procrastination.

Let us say that you are a web developer who has been given a fresh project to work on by a very reputable tech company at Silicon Valley. When such companies give out jobs like that, they expect that the individual finishes it on time. Now, let us assume that you have a group of friends who call you up and complain that you have not been frequent at the spa and wished to come to your home to pick you up. The immediate thought that may come to you is "Why not?" and then you may mentally begin to shelve away the plans that you have during the night while relishing an opportunity to be among friends. However, a truly successful person would have to politely say no to the invitation and stand firmly by her decision because she recognizes the fact that she needs to engage in a grueling session of coding so as to finish up with the project given to her.

Let us say you have just become a parent, and you are at home with your newborn. At that time, you may feel the urge to go out for a period of time and come back to attend to your baby's laundry. If you give in to such thought, you would only be piling up the jobs that you need to do, and you may not get to perform such jobs perfectly. The most successful people have cultivated the habit of being lonely because they realize that they get most inspiration at such moments and are able to cheer themselves the more. If you are a sports player who enjoys the cheering and the company of people who adore you, you may need to begin detaching yourself from them at some point because they may keep reminding you of your unique abilities while you forget to perform the activities that got earned you the top spot in the first place

Get Rid of Indecision

There has been no other pathetic sight that I have seen than a person who is seen to take much time contemplating if to take one action or not. In the classic film, A man on a Ledge, the protagonist finds his way through to the top of a high building and then stands on the ledge with the threat to jump to his death more than 60 feet above the ground level. Like all suicide attempts, a crowd began to gather, and most of them urged him not to take his life. Rather, they appealed that he should look on life with fresh vigor and come down. As the hours passed by, the pleas that he should not commit suicide, eventually turned into angry chants that he should jump to his death since he was taking a long time in deciding to jump. At the ending part of the film plot, however, viewers saw that he had no intent to die as he served as a distraction while his gang engaged in the theft of a diamond from a new-by office. However, the immediate lesson learned is that people get impatient over the course of time when you exhibit indecision.

In the same vein, indecision can cost you a lot of opportunities because people will get frustrated and end up passing you. To a pressing extent, indecision is the cause that causes procrastination, and you can easily see it among college students who are in their finals.

Many of such students begin to experience panic when they are told to state their future career path and when they exhibit indecision, they begin to procrastinate in engaging in the right set of activities that they need to take.

For example, a college student who has not yet decided between choosing to pursue a legal career or follow through with her passion of photography will continue to postpone the decision of getting a professional camera and applying for summer internships at reputable photography agencies. The line of thinking that often spurs such indecision is that there is enough time. However, you should learn to attach maximum importance to every second of the day so as to avoid indecision.

Imagine that you were thrust into the setting of a horror film where you are presented with the opportunity to either use a chainsaw to fight off zombies or run away. I am very sure that you would carry the chainsaw without waiting for any second. That is the sense of urgency that you must try to adopt at all times. This doesn't mean you should not think through any action before you take it. However, thinking about the action you wish to take must not take long as there are many lives hanging in the balance. To ward off indecision, you should adopt the motto which states that "the earlier, the better." This will enable you to start off with the right decisions at an early stage.

Make Use of Productivity Hacks

In order to be able to defeat procrastination, you can begin to engage the use of some productivity hacks that have been tested and trusted. Two of such hacks are discussed below and are still being adopted by highly successful people.

Time Chunking: According to the seasoned guru, Tony Robbins, chunking is the grouping together of information into ideally sized pieces, so they can be used effectively to produce the outcome you need without stress or shutdown. The idea behind chunking your time is that you are dedicating particular periods of your time in solving the much-needed tasks that need to be done. In most occasions, people tend to run their life tasks in a haphazard format with no thinking considered for chunking. With Time chunking comes orderliness and with orderliness comes precision.

Let us see how you can be able to chunk your time in a wise format.

The first step is that you must be able to capture all your tasks on paper. Your tasks may include, spiritual exercises, health exercises, career building, relationship building, and the list is endless.

When you identify these tasks, you can then proceed to the next stage that is carving out time for all of them in a way that balance will be ensured. To carve out time, you can choose tasks that are complementary in nature and then lump them together

Let me quickly give a quick example of how you can chunk your time.

You can designate certain days of the week to be set aside for jogging so that you do not feel the need to always engage in an early morning jog. Such days can be devoted towards going to the gym and also family building time if you are in a relationship.

On such days, you can totally ignore anything about advancing your career in order to focus on the activity. This makes it less difficult to procrastinate when the days for other tasks arrive because you would be mentally ready to engage in such a task.

For dads and moms who have been postponing the time of bonding with their children, they can set aside particular days and time where they will totally ignore other things and focus on playing with the kids or solve challenges with them. The same applies to pet owners who are noticing that their pets are becoming restless. You can craft out a time that would be beneficial instead of clogging up your time.

However, when you are chunking your time, you must learn to be flexible to make room for activities which may come up at unexpected times.

The Pomodoro Technique is a unique time management technique that is used to break tasks into intervals which is traditionally 25 minutes in order to allow for short breaks. People who tend to go on a long stretch of activities usually end up exhausted at the end when they do not create any kind of interval when they can rest. If you have ever hiked, or engaged in skipping, you would understand what I mean because the two activities can easily start up as enjoyable.

However, when you do not take short breaks to regain your strength, you may find out that the task is terribly boring to you and when the thought of doing them crosses your mind on another day, you will not consider them. Within every task that you are engaging in, learn to break away for some minutes so that your brain can refresh itself with a purpose of attacking the task anew when it returns

Adopt A Mentality That Conquers Fear Of Success

The first step of success usually begins at the doorstep of your mentality. At that door, you will find an entity called fear and your task will be to replace it with boldness. This is because everything you are going to be successful in requires you to picture it.

Every great Athlete who has ever won the Olympic gold medal began to dream of having it and then dealt with the problem of fear.

How then do you deal with the problem of fear and build the right mentality?

To answer that, you have to learn to build up a mental toughness that will later transform into your character. A great pianist like Beethoven had already begun playing at an early age, but he had to develop a mental toughness because of the fear that he may not become the best composer in the world. That is why he was always engaging himself in visualization. Ultimately, what you visualize becomes your reality. If you harbor the thoughts of becoming the best cook in the country that is sought after by 5-star hotels in Las Vegas and Paris, you will have to keep up that image in your head while mentally telling fear to keep quiet.

That fear will whisper everything that could ever go wrong on the path to becoming the greatest chef.

It would remind you of your poor background

It would remind you those moments you cooked and was not appreciated by friends.

It would remind you of the lean pocket and your inability to get enough funds to apply for a cooking show.

That fear may even go as far back as ten years to remind you of an incident when a friend said you would never reach the top.

Fear can be really terrible, and that is why you will have to adopt a mentality that tells fear to shut it. That is the kind of mentality that sees a successful path even within the thick Amazon forest. That is the kind of mentality that sees the impossible and laughs it off. This is the kind of mindset adopted by top researchers at NASA. And top Fortune 500 companies pay a lot of money to hire people with such mentalities.

So What If I Fail?

You should be ready to ask the "*What if I fail question?*

Failure has never meant total closure, and most times, Networkers have often interpreted NO to mean Next Opportunity. Throughout history's course, there have been numerous people who failed and have still gone on to achieve great things in the course of their lives. A classic example of a person that embodies this was Abraham Lincoln who ran for the position of the Presidency on more than one occasion and lost. He was not deterred when he lost but took it as a means to regroup and strategize.

At a point in time when other people were not bothered about the future, Thomas Edison was within his laboratory where he was experimenting with a new invention that was the light bulb. Being a visionary along with Nikolai Tesla, his contemporary, Thomas Edison worked at the light bulb invention for more than a hundred times and kept failing. He could have easily decided to walk away without achieving what he set out to do, but he remained and continued testing. He was finally able to come out with a working design as his name is in the history books now.

Take a drive across your neighborhood, and you are sure to come across a restaurant with the logo of an old man who met with failure in numerous ways. That man was Colonel Sanders, and the restaurant is the Kentucky Fried Chicken that is the fourth largest fast food restaurant chain with over twenty thousand branches across the work.

Colonel Sanders started out late and still encountered numerous rejections for his recipe. Still, he was the kind of person who took NO to mean the next opportunity, and he brushed himself up and went in search of more opportunities.

You may have watched Films like Going in Style, Mandela, and Now You See Me and seen that one of the main actors within the film is an old man nearing his sixties. That man is Morgan Freeman, and he was someone who came to encounter failures till he was reaching his forties. At that period, it was always going to be difficult for him to break into Hollywood but Morgan Freeman's persistence paid off.

If I could go on listing examples of stars who encountered failure. Stars like British Born Andy Murray who had to wait a long time before rising to top the men's tennis world. Stars like JK Rowling who had to endure several rejections until she was able to publish Harry Potter that has become one of the bestselling franchise ever produced. The most important thing you should take note when looking through these examples is that failure is an inevitable part of our lives. Oprah Winfrey did not start off as graceful as she is now but she was ready to fail.

You cannot keep holding on to so much fear of failure that you run away from every attempt. If you are afraid of failing in your relationship, take a risk and begin. You would surely have issues with the guy that you enter the relationship into, but those challenges are the bonds that will unite you both in a more intimate fashion. Most times, failure serves to show you what you did not do right and what you can avoid doing in the next time you try. The right attitude is needed if you are ever going to learn from failing.

Have A Mind Map

Your mind is a unique tool that you will have to train and condition in a certain way so that it can help you in the fight against procrastination instead of working against you. The most successful people have also been the ones who have mastered the art of controlling their minds because they realize the kind of potent weapon it can be for them.

How much have you researched on the human mind? This is vital for you since you need to understand its limits and the best way it can function for you. One of its functions is mind- mapping, and this means the ability of your mind to organize its tasks and then track them mentally. Most people's minds are in a state of chaos with the physical result being the disorganized state that they are and the nature of their procrastination. Being a reader of this book, you should begin to train your mind by engaging in exercises of calm. When you are able to calm your mind, you can beg the process of mapping out the tasks that you wish to do and breaking them down. This brings order to the chaos up in your mind, and the path is paved for concrete directions.

Begin The First 10 Minutes Of What You Have Been Procrastinating On

Since you have been able to identify that fear is inevitable, the next step that to take is to delve into what you have been procrastinating for a period of ten minutes.

Every workshop organized for fiction writers or writers from any other genre always has a session where the lead speaker tell the participants to organize themselves into groups with the intent of putting what they may have learned into practice. After they are spilled, they are given sets of different themes such as "Love," "Betrayal, "Death, etc., to work with, and they are told to be writing everything that comes to their mind for a period of ten minutes without interrupting for any purpose.

This particular way has been known as the freestyle method wherein the writers get to engage in a kind of furious writing of everything that comes to their mind. It is at this point that they allow their subconscious minds take over and this subconscious mind helps to break through the feeling of fear.

This same thing is applicable to budding public speakers who have stage fright and are afraid to speak to large audiences. In order to help them break through this particular fright, an audience may be simulated in a way through technological applications or a live audience may be gotten and the speaker would have to speak for ten minutes. Generally, the ten-minute barrier is set because at that time, you would have begun to gain some form of composure and you would wonder why you had not engaged in the activity beforehand.

Are you part of that group of men who find it difficult to talk to a lady? You do not need the help of intoxicants to dull your senses and embolden you to initiate a conversation. Simply walk up to the lady, say your greetings, and manage a conversation for a period of ten minutes. What you notice is that your mind would stop ticking down to the expiration of the ten minutes and you would flow better.

You can easily adapt this same approach when you are engaging in preparations for an important board meeting where you have to pitch your ideas. Take a deep breath before entering the boardroom. If possible, you can engage in some mind-calming exercises and then walk boldly into the room. Before you begin, scan the room and then begin to speak without pausing for ten minutes. Generally, if this is your first run in the park, the board members may offer a few reassuring smiles as they know what you must be feeling. Keep going for the ten-minute mark and then realize that your fear is nothing but an illusion.

Embrace Imperfection Of Things (For Perfectionists)

One of the most upsetting things about our societal culture is that we tend to esteem perfection a little too much.

We hold these elaborate pageants events where we hand the crown of perfection to one person who we call the most beautiful as though others are not worthy to hold the crown. In the same vein, magazines such as Vogue and others continue to bring out their lists of Sexiest women in the world with the undertone that some women are not beautiful.

On a daily basis, new products are being churned out with the claim of being the perfect cure for this or the product to help you achieve the perfect that. Hence, we begin to see products promoting finer hair, smoother legs, smarter beards, and others.

The Perfectionist culture would be the apt description that we can give to our society. While it is okay seeking perfection, we must understand that we may never achieve such perfection in many areas of our lives.

Why this may seem like a mentality that promotes mediocrity, it is one that would help you enjoy the life you life while being content. The idea that someone is perfect does not necessarily mean that the person is perfect. This is because the word "perfect" is a relative word that differs according to location. While the culture of America may esteem the slim, pretty model as the ideal of perfection, other cultures of other parts of the world may esteem other features such as the length of hair and also the wideness of the lips.

The idea that is being espoused here is that you should be the one defining what perfection for yourself is. If you allow the society to define perfection for you, you may end up chasing after a shadow that you may never catch up with all throughout your life. The ideal image of an extraordinary life as painted by the media is when you are rich enough to own your personal jet and yacht which you can use to ride off to your personal island. The message they sell is that everyone can reach that kind of success and become extra-ordinary while forgetting that no one is superb when everyone has the same kind of wealth.

It should be taught to children that they are awesome even if they come second place at a spelling bee competition and they still retain their charm if they do not come within the first three positions when they are in their ballet classes.

Every reader who understands this principle will recognize the need to take a pause on most of their aspirations because such aspirations arose as a result of what the society defined as success. Parents who innocently tell the kids to face the 'real world' and look for 'real jobs' have killed the dreams of many kids. Many a dream have died because the parent refused to support the child in the career path since the job does not fit into the traditional kind of jobs that bring in the big bucks. At the moment, there are people who make money from being professional video gamers. These top-notch video gamers began to follow their passion at an early age and did not listen when society told them to "grow up." Some of the gamers are hired on a multi-million dollar commission by video game companies, who contract them to test their games and give positive reviews to the millions of video-gamers who follow such professionals. They recognized early that they were never going to fit into other people's definition of 'perfect' and began to follow their own passion.

The question this book is asking you today is,

Are you following your dreams or trying to achieve the perfect dream of society?

If your answer is Yes, then you will not feel the need to procrastinate since you actually love what you are doing. On the other hand, you will often procrastinate if you are chasing what society has defined as perfection.

Learn To Reward Yourself For Small Achievements

People who tend to work themselves into becoming tired without rewarding themselves often find themselves frustrated and begin to engage in procrastination if such a task comes again.

Why is this so? The answer relates to the fact that everyone loves to be rewarded.

I want you to try an experiment with your canine friend if you have one as a pet. First, set up a doggy course for her and then do her work towards scaling through every hurdle. Try and maintain silence when she comes back with the prize and then note her reaction as you walk away. Then, the next day, set up the same task and when she comes back with the same prize, shower her with lots of praise words as well a favorite and then take notice of her reaction once more. What you will immediately notice is that she would exhibit a better reaction than the previous day because of your reward for her efforts, and her confidence levels will rise.

The reason why you are probably being frustrated and postponing stuff is that you do not appreciate yourself enough. When was the last time you truly had a vacation and went with your family?

Your answer to this either showcase why you have been so grumpy and procrastinating stuff OR why you have been brimming with much confidence and attacking newer tasks with confidence.

In this age of technology that can link us in a second and make us feel as though we never left office, it is possible to be on vacation and at the office at the same time. That is why you should learn how to be on vacation truly and then switch off your devices.

If you have been procrastinating on building your love relationship and it is deteriorating, I believe a vacation should be in the cards from this time of reading. Now, I can feel that your mind is beginning to conjure up a million and one reasons why you will not be able to go; procrastination at its destructive best.

I can vividly hear those thoughts telling you,

You cannot go on a vacation at this point in your life

You will not be granted an audience when you approach your boss for it

Where would the kids stay?

That co-worker of yours at the office would bungle stuff and give trouble

Your bills are too much. How can you afford it?

You would not look good in the sun with your body out.

Would your partner accept this offer of vacation?

I can doubly assure that these thoughts if you allow them to linger, would discourage you from ever taking the step to vacation. The problem is that you think you will be richer if you shelved this kind of vacation at this time, but you are not considering the extent of refreshing that would occur if you choose to engage in this line of action. You may even be working with the wrong assumption that your superior at the office would refuse your request.

However, what if your boss at the office takes a long look at you and decides to add one more week to your vacation request? You have not thought of this because you do not understand the values that top managers place on vacations. Top Fortune 500 companies place a high premium on organizing vacations for their employees and Amazon in recent times built a gigantic edifice that they now use as offices. In the revolutionary office setting, they simulated the Amazon rainforest with the air as well as some of the animals. The reason for this is that they recognize the benefits of vacation on their employees' mindset.

If you take a vacation today as a reward, you will be physically revitalized and mentally refreshed to attack your office tasks when you return. Do not listen to the tones of negative thoughts that are encouraging you not to take a vacation. Just take a leap of faith by putting your foot on the pedal of the request.

No one who has the aim of becoming successful can continue to shun the necessary first step that needs to be taken which is planning.

The Great Wall of China was first a line of thought in the mind of the Chinese emperor who began its construction. The thought must have intrigued him at the point of thought conception, but when you walk on those ancient walls, you recognize that he did not procrastinate further. Instead, he chose to write it down as well as making a list of what needed to be done. Afterward, he would have called his advisers, empire architects and every other professional who would have worked to bring the list into the reality we have at the moment. The same is obtainable for all the ancient wonders of civilization such as the Great Pyramids of Egypt, the Hanging Gardens as well as others.

Let us take the example of Facebook. While in college, Mark Zuckerberg, who was obviously a nerdy guy, identified a need that was in the community. He identified that many guys needed a medium that they could use to determine who was hot or not. This was the product that he had in his mind, but it did not stay in his mind like many ideas are lying fallow within many individuals today. Instead, he took out his paper and began to make a list of everything he needed to do before calling the necessary individuals who would provide him with the services needed in bringing Facebook to life.

Everyone has many ideas that they sometimes dismiss as not important or not feasible. As you are reading, I know you have this mind-blowing idea that you think cannot be brought into reality by the sheer grandness of it.

It may be that you are already envisioning a future where dog thoughts can be transmittable to speech and they can effectively communicate their thoughts.

You may even be thinking of a future where human beings can get an alternative source of beef that would replace the traditional cows, thus preserving the lives of animals.

There are even some individuals who have envisioned revolutionary changes in the educational sector along with revolutionary techniques that could make homelessness a forgotten reality.

For people who possess this kind of revolutionary ideas and more, there is a vital need for them to begin to put down their ideas into lists. If you took note of the examples I gave, you would notice that both the Chinese Emperor and Mark Zuckerberg began to see artists, architects that could bring their dreams into reality. The reason why it seems that you have not seen anyone that can bring your dream into reality is that you have not written it on a list. The process of doing this automatically begins to open your eyes to the possibilities around you that you may have never noticed.

For example, if you plan on developing a device that helps spinal cord victims regain their ability, you could make a list a list of what you need and then, you would be exposed to a research being carried out by NASA and some scientist using nanotechnology to help disabled soldiers regain the use of all parts of their bodies that are non-functioning.

Make Sure Your Calendar Is Filled

Calendars can become a priceless gift if you understand the best way to utilize them for your benefit. There is a wealth of functions that your calendar provides for you more than the usual reminder that it is Friday to go out with friends or your baby girl's birthday is coming up by the 10th of August. While these functions are cool. They do not encapsulate the totality of what your calendar can do. By filling up your calendar, you can be able to overcome the procrastination that is usually present when there is nothing on the calendar. This filing up of calendar remains one of the attributes of numerous high profiled professionals because they understand that a quick glance at their calendars can give them the necessary motivation that is needed to push them through the daily activity.

Beat Back Negativity With Your Thoughts

Beating back negativity will require you to build your ability to say no. It would also require you to learn the best way to engage in building up your confidence. Make no mistake about this: when you begin to succeed, the negativity will come like a storm especially from people around you who may not know your beginning. If you allow yourself to be swept by their negativity, you will end up procrastinating and not doing things that will make you rise higher. Have you ever wondered how many celebrities have remained standing despite the negativity that comes their way? It is because they were able to build a thick skin against what people said and continued to work towards getting better progressively. Often tagged as the 'Queen of Hip-hop,' Beyoncè Knowles has been able to develop a thick skin to many allegations leveled against her and Jay Z, her husband who happens to be regarded as the King of Rap.

The Power Of Positive Self-Talk

The process of avoiding procrastination involves a dire need to learn the power and pattern of positive self-talk. People who have often emerged victorious are the ones who have learned how to stimulate themselves starting from the beginning of each day. The process of saying, "I am the best" is one that is potent enough to trick your mind and position it in the right frame to face challenges. The principle of positive self talk is something that has been proven to help boost the morale of everyone when it is time to engage in a task that seems frightening. Let us go back in history and see how Positive self-talk would have worked. Gladiators who usually fought each other would wake up on the day of the fight and begin to remind themselves that they are the best because their lives depend on it. Remind yourself that you are the best today because your future lies in it.

Letters Of Encouragement

How often do you write letters of encouragement to yourself? While that question may seem odd, it is very vital for you to ask if you are going to overcome procrastination. You will need to pen unique words of encouragement to yourself on the achievement of big milestones, and while you are chasing a particular goal. The letter format could be,

Hey Mary.

I can see that you have been putting every effort you have into finishing this project given to you by Amazon. Though the deadline is a few weeks away, I know that you can be able to pull it off because you are the best. Remember that period you were in college and completed that project for your class? Yes, you completed that project without procrastination and then ended up becoming the best in class. I know you can do it.

Go, Girl!

From Mary.

This kind of letter can be placed on the door to your fridge, or you can go to mail it to yourself if you are feeling a little bit creative.

Take Small Steps

Little drops of water make an ocean. Many have quoted popular sayings like this without understanding the meaning that is implicit within. The idea behind the quip is that you will have to start from small steps when you want to reach a goal.

If you were confronted with the task of erecting a hospital for maternity purpose in a Third World country, you would not immediately begin to erect bricks on the property you have gotten. The first step would be getting an architect who would design a structural plan for you. Often, people end up procrastinating because they took huge steps that they are not able to complete at the time and set enormous targets that are too lofty to attain. You should recognize that building anything takes time and patience. Though it looks like you are slow, take one step at a time in reaching your goal.

Self-Introspection

The process of self-introspection requires that you look inward and ask some vital questions about yourself. You can choose to engage in this process of introspection at any place provided that it is silent because noise has been proven to disrupt the quality of answers that you will arrive at.

The first set of questions that you have to ask relates to who you are and what you are going to contribute to mankind. You should be ready to answer those questions as truthfully as possible, and if you are coming up short, you could decide to go on a tour of self-discovery which should lead you to research why you were created. When you are able to ascertain your origins, the next question will be your purpose and your destination. What are you planning on giving back to mankind and where do you see yourself when you reach an advanced stage.

Eliminate The Unnecessary Task

There are a million tasks that you can do, but not all of them are important. To achieve this, you must first get a sheet where you will write out a list of the necessary things that you need to engage in order to reach the goal you wish to achieve. If you have been thinking of the best way to mend a broken relationship, you can begin by identifying the list of tasks that are going to help you. That list may go like this,

I will create time to go to the cinema with my partner.

I will ensure that I listen intently when she is speaking and respond accordingly.

I will attend counseling sessions with him.

I will make out time for the kids and help out more often.

Now, these are great tasks that will be beneficial in helping to repair a broken relationship. However, if you don't have sufficient time, you can easily scrape out the item that says that you will go to the cinema with your partner. This can be removed because the other tasks are equally important and have been proven to repair strained relationships.

Explore The Consequences Of Being Lazy; It Is The Best Mental Whip

For a long time, we have explored the possibilities and benefits of finishing a task. However, have you tried to explore the consequences of being lazy? The result of this line of action has become a better whip that drives many successful people. The reason why you are mainly procrastinating is that you do not think that your task is vital to humanity because if you do, you will realize that a lot of things will go wrong if you decide to be lazy.

It might sound pompous when we talk about humanity and procrastination in the same line but honestly, this technique will be a very very powerful one with which you will be using to displace procrastination from your daily life.

When you think about what your consequences of procrastination will be, as in like truly think, you will achieve a few things.

First, you will realize how important that task is, however odious and hateful it may be, because it impacts you and your life so much. That is the mental whip we are talking about because it becomes a propeller for the positive, driving you forward to clear what should have been cleared.

Second, you may realize, hey, that task if not done is actually not such a big deal. You will then be able to rest easy and clear that mental drag of needing to do that task away from your mind. This lets go of the accompanying guilt as well because you realize that you can effectively place this task safely in another day without procrastinating it.

Third, you may actually gain a spurt of energy and look upon the task with new lenses because of this mental practice that you just did honestly. You realize it has far reaching effects if the task is delayed, and hence your approach to it changes. Sales people may oft face this issue. Sales is always almost a weekly or monthly, perhaps yearly struggle with numbers. The salesperson needs to clock in certain numbers to qualify for commissions or even just to keep the job. However, it becomes easy to procrastinate working hard on a daily basis because a month has thirty long days. That's plenty of time isn't? And so it becomes easy to just take a break or go off early, and before you know it, the month or year is up and the numbers are shown to be lacking. If our erstwhile salesperson did this deeper introspection on the consequences of not achieving the sales, then he or she may realize that the job as well as financial rewards are at stake. Family and job security are actually on the line and this is a super important reminder daily that acts as an effective stave against procrastination.

Let us again presume that you are a doctor in an Internal Displaced person camp in a country like Somalia where there are incidents of terrorism which have led to thousands of children dying. Imagine that you choose to be lazy for one day by not attending to the dying children who are brought by their mothers. The consequence of such laziness is that many would die, and the thought that you caused it would prick your heart for a lifetime. Other consequences for people who decide to be lazy are a failure in reaching their desired goals and also shame as well.

Explore The Benefits Of Completing A Task

This is one of the best ways of beating off procrastination. When you complete a task, the first reward you get is a sense of mental ease wherein your brain is flooded with a feel-good hormone. This is the exact reverse of the above technique using the mental whip. This is actually the mental carrot so to speak.

It is invariably the thought of success and the feeling of completion of the task that will engineer feelings of happiness and fulfilment. These aren't to be scoffed at. Even if you were to just visualize doing up the task on hand, it helps with the mental picture and actually triggers the impetus to achieve it.

Humans are often visual creatures, so painting that mental picture of task accomplishment will invariably lead to a higher chance of getting it done. This is then particularly reinforced when that feeling of satisfaction and happiness on getting the job done and seeing something completed is felt. This acts as a positive anchor and again, leads one on a positive spiral away from procrastination.

Imagine how scientists feel when they come up with the final antidote to a vaccine that has been ravaging humankind like malaria? That feeling of happiness cannot be recreated in any other occasion.

Another benefit that you stand to get is that you walk gallant with a feeling of self-pride. The ability to stick to a task, from the beginning to its very end, showcases a sign of mental maturity that brings you immediate respect from everyone around who may have seen you during the course.

Shorten Your Daily To-Do List

Why do you need to clog your daily To-do list with numerous activities that you may never get to finish? Many people often make this mistake of filling their list with wonderful activities they would love to attend to during the day, but they end up frustrated when they do not finish up with such activities. When such people finish such activities, however, they become so much physically and mentally fagged out that there is no fresh vigor that remains for them to face the next day. Instead of filling your day with numerous activities which may be awesome and burdensome, pick out a few and make sure you attend to them fully while leaving the other tasks for the next day. In this way, you would have conserved your energy for attacking the tasks the next day.

Have An Accountable Person

To avoid any kind of Procrastination, cultivate the habit of having a person that you are accountable to. Accountability is a culture that is fast dying out in the present day because numerous persons do not want to hear the truth in its ugly form. Most people are developing applications that would show the popularity of other people such as Instagram and this continues to fuel a mentality that shuns criticism.

You need to get someone who will not hesitate to tell you the truth about your laxity in fulfilling your dreams. The accountable person must already be someone who cares enough about you and knows your dreams, but the likeness should extend towards chiding you when you are wasting time. In most occasions, I have found out that parents prove to be very accountable people because they do not hesitate to say the truth to their kids when such kids are lazy.

Seek Different Ways To Do A Task Better - Research To Counter Boredom

Do you find yourself repeating a method all over again without making any headway? Leave it! You do not have the luxury of time to keep on sticking to a particular method that is not working for you: rather, begin to devise new means of getting things done. If you are a kindergarten teacher who has been trying to make your kids behave without encountering any luck, you should begin to think of dynamic ways.

In order to adopt new ways, you will have to research wide: begin with academic journals that are available online and at the local libraries, discuss with psychologists and also read parenting books of people who have passed the hurdle of training children. You should not keep learning until you get what you desire and even when you do, you should not stick to a single method. Successful people always look for ways to make something better, and that is why they hardly have the opportunity to procrastinate.

Trick The Mind; Turn Your Task Into Play

When you watch many films on hypnosis and magic, you get to understand that the mind can be tricked and some people have actually mastered the art of doing so.

The need to trick the mind arises from the fact that it recognizes work and tags it as a boring chore and while you are working, you will recognize that some parts of your mind will urge you to go and play. To combat this, convert your work into play and begin to have a nice time.

The first rule in converting your work into play is that you should chase what you are passionate about doing. For example, if you love to play the violin as a passion and then proceed towards becoming a violist by profession, it would be easy for you to trick your mind since you would easily enjoy the thrill of playing and getting people to appreciate your art

Learn the rubrics of hard work

Learning the rubrics of hard work is an important step you have to take in order to defeat the enemy of procrastination. What exactly are the indices that make up hard work?

Firstly, you have to understand the "No Pain, No Gain" rule which states that there cannot be any success without any pain attached. Selfies taken at the peak of Mount Everest may look awesome, but they do not tell the story of the grueling journey that was taken to reach the top. Numerous pop stars who show off pictures of their cars as well as magnificent mansions on 'My Crib' that is aired on MTV Base, usually do not tell the stories of the pain they underwent in order to gain their wealth.

Leverage On Your Best Ability And Skills

We have reached the section on leveraging, and we are starting off with the principle of leveraging on your best ability and skills. Leveraging is from the root word 'leverage' which generally means to take advantage of something.

You have been born with a unique set of skills that you will have to discover on your own, and early discovery of these skills will help you leverage on them. Most people procrastinate because they find themselves engaging in jobs that they are not making use of their best skills: It is just like a lawyer who is stuck on being a janitor.

When you discover your skills, you will have to use it in advancing your career and not merely sit at one spot while life walks past. If your best skills are in Networking and business, you should not remain any longer in the teaching profession because you will grow increasingly frustrated while not achieving anything.

Optimize your environment

The environment you are could make or mar your productivity and your ability to beat procrastination. More attention should be placed on social media and technology that may prevent you from doing what you need to do when you need to. For instance, your email or messenger keeps beeping to alert you of an incoming message. Social media could keep you off track of your goal, and receiving phone calls when you ought to perform a task can lead to procrastination.

Instead of this, you should schedule a significant amount of time for working on a particular task, close your IM and email, and switch off your phone (or you could turn on the "Do Not Disturb" mode and put it out of sight). Transform your environment to the one that encourages you to complete the task at hand, not the one that promotes distractions. So, don't get on the web until the task has been completed.

Leverage On People By Building A Network

The second step is leveraging on people. To leverage on people, you must first understand that you cannot do everything on your own even if you have all the skill set in the world.

The concept of leveraging on people is that you reach out to people who are good in other aspects of life and then get them to help you deal with the same challenges that you are facing. Steve Jobs understood the principle of leveraging perfectly as he was able to build teams of coders while he was not a coding genius.

The Network Marketing industry runs on the principle of leveraging because they understand the need for humans to build teams that are channeled towards success. Get out of your comfort zone and begin to network today: thankfully, LinkedIn remains one of the best platforms that you can meet professionals in order to network.

Chapter 4 :
When Is Procrastination Good?

This question may sound quite odd to a large number of people. First, because it assumes that at some point, procrastination is good; and secondly, because it suggests that since procrastination can be good, it shouldn't be totally disregarded. Most of those in this category have, at one point or the other, found procrastination to be a helpful tool but may not be able to attribute those incidents to procrastination. For most, procrastination is a means to an end. However, the end determines whether or not procrastination is good or bad. While some people would naturally avoid procrastination generally and seek ways to truncate it in their life, there are people who seek ways of harnessing procrastination to accomplish certain goals effectively.

Life comprises of ups and downs, and in life, there are no absolutes: the peculiarities of what we encounter daily determine the best approach hence there is no one solution fits all. There is a generally negative perception about procrastination which is unwholesome as most of the evaluation of procrastination as a concept is lopsided. Procrastination has a lot of benefits that many often overlook due to their personal bias or perhaps an oversight. For instance, procrastination stimulates creativity in a person. This is obvious because you process information faster when you are quite comfortable. You tend to really get the best out of yourself when you are "put under the spotlight," i.e., when the deadline is rapidly approaching; an individual who has a strict approach against procrastination will likely not really get to see himself in the full extent of his creative capabilities. If you are conversant with sports for example, you would realize that the urgency and intensity of the losing team gets higher as the match draws to a conclusion and need I say that there have been many instances of the losing team turning over the outcome of the match after being in a losing position earlier in the same game!

There are indeed times when procrastination is good. In fact, there are certain times when you necessarily need to procrastinate on some activities in order to be taken seriously. Imagine turning in your final year research project in college 4 weeks after commencement, no matter how brilliant your findings are and no matter how authentic they are, be rest assured that even if your supervisor would accept it, he would do so with a lot of skepticism perhaps thinking you might have simply gone to plagiarize someone else's work; even if you had produced exact findings 4 months later, he would have been more convenient with the submission coming in after 4 months than it coming after 4 weeks. Procrastination is certainly not as bad as people make it seem. Procrastination forms a huge part of leadership. Imagine a leader who makes a decision at every possible second without ruminating over the possible consequences of his decision! Certainly, a lot of hush decisions would be taken which the individual will later come to regret later on in life.

The principle of procrastination is directly connected to the principle of patience. Certainly, if you ruminate over the decisions you have taken in your life over the past few years, there would be some you have wished you have exercised a little patience over. It is easier to make bad decisions in a hurry than it is to make good ones. This is why procrastinators tend to make better decisions than those not given to procrastination, after all, they have more patience. Have you ever sat to reason about something and after a while new perspectives about that which you were thinking about begins to surface in your mind? Am sure you must have encountered this experience before. Indeed, there are times in life decisions have to be made in split seconds, and there are times when decisions have to be made in patience. However, the bigger decisions in life such as who to marry, where to live, how many children to have, what job to take up, etc. are decisions that necessitate deep thought because they would certainly have major impacts in your life both presently and in the future.

In this chapter, we would consider several instances where procrastination in doing a particular thing or making a particular move has proven to be productive to the individual.

Work-Related Procrastination

While we have agreed that procrastination may result in a loss at work or distrust, it is also important to point out that procrastination usually has its perks as well, especially in work environments. For example, intentionally delaying the submission of a report in order to perfect it could result in the detection of a miscalculation or a mistake that may have affected the general performance of the company. In this case, something naturally considered being a bad trait serves a good purpose and functions well in the collective growth of a work environment.

Also, putting off for later what can be concluded today, has its own way of keeping open an opportunity for adjustments and corrections in that particular work. For example, while working with data which is immediately computed once a particular button is clicked, an individual might decide to put off the clicking of that button to later and may, in the long run, find that there are other parts of the data which he did not enter initially and enter them promptly before finally clicking the button. We find that this saves one a lot of stress and time and helps to ensure that one's work is always accurate when crosschecked.

Academic Related Procrastination

Quite a number of times, procrastinating on the execution of a particular task resulted in the discovery of new data or detail related to that task, which in turn contributed to the betterment of that particular task. For example, a student who is writing his thesis and decides to put off the writing of the abstract until later, may find that writing the abstract by the time the entire body of work is complete is a lot more efficient because, this time, it is easier to make reference to the work which has been already completed and be accurate with it. Many students would testify that at several points through their educational process, they have found additional information to make their work better just because they delayed a little bit. In the long run, it boils down to how one manages procrastination and the possibility of harnessing procrastination to work for you successfully.

Procrastinating the Setting up of a Business

We all have that one friend who has had a business idea since we have known them but have not set up that business, largely because of procrastination. In some contexts, it is bad procrastination: for example, when the procrastination is out of fear of failure or lack of self-confidence. In other contexts, like in this one I am about to elaborate on, procrastination can be harnessed to ensure safety and effectiveness. For example, an individual who has amassed all the necessary tools and machinery for setting up a business but procrastinates the setting up of that business may be considered to be foolishly frightened. However, it could be a wise decision, especially when you consider why the individual is holding back. It might be that they do not feel like the research they have carried out on the business is not sufficient and as such need to go back to the drawing board and rectify most of the calculations made. Also, in the time of the procrastination, the individual could carry out necessary investigations and research and come up with a more failsafe solution to the problems the business seeks to solve.

Especially in business, people need to learn to harness procrastination as a tool and instead of using the term "procrastination," they could be making "calculated decisions." When people learn to harness procrastination and come to the point where they know the fine line between disinterest and bidding time, then things begin to flow a lot more easily.

In this context, there is the possibility of contrasting this reality of careful decision making with hurried executions. Both are effective ways of establishing different businesses, but one is a lot more carefully thought out and pays a lot more attention to detail.

Procrastinating Romantic Relationships to pursue Business or a Career

For some, nothing is more important than a successful career or establishing a successful business. Not even a romantic relationship. Throughout history, we have seen examples of people who were so focused on their grind that they didn't really see the need for a romantic relationship. Worthy of note is Jesus of the Christian faith which is even quoted to have said: "My meat is to do the will of him that sent me…" (John 4:34). If you follow the story of Jesus closely, you will find that he spent all of his time spreading his gospel, teaching, feeding and healing the sick, poor, dejected and lost and yet, when he was once told that his mother and brothers were looking for him, he replied that his family was every one of the people who followed him everywhere.

In our modern world, there are a lot more relatable stories or instances similar to that of Jesus, in which people have verbally or mentally declared that they would rather dedicate their life to grow a personality or brand or a business than to settle down and build a family with someone they share an emotional feeling with.

While some of these people are just worried about being unable to combine work and romance efficiently and equally scared of the prospects of breakups, some others just do not care for any of those and have successfully convinced themselves that this path requires them and them alone (or them and the few people who are willing to build with them). These last set of people work assiduously, week in and out and return home after several long hours out, to an empty apartment and a constant reminder that the life they are building doesn't require a crowd to build.

In the same vein, there are some in this category who find romantic relationships very endearing but are unable to sustain them. A typical example is Elon Musk of SpaceX who has divorced his wife with whom he had five sons and broken up with two other girlfriends. According to Musk, he needs to feel and express love in order to be at the top of his game. However, Musk hasn't been the best of the best as a romantic partner or a father, especially with making time out to spend some quality time with his loved ones. Once noting himself that he handles relationships almost perfunctorily like business meetings, Musk may have successfully procrastinated emotional feelings which are a normal human trait in exchange for a successful career or business.

Some other celebrities and big names fall under this category of people who procrastinate settling down in a relationship or in marriage because of their need to focus entirely on building their career or brand to its peak. Some of them may give the excuse of being unable to fit their attention span into building their career or business or brand and building a relationship. For some, combining the two means, one has to be boring, and when one is boring, they may be tempted to procrastinate in the boring one. And it's usually the relationship that suffers. Quite a number of female celebrities have outrightly declared that they do not need love because they were focusing on building their career and in context, they may be right. A relationship may be too much distraction for them; a relationship may be too cumbersome for them and, as we have pointed out earlier, most cases of procrastination results from the fear of venturing into something because it may be too tasking. It is safe to say that these people have mastered procrastination whether consciously or subconsciously to their benefit or to the benefit of building their desired enterprise.

Sixty-four-year-old Oprah Winfrey, for example, has been in a relationship with her partner Stedman Graham for over twenty-five years after having dated Roger Ebert in the mid-80s. To many relationship experts, this relationship hasn't been progressive for the obvious reason that it has not led to something more elaborate, like a marriage. However, we all know how successful Oprah's career has been in that time. In contrast with her relationship, her career has grown exponentially by more than one hundred and fifty percent. While it can be said that Oprah Winfrey has been unable to make reasonable headway in her relationship with Stedman Graham, it can also be said that she has successfully procrastinated the prospect of getting married for the purpose of focusing her time, attention and energy on building her brand. Whether consciously, subconsciously or unconsciously, Oprah's is another wonderful example of putting procrastination to good use.

However, we are faced at this point by the question of "who defines what is a good use?". And, even though the answer is a straightforward "the person(s) directly involved," it may still require a little or a lot of explanation to put it in context. For example, who determines that Oprah's decision is the best decision for her? And the simple answer is; herself and anyone else directly involved (in this case, Stedman). In this sense, we can bring in the question of who decides when it is right to get birth control in a marriage between a man and his wife? And the simple answer is, the persons involved. As a result, we can queue in the man and his wife. If a man was to blow up in anger due to his wife making that decision of her own accord, he wouldn't be acting out of place.

Another classic example of people procrastinating relationships in order to focus on their career is Trey Songz, who is most popularly known for his incredibly composed love songs. Trey is recorded to have mentioned once that when he is in love, he prioritizes all of his attention to loving and procrastinates his musical endeavors. Speaking with Madame Noire in 2014, the singer noted that he was all about the music and was putting all of his attention into making wonderful music.

With over 50 million albums sold, nine Grammy awards and performances with some of the best in the world, including Michael Jackson, The Rolling Stones, Prince, Kid Rock and Eric Clapton, one would wonder what it is that makes Sheryl Crow unable actually to settle into a relationship or marriage. While she has been involved in some high profile relationships, the 54-year-old has been single since she ended things with Lance Armstrong whom she was once engaged to in 2006.

Sheryl Crow, Oprah Winfrey, Elon Musk and every other celebrity or business mogul out there who have sacrificed a thriving relationship or the prospect of a thriving relationship to procrastination are examples of instances where procrastination can be used to a good effect. As long as we agree that good in this context is subjective to the persons involved.

In quite simple terms, many people want to focus more of their attention on building their brand or career, and when anything comes up that may portend a threat to the success of their endeavor, there is a subtle desire to procrastinate the development of that thing in order to keep on track with their desired endeavor.

When you have to choose your relationship over your workplace

The decisions you make determine your life outcomes. We are all a bundle of decisions, and our present state is a direct reflection of the decisions we have taken in times past. For instance, a doctor is so called because he/she had taken a decision to enroll in the medical school several years ago to obtain the necessary training and instruction relevant to becoming a doctor and likewise an engineer is so called because he/she had taken the necessary training in becoming an engineer. Two of the most important aspect in life are work and relationships. Somewhere along the life of every individual, these two factors must feature.

Man is a relational being and naturally craves affection from another member of his species. Likewise work is very important because it is a means of acquiring the resources relevant to survival in life. This is why who to marry and where to work are very critical decisions that cannot or shouldn't be taken in a hurry. At some point, it is normal for an individual to crave the emotional or romantic feeling of another individual usually a member of the opposite gender. At some point as well after school It Is expected that the Individual begins to seek gainful employment from which he would seek to make ends meet and finally secure financial and economic independence from his parents, caregiver or benefactor; yet as critical as these two decisions are to a person's overall welfare and wellbeing, at times there may be a conflict of interest arising as a result of a dissonance between these two important decisions.

What this means is that your relationship at times may impact your performance in the workplace and vice versa. While it is true that society places a lot of expectation on the individual particularly along the lines of our specific gender, it is, therefore, normal to be influenced by others while making decisions about our own lives while ignoring a very important principle of life which is human differences. For instance, a young couple with a kid who is just 2 years old both working at places that warrant they leave home in the morning and return later in the evening. At one hand, they are making good money which would afford them the privilege of obtaining a higher standard of living for themselves and their child, but at the same time, the demands of their jobs condemn them to be away from the child so much that they miss out on the formative years of the child.

In this instance, there is a need for deep introspective thought about the right step to take because this is a big decision that does not just affect themselves as a couple but now affects their child as well and they would be aware that whatever decision they settle upon then there would be some sort of sacrifice to be made because it is either one of the couples resigns from work to be able to spend time with the child and this would certainly result in lesser income for the family or they both maintain their work while they sacrifice the quality time they could have spent with their child in return for more money to afford the good things of life for themselves and their family. In instances like this, there are no definite answers and certainly no hasty answers. The pros and cons had to be weighed in the balance and whatever conclusions reached and decisions made would hitherto lead to happiness or regret later on in future. In situations like this, what is most important to you, therefore, takes prominence.

Scale of preference

This is perhaps the most important in economics mainly not so much because of its importance but rather because of its relevance. Even if you are unfamiliar with the concept of the scale of preference you would still have to utilize it unconsciously at some point later in your life. Getting a car is one of the dreams of everyone especially the young folks. It is such a big aspiration because it represents an upgrade in the perceived social, economic status of the individual. By all means, having a car is good because it gives you comfort and with the possession of a car, you are able to determine your own movements without recourse to anyone. Many see buying a car as a personal reward for themselves having toiled and worked for the money with which they purchased the car. However, there's something I have noticed among young employees, and that is the confusion in whether to go for real estate or to purchase a car. Without a doubt, both prospects are enterprising and are both money well spent in both instances albeit depending on the particular circumstances going for a car might be better than going for a house and vice versa.

Should I get a car now or should I just invest the money in real estate? These two options are quite okay in their own rights and depending on your age and experience; one option may appeal more to you than the other. However, I always recommend procrastination in the case of buying a car, rather than going for a car; the individual might consider investing it in a way that it can yield even more profit for the owner. The difference between the rich man and the poor man is the decisions they made in times past. Majority of the current billionaires especially the young ones had the opportunity of just splashing the cash on expensive trinkets and showing off, but they rather invested in order to have more because investment is far better than a liability. There is a need to picture yourself as a CEO, and your life is the organization you are running and then begin to make decisions that are designed towards meeting your goals; if you can adopt this mindset, certainly there will be a positive difference in your life. The major reason for my preference of real estate is motivated by the fact that it can appreciate which a car is more likely going to depreciate in value in the coming years.

Furthermore, the real estate industry is seasonal in nature in that there are times where properties come at an appealing, i.e., lower price, and this price fluctuates hence if an individual encounters such scenario, the best thing is to invest and possibly sell when the price is higher. This implies that financially, real estate appreciates while vehicles depreciate in value. Vehicles have no such season because their prices are more stable over a period of time as compared with real estate.

Go for that vacation now

We all have an option at every point in our lives. The student has an option whether to participate in tests and examination or not. The employee has an option whether to report at the office or not etc. However, the big part of it all is that no matter the decision we adopt there will be consequences at the end. I believe life is meant to be enjoyed and whenever the opportunity beckons to rest or go on vacation, we should take it with both hands. You have only one life to live, and it is better than you make good use of it. Every day as you go to work or school or whatever activity you are engaged in, your brain goes to work as well. Remember that the brain is the site of thinking in the brain, vacation gives us an opportunity to rest and recharge, to de-stress and replenish lost energy.

Vacation is one of the things that should not be procrastinated on. We all need money, but some in desperation continue to work while they were supposed to be resting. The body may not react now, but by the time it reacts, later on, the consequences may be so sudden and tragic. You might not know, or you know and perhaps don't attach more significance to it but health is wealth, treating yourself right entails you have time for work, and you have time for relaxation. The love for money must not supersede the love for self because if something inimical or untoward should happen then even the organization would easily employ another person to take your place. Such is life, and this is why I always recommend that we put ourselves first at all times. Enjoy life and have fun. Work and play!

Chapter 5 :
FAQs To Halt Procrastination

Right now, I'm sure we are all aware that man, i.e., the human being is in a constant struggle, not with anyone but with himself. The struggle is with his instincts and desires. Procrastination occurs whenever there is a clash between the instincts and desires. Indeed, we have all procrastinated at some point in our lives; either due to stress or laziness, we have all at some point put off activity or two which could have done now till much later. Procrastination is not age specific as everyone is prone to it regardless of socio-demographic factors such as age and gender hence the prevalence of it is general and not skewed in any way. There is no one solution fits all approach for ending procrastination. It can be a sign that you are currently engaged in an activity that you are not particularly interested in because when you are passionate about a thing, the tendency to engage the activity on time is high. This is why it is a statement of fact to posit that our level of procrastination is a reflection of our preference and sense of value and interests in life.

A lot has been said procrastination which certainly would throw up some questions. Here are some of the most frequently asked questions on halting procrastination.

1. Are there any benefits to procrastination?

This is a somewhat tricky question, but I will say YES: Procrastination does have a benefit as it helps you reduce anxiety! However, procrastination in helping you reduce anxiety about a particular activity only ends up delaying the evil day. In most cases we procrastinate because we are anxious about a particular activity we should have engaged in right away, or we procrastinate because we feel the deadline for that activity is still far away or perhaps the activity in question is a personal one hence we are accountable to only ourselves in getting the activity done. Whatever the reason for procrastination, it helps us reduce our anxiety for that activity but what we get is only a temporary reprieve as the activity postponed will not go away and by procrastinating it the task to be done might get bigger as the days go by. Take for instance a student who should read daily but will rather procrastinate reading till when exams are around the corner, then the bulk of what to be covered then keeps increasing, so much that he might not be able to effectively cover every aspect of the lesson note which would have been possible had he started reading earlier.

In some cases, it has also been reported that procrastination helps improve efficiency and performance. The awareness of deadline for an activity automatically boost the concentration levels of some people and ultimately increase their concentration and output in the said activity. However, as stated earlier, there are tasks that tend to increase further if delayed hence an individual who is attuned to always procrastinating may eventually encounter a task that will overwhelm them in the nearest future. I once witnessed a situation whereby a student collapsed during the examination period. Obviously, he had taken up too much work more than he could handle and his system couldn't process it all hence he had a total breakdown. In short, procrastination helps reduce anxiety, but it is merely a Greek gift to yourself that will only come back to affect you in the nearest future adversely.

2. What is the source of procrastination?

There are many factors that could evidently trigger or motivate you to procrastinate. For instance, you are likely to procrastinate when you have no interest in an activity. The lack of interest in that activity kills your motivation and interest so much that you continue to postpone the activity until the last possible minute. In some cases, you may be overwhelmed by the size of the project that you don't know how to start and in yet some cases the perfectionist mentality in you may motivate you to wait for 'the perfect time' to begin and in anticipation of starting at best possible moment you may find yourself delaying the task.

Furthermore, nature and nurture can be complicit in the explanation of procrastination. It may sound a bit weird, but it is true that procrastination can be inherited. A person does not just inherit the biological components of their parents alone, a person may also inherit the behavioral tendencies of such parent(s) as well, and these tendencies could possibly include procrastination. The environment a person is nurtured also plays a role. A child brought up by a permissive parent is more likely to procrastinate because he/she is raised in an environment whereby there is no consequence for the adverse behavior. Hence he develops the tendency to lay off tasks meant to be done now till much later. Psychologically, the behavior is motivated by reward or reinforcements while behavior is discouraged by punishment. In a scenario whereby a child is reprimanded for procrastinating all the time, he will likely seek to do things a little bit faster just to avoid the reprimand of the parent, teacher or caregiver. Where there is no consequence for procrastination, then the behavior tends to continue unabated. This is why in seeking to investigate the reasons for your procrastination you need to evaluate the source of it.

3. Is there a link between self-control and procrastination?

Absolutely! A big part of procrastination is lack of self-control. They are like Siamese twins that cannot be separated because they go hand in hand. A chronic procrastinator has lost control of his or her own actions. The normal thing is for an individual to master himself at all times. In fact, regardless of the activity or endeavor, an individual is engaged in, self-mastery is a necessity for success and achievement. It is a necessary attribute and requirement for success because in most cases success involves self-denial and this can only come through mastery of self. Procrastination comes naturally to people who do not have the discipline to complete tasks on time. This is why any curative or preventive remedy for procrastination needs to develop a viable way of helping the client gain mastery of his own actions. This is simply non negotiable in the quest to combating procrastination.

Every form of addiction is invariably a lack of self-control. This is why the danger of procrastination is great because since procrastination is the aftermath of lack of control which is also a strong causative factor for addictions, it, therefore, follows that an individual engrossed with procrastination will likely have an addiction. Every addiction starts with a step and the individual upon realizing the danger in the activity he is engaging in could easily have stopped successfully but rather than stop straight away, he/she postpones stopping till later on until they eventually develop a dependent relationship with whatever substance or activity they are addicted to. Procrastination is also significant because it can mess up the psyche of a person and affects other aspects of their life.

I have discovered that one of the best ways to live life is to set targets for each day and work assiduously to achieve all the targets set out for the day without exception. I have discovered that the easiest way to gauge the level of control you have over your own life is to set daily targets and see how you are able to perform in the actualization of these targets. Self-indulgence is an enemy of progress because it absolutely adversely affects a person's output in any given activity. A self-indulgent person will always perform lower than expected in tasks or where they perform reasonably well in the set tasks will ultimately find it a bit difficult to meet p with the deadline set for the task. Success is strongly connected to control, and every individual must seek to take control of his or her own life and actions on a daily basis.

4. Can procrastination affect my relationships and personal life?

Behavior is transient; this is why a behavioral disposition of an individual in activity will always reflect in the other aspects of their lives. It is true that procrastination can cost you relationships with people especially loved ones and associates at work or at school, How many homes have been broken due to lack of quick resolution when disagreements arise between the couple? How many careers have been lost due to lack of quick resolution? Heck, many have even lost their preferred romantic partners due to their inability to declare their interest on time. Procrastination is so significant it can break down key relationships that could have been helpful to the individual both in the short and long run. When a partner in a relationship be it romantic, or business relationship often procrastinates, the effect is mostly that the other party feels unimportant and undervalued and they may, therefore, determine to seek an exit from such relationship. The relationship is hard work because it requires regular input consistently for it to stand. It is like a building. It requires regular input before it can grow to the desired level but unlike a building which can be stopped whenever it is complete, there is always need to put in more effort into a relationship at all time because the day you stop putting in effort into a relationship is the day you're your partner begins to lose value and worth in your eyes and is the day that relationship begins to die.

Every activity or task we engage in daily so far as it entails interaction with people, we build a relationship. You must have heard the quote first impression matters a lot. Picture a situation of a job interview whereby a particular applicant meets all the criteria's listed out as a prerequisite for the job, but the individual comes late for the job interview. While the fellow might have cogent reasons for his lateness, he or she has ultimately created a wrong perception of himself and has therefore started out a potential relationship on a wrong footing. There are many qualified applicants who are discounted merely on the basis of punctuality yearly. This is why it is very true that procrastination can affect not just a person's life but also their relationship with others. I guess it is, therefore, safe to say that your happiness may be connected to the promptness at which you take up tasks.

5. Are Procrastinators bad people?

Procrastinators are not necessarily bad people. In fact, in most cases, they often turn out to be nice and caring people who are easy to mingle with and relate with others around them. On a personal level, procrastinators, are merely those who like putting off tasks till much later, and this does not in any way tamper with their relational or interpersonal skills. They are just like every other person. They are as easy to mingle with, and just anyone could readily relate with someone given to procrastination. Strangely, procrastinators are always fun to be around. They are mostly calm and collected as they have a relaxed approach towards life. They are the ones usually cracking jokes and bringing about a relaxed atmosphere when there is a task to be done. They emphasized work and play which is why they are usually nice to be around.

However, on a professional note, they may not be the best of partners to have whether as a colleague at work or as a partner working on a group assignment in school. Procrastinators always contribute little to the group task and group goals. The reason for this is pretty obvious. They are less productive at what they do and in the most cases always exceed deadlines hence while they may be friends with everyone on a personal level, they may not necessarily be the darling of everyone when it comes to official or professional assignments. This is because they may weigh everyone down with their laid-back approach to work. At times, they are perfectionists, and they influence people around them with their calm demeanor.

6. What are the dangers of procrastination?

You must understand that overindulgence in procrastination often come at some costs to the procrastinator. It can lead to broken relationships because it can throw up a feeling of lack of worth or relevance in the mind of the other party that can make them unhappy and perhaps seeks a separation. This I believe is the biggest danger of procrastination. This is because they may feel that perhaps the other party is cheating on them since they don't seem to value them again hence there must be someone else in the picture even if he or she is hidden somewhere. A simple analysis of some of the divorce cases around today has elements of procrastination in them not just because in terms of their refusal or inability to settle rift on time but also due to their oversight generally on issues pertaining to themselves as a couple. Issues on love and relationships are quite important in life; it is a huge emotional investment which we will all make at some point in life which is why both parties involved must always keep the other happy by putting their interest and happiness at the top of their own agenda.

It can lead to career setback because a procrastinator will likely have issues with punctuality at work as well as complying with deadlines on a particular issue. All of which can affect the reputation of the employee with his/her employers. In fact, it can lead to isolation in the office especially when it comes to tasks requiring collective effort; past history of abdication of duty often comes to mind and may lead to the person being sidelined by others around them. Career-wise, it may be unwise to have the habit of procrastinating. The truth is that consecutively missed deadlines will always have a negative impact on the professional life of the individual whether in the short run or long run.

For a student, procrastination can negatively affect academic performance. When the students continuously postpone reading and resolving assignments; the end result might not be good enough. For the entrepreneur, procrastination can result in an inability to meet up with deadlines and targets, and this could hamper the relationship between the entrepreneur and client and this can eventually lead to a decline in income. For the average individual, procrastination can lead to deterioration in health when the individual continuously put off the healthy foods, exercising and sleep till much later, it could lead to deterioration of health and even sicknesses and disease as well as death in some extreme cases. The essential point to note is that procrastination affects output because for example, when an assignment is given in class and due for submission within the next 24 hours, procrastinating on getting the assignment done will result in the time left continuously shrinking and decreasing so that when the individual is ready to tackle it he will have to do it in a hurry, and this will certainly affect the quality of work done.

Procrastination can cause anxiety as well. Take the instance of household chores, for example, you put off the task of washing dishes till much later say the next day, the dirty dishes will keep piling up and other tasks will keep joining until such individual is in a frenzy on how to clear the dirty dishes. Time is an illusion; we often think we have time when in reality we don't even have much time left again. Doing things as early as possible makes one attains some level of rest and calmness rather than running around to fulfill the task later on. It is imperative that the individual understands self and refuse the urge to compare themselves with others when it comes to their approach to resolving tasks. For instance, there are students who have the habit of reading for the exam when it is very close by and as weird as that seem they perform quite okay and excel in it, and there are yet others that don't perform well with such scattergun approach.

7. Are there ways to overcome procrastination?

If you find yourself frustrated and in desperate need of overcoming the problem, the good news is that procrastination can be overcomed. Certainly, procrastination can be conquered if you really do set your mind to do it. I must confess that it might be hard especially if you have been on it for quite a while. Speaking from experience, merely verbal confession of willingness to end procrastination is not enough. It takes concerted willpower from the concerned individual to effectively conquer procrastination for good. There are certain steps you can practice to overcome procrastination quickly, and some of them are enumerated below;

i.   The first step to overcoming procrastination is the admittance that it could be bad and has a negative effect on you as a person. You cannot conquer what you do not see as bad in the first place. You must simply come to the acknowledgment of the issue as a problem and challenge that is not beneficial to you.

ii.   Identify the lost opportunities and deadlines missed due to your procrastinating on some activities in the past. Doing this will give you more basis to be angry at procrastination and infuse you with the necessary strength and fortitude needed to overcome the problem.

iii. Forgive yourself for past issues that must have arisen as a result of procrastination. You need to let go of past hurts and mistakes, wipe the slate clean and start on a new page.

iv.   Set daily targets: Rome was not built in a day; it was built gradually until it was eventually completed. Every big thing starts small, so if you want to overcome such a big problem as procrastination then you must start setting daily targets which you must strive to actualize; doing the small daily tasks consistently would equip you with the self-belief needed to help you to conquer the bigger tasks. Have a to-do list which would be written daily and placed at a conspicuous place where you would always come in contact with it regularly and be reminded of what still needs to be done. Approach your daily targets with accuracy and precision and ensure that no day passes by without you ticking up every item on your to-do list.

v.   Reward yourself: The concept of reward is central to the principle of motivation. As you seek to drop the habit of procrastination, you should learn to reward and motivate yourself for every achievement made along the way to overcoming the problem. The reward will keep you motivated. However, due to the fact that you are the one administering the reward, avoid the temptation to abuse it by giving yourself the reward even though there are still other items on your list waiting to be achieved for the day.

vi. Minimize distractions: Distraction is the archenemy of activity. When distracted the tendency to procrastinate till when the distraction is gone often arises. Hence, in order to fully overcome procrastination; move away from people or things that form distractions to you. You need all the focus you can garner. Hence you must eschew the company of those that affect your concentration.

8. Is procrastination a reflection of my level of motivation?

Not really. Procrastination is not necessarily a good reflection or gauge of your level of motivation. At times you procrastinate out of confidence, and at times you procrastinate out of doubt about something. If as a student you are given an assignment with duration of 8 days, yet the questions seem like what you can accomplish in a day, it is normal to want to set it off till much later. Likewise, if an assignment is given which seems cumbersome and difficult, it is likely that the student will delay on the project rather than getting it done right away. In the first instance, overconfidence was the complicit factor in procrastinating the time for resolving the assignment and in the second instance lack of confidence was the factor responsible for the lack of interest in the task.

There are certain theorists that view procrastination as a personal weakness in individuals but it is clear enough in recent times that procrastination is dependent on the individual as a person and has nothing to do with it being a weakness because there are those who procrastinate and have been able to achieve as much success as even some of those who do not procrastinate. However what can be truly said of procrastination is that it is a reflection of an individual's orientation on personal enjoyment and wellbeing. A person who feels life must be enjoyed will likely value rest more than work if put in a position to make an option out of the two. This is why it is said that procrastination is a function of a mismatch between current engagement and the motivational structures that is situated in a person.

Why do you do the activity you are engaged in? Is it due to your personal interest or the expectation of parents or society? We reside in a world where you are compelled to take on some roles and activities regardless of your interests in them. You are forced to be who you really are not and is not interested in being. This often brings about a lack of motivation which usually culminates in procrastination. Interest and activity are intertwined. When you are really interested in an activity, you tend to love engaging in it naturally. This is why little children do not really need much pacifying before they play with their toys. I have realized that at times the difference between the best and the worst student in a class is not necessarily a function of the intelligent quotient levels. At times it is just out of interests. The interest one has in the course makes him read regularly even wider than the syllabus covered by the instructor while the lack of interest of one makes him disdain the studies that he merely reads and even though he possesses the capacity to be brilliant in that course, he is simply unwilling to exert himself towards becoming the best he can be.

9. Are there types of procrastinators? If yes, what type do I belong to?

Ideally and truthfully, every human being walking the earth has procrastinated at some point in his or her lives. However, the frequency at which we procrastinate is what varies. This, therefore, begs the question is there types of procrastinators and what are the types of procrastination available? This question is important because knowing your type of procrastination will certainly be of huge help in the quest to overcome the problem. There are six known types of procrastinator, and they are enumerated below;

i. Dreamers: These are the categories of people who have a laid-back approach towards life in general. They are usually narcissistic in nature and have a heightened sense of self-importance. Just as the name implies, they so much love to fantasize rather than put in work needed to achieve their often-lofty dreams.

ii. Defiers: These categories of people just like the dreamers also have a delusion of self-importance because they find it difficult to comply with instructions from a superior. They often put off tasks due to be done in the present till much later simply because they always seem to go against authority. Defying authority instructions gives them some level of intrinsic happiness within themselves because by their defiance they derive a feeling of power that serves to only boost their ego.

iii. Worriers: These categories of people are those that worry a lot after a task is given. They merely procrastinate because they feel like they are not in the best possible mood or scenario to begin the implementation of a task. Rather than begin on time, they often begin later and at times may not get to complete the task at hand. This behavior often makes them underachievers in some way because at the very end they mostly get their tasks done under duress due to the fear of impending deadlines hence they may not be able to give their best before all is wrapped up.

iv. Perfectionist: These categories of people are usually very slow in taking off. They always don't start on time. They are very similar to the worriers but their own refusal to start earlier is not down to worry but due to overconfidence or pride. They see every task no matter how insignificant as a direct reflection of their abilities hence they want to give out the best but rather than start early; they often prefer starting later.

v. Overdoers: These ones lack concentration. They have a short attention span yet they take on multiple activities simultaneously. Rather than give a task their undivided attention before moving on to other activities, they juggle multiple activities together concurrently. At times as a result of taking on multiple tasks at the same time, they may not be able to deliver on their tasks as at when due. They are mostly members of the Sanguine temperamental class that we discussed in chapter three and one profound thing about them is that they need to research in-depth to know how to be fully focused in the tasks they are given.

vi. Crisis makers: This is the category of chronic procrastinators. Their procrastination is so severe that they want to achieve what they naturally should have taken about 2 months to achieve they often seek to achieve it in a few days. Majority of those who fall within this continuum are students as it is not uncommon to meet a student trying to juggle reading his class notes and textbooks just a few hours to the exam even though he has been aware of exam coming up.

CONCLUSION

As we know and can collectively agree, everything which has a beginning must come to a close at some point. For this reason, it is imperative that this book comes to a close. However, before I walk away from all I have shared in this collection of advice and direction, let us take a few minutes to refresh on the contents and points I have considered so far.

It has been established that procrastination isn't exactly a wonderful trait to have. For this reason, anyone who suffers from any form of procrastination or from the effects of procrastinating may find resource herein to help them get by to change or get better. In defining procrastination, I find that it implies putting off for later what can be done now. In a lot of situations and events, there are very visible effects of procrastination. For example, it is easy to notice the effect of procrastination in the making of laws relating to security or gun control. At the same time, it is easy to notice the effects of procrastination in making traffic and/or immigration laws. The effects of procrastination in these scenarios would show up almost immediately.

However, there are situations in which the effects of procrastination may not present themselves immediately. In some such cases, the effects only show up after severe harm has been done and to some irreversible extent. Examples include procrastination in work-related contexts, romantic and business relationships and health-related circumstances. For example, when a romantic relationship breaks apart, people without relationship experience would easily assume that the relationship broke apart by occurrences which occurred immediately before the break. However, in most cases where relationships break apart, the reasons for the break are usually more far-fetched than a simple fight the day before. Sometimes, the reason is a long overdue apology expected from a partner, or a habit which should have been rectified long ago but wasn't because "there's still time to fix this" is a common excuse people give.

In work related contexts, procrastination can have far-reaching effects years after the actual act of procrastination occurs. For example, a document a manager was too lazy to file adequately 3 years ago may get damaged over the years and cost the firm a fat contract which requires that document. In situations like this, it is safe to say the effects of procrastination are more long term than short term.

In this book, I attempted to identify procrastination, its allies and manifestations, and the overreaching effects of putting off for later, what can be done today, and the instances where procrastination can aid and lead to productive growth either in business or career. With this information, I attempted to create a reasonable solution to the problem of procrastination, through suggestions and simulations of workable and practical formulas for managing procrastination professionally to suit a specific ambition and aid that ambition to grow into a real benefit.

Some of the causes or reasons for procrastination identified include: laziness, boredom, tiredness, fear of failure, desire to be absolutely perfect, fear of success, the feeling of being overwhelmed, waiting for the right time, feeling of negativity, negative self-talk and declaration, lack of stoicism, uncertainty on whether or where to start from, indecisiveness, fear of hard work, etcetera.

Some practical case scenarios of these in work-related and general contexts include laziness to finish reports at work which may eventually lead to clutter in both your work schedule and your work table. This could, in turn, result in a loss of confidence in one's ability to execute tasks by the boss or a loss of data due to the eventual rush to complete the task later on. Either way, laziness results in procrastination which in turn results in a terrible outcome.

Similarly, a feeling of boredom may result in a severe case of procrastination. For example, a writer with a deadline for publication may be too bored with the process of writing the particular text and seek excitement in doing other things which may, in turn, result in a delay in the execution of the writing project. In the same vein, much procrastination is as a result of a lack of stoicism or a feeling of uncertainty on whether to start or where to start from. Any feeling of uncertainty could be classified among the more frequent reasons why many great ideas are not birthed. This feeling of uncertainty comes from several discouraging pointers in the process of planning for a particular idea or for the execution of particular inspiration.

Also, in this book, I outlined a number of ways through which procrastination can be beaten to the back seat or used effectively to achieve a responsible ambition. Summarily, these include; adopting a "so what" mentality in situations involving the feeling of fear of failure or fear of success. The "so what" mentality is a mechanism of the mind which sounds a rebuttal at the voice inside the head which projects the many challenges that may present themselves in the process of accomplishing a particular task. The "so what" mentality is preferable because it is a psychological response which both counters the question and reassures the mind of the individual who uses it. This mentality gives one a kind of confidence similar to the confidence gained from taking alcohol or some kinds of drugs.

Another way of combating procrastination is to make a mental or physical note of the various things you may have to do for each day and develop the habit of following through with that schedule to accomplish the tasks outlined within. For people who have to procrastinate as a result of a craving to be perfect, it helps to convince yourself that imperfections are regular and normal traits of the human nature and as such, there is nothing terrible about having imperfections in your work. Convincing the mind to believe a particular thing is easy, all it takes is an agreement to continuously remind the mind of that particular thing until it becomes a part of the mind. Another way that works is rewarding yourself for accomplishing small feats from time to time. This way, you can successfully convince your mind that accomplishing tasks at the proper time is rewarding and in turn successfully convince your mind to take new tasks seriously and work assiduously on completing them.

In this book, I also found that seeking different ways of doing things helps to keep us on track and counter boredom in work-related scenarios. By choosing more interesting ways of working on a particular task, you may find the right inspiration to execute that task. For example, someone who finds music interesting and engaging may find that listening to music while working is a very efficient way of making work a lot more interesting. In this vein, when the individual feels bored with work or a particular task, they could help the situation by listening to music alongside completing the task. However, when employing this solution, be sure to remember that if what makes the individual feel interested or engaged also serves as a form of distraction, then it shouldn't be considered. For example, someone who is wont to bob his head to a song or sing along may consider using something else to avoid the distraction of pausing in the middle of completing a task just to bob to their favorite song or sing a particular line from their favorite song.

I also considered in this book that, one sure fire way of solving procrastination might be to get to the root of the actual reason for the procrastination. Many would suggest that this should come first before anything else. As we know, the quickest way to a solution is first identifying the problem. Once you have been able to point out that the problem or reason for your procrastination is laziness or disinterest or a fear of success or failure, you can then proceed to determine whether the more practical solution is a psychological approach or a physical approach (e.g., taking notes or setting reminders and creating to-do lists).

I also pointed out that another sure-fire way of overcoming procrastination is to join up a boring or monotonous task with another more interesting or pairing up a difficult task with another more pleasant or less strenuous. When very difficult and not so difficult are executed side by side, results become a lot less difficult to get.

I pointed out also that some people usually seek the help of a mentor or someone who can be considered a coach to help them with guidance through the process of executing a project. Once there is someone who cares about how much time it takes you to accomplish a task, it becomes less likely that you will procrastinate on that task. Also, mentors and coaches help you get rid of distractions and lazy man excuses and, as a result, help you achieve your set goals on each task at the estimated time. From this point, a mention was made of the importance of goal setting and goal monitoring. Setting a goal is one thing and making the conscious effort to monitor the progress of that goal is another thing. While some people complain that they find it difficult to reach or achieve their goals, they fail to realize that just setting a goal doesn't mean you won't procrastinate during the process of execution of that goal. Putting measures in place to monitor the progress of that goal is as important as setting the goal itself. Whether in the form of human reminders and watchdogs or technological watchdogs, it is important to have a contingency which keeps you in check during the process of completing a task, to avoid procrastination. Still, wonder why so many firms have project supervisors?

In chapter four, I touched on a very dicey aspect of the general topic; when is procrastination good? In the process of trying to answer this question, I first answered the question: is there any good in procrastination. While dealing with this, I find that while procrastination is popularly labeled as a bad trait, when adequately managed, procrastination can be harnessed positively to achieve a specific ambition whether in work or in a general aspect of life. I find that what most refer to as terrible human trait, others have trained themselves to use as an excuse to achieve certain levels of success. Some examples given in this chapter include the lives of successful businessmen and women or career men and women who procrastinate the notion of getting into a relationship or settling down to marriage, mostly because of their desire to attain a certain level of career and business success. I find that many such persons are considered to be romantically shut off from the rest of the world and only focus on building their business or career, when, however, they feel emotional attachments like normal people. For some of them, this procrastination isn't intentional; they just find that they keep putting off for later, an emotion that needs to be expressed now.

While I reviewed examples of people who fall into this category, I considered that for most of them, there is a more pressing urge to accomplish a work-related task than to call a loved one. As a result, there is a lot more focus on work than there is on emotional attachments. Also, I find that for most of these people, it is not the absence of a loved one but the laziness to express affection towards that person that leads to this procrastination. Also, I discover that some people have successfully learned the subtle art of postponing emotional attachment in order to reduce the burden of the individual and focus more on what adds to the achievement of their ambition. I can say these are skilled in the art of procrastination (if we agree that procrastination is basically postponing things you can do now to later).

I am sure that this book has helped you in understanding the concept of procrastination, the pros and the cons that are attached to it as well as broaden your knowledge base on how to overcome it or help others who may need to overcome it. Without a doubt, procrastination is the biggest challenge of our time. The advent of civilization has brought about widespread technological advancement that has made procrastination so appealing that it is fast taking up endemic proportions among the old and young alike. How do you feel when people delay the performance of a task you gave them until much later? Your feeling should determine your approach to procrastination. Procrastination is not absolutely bad neither can it be absolutely said to be good because it has certain benefits as well some bad sides. If you manage it well, procrastination can pretty much work well for you. The reality of life is that everything no matter what it is if done in excess will adversely affect the doer. Certainly, it is imperative that you show dedication to any task we are saddled with, and this means. The life of a human being is like a car, and the individual is the driver himself, excessive procrastination takes over the control of your life because control is at the root of procrastination.

It is quite easy to overcome it. The human being has been naturally equipped with the capacity to overcome any behavioral disposition they deem unfavorable. The possession of willpower is the biggest tool in the arsenal available to us in defeating procrastination. There are various ways in which procrastination can be overcomed, and a lot of it has already been examined at length earlier in this book. If you have been adversely affected by procrastination in the past, I am here to tell you that you can overcome. It is a fight that you can win if you are willing to fight it smartly. You can overcome, and I believe you will. However, I will advise that as a matter of urgency right now every time you wake up to set a to-do list for yourself and try as much as possible to fix a deadline for the achievements of the tasks. Make sure that you ensure due diligence in achieving the tasks. Overcoming procrastination is a battle that requires utmost discipline if you must win. If you list out your daily tasks and are able to achieve them, then you will be strengthened in your resolve to winning the grudge battle with procrastination. Ensure you reward yourself as well when you have achieved your tasks for the day. It will serve as a major motivation that will fuel your passion towards overcoming it forever.

There are people that procrastinate their efforts towards ending procrastination! It is really compelling how you can procrastinate ending procrastination itself! The fact is that the best time to start if you must end procrastination is now. There is no better time or day to start than right now. If you decided to read today, after reading this book, go and read that which you planned reading earlier. In fact, if you have successfully read the contents of this book from the beginning right to this concluding part, then it is a testament that you are already half way towards overcoming procrastination and gaining back the control of your life. As soon as you set your tasks for the day, try to start immediately. You do not necessarily wait till nightfall before completing the tasks on your to-do list. Imbibing the culture of starting out a task early is very good as it helps the individual enough time to ruminate and reflect on other aspects of that task and possibly make some improvements and modification if need be before the end of the day.

Those who are used to procrastination often report their likeness for the adrenaline rush they feel like the main contributory factor towards continuing the trend. While you might develop a feel-good feeling at the prospect of achieving your tasks within a short while, it is not good to live life this way as your recalcitrant attitude will eventually catch up with you whether now or later. Save yourself the unnecessary stress by accomplishing your tasks earlier rather than waiting for much later when the time would no longer be on your side. You can compensate yourself by engaging in sports or any other similar activity that can bring you the needed adrenaline rush.

Also, you must learn to say no to distractions if you must overcome procrastination. Browsing the internet, mingling with friends and watching television have all been some of the most common distractors around. You must learn to avoid these distractors if you must accomplish your wish of overcoming procrastination. If need be, these distractors can be fixed as the medium of reward you give yourself after accomplishing your tasks for the day. Believe me; it is such a great feeling to overcome procrastination and gain control and mastery over yourself.

So far, this book has served to satisfy the longing to beat procrastination or, at least, use it effectively for a beneficial goal. What have you gotten from this book? I implore you to utilize the steps you have learned from this book as soon as possible. Also, consider picking out 9 proven ways of curbing procrastination which you most identify with and write them out on your journal or iPhone or anywhere you can easily see it to remember or as a daily reminder. This way, those tips would remain with you and find expression from within.

Use the strategies highlighted within, any of the 36 proven steps with which you can utilize to beat procrastination. Or at least turn it around such that you aren't adversely affected by it.

It is here that I have got to bid you a short good bye. And I hope to see you again in my other books - that is if I do not procrastinate on writing them! That was indeed a joke and jibe at myself.

At this juncture before you go

I would like to seek your help on a single matter of some importance.

Would you be able to share with the good folks that shop on amazon what you have picked up from this book? Any single 1 of the 36 stratagems which you took up and found particularly effective?

It would be great to let the other folks know and also to help this budding writer out a little! Actually it matters quite a bit

So here's a big Thank You in advance for this

And have a great day!

Cognitive Behavioral Therapy

The 21 Day CBT Workbook For Overcoming Fear, Anxiety And Depression

How To Use 30 Proven Techniques To Get Measurable Relief And Improve Your Daily Life

Jacob Greene

Cognitive Behavioral Therapy
The 21 Day CBT Workbook

Introduction

Problems.

That is a definite common denominator for everyone on planet earth. Whatever we want to coin it as – challenges, milestones, issues, and a whole myriad of other colorful terms. One thing is for certain. Everyone would have problems. Problems of the material sort, problems stemming from the mind and emotions. The question here is what would you choose to do when faced with them?

For the issues that originate from the mind and emotion, the contents of this book would be well suited to help you with tackling those matters. For folks suffering from phobias, anxiety as well as the more common than thought incidences of depression, the good news is that you can be empowered with the right tools contained within this book to help with handling those issues.

So much of our lives is determined by our thoughts and emotions. Even the most rational and logical of us would sometimes let our hearts rule over our heads. They say that the secret to the Universe is this: our thoughts shape our realities. We attract what we think, and through our thoughts, we manifest what we fixate on.

This means that if you're a pessimist who always sees the negative side of things, you'll only attract more negativity into your life; whereas optimists are positive thinkers who are grateful for everything that comes their way, and in doing so, multiply their blessings and become more abundant in goodness.

Whether you believe in the magic of the Universe or not, the power of our thoughts and the actions they invoke in us is undeniable. Just imagine what you could do if you had complete, masterful control over your own thoughts, actions, and emotions. The possibilities would be limitless. This is why Cognitive-Behavioral Therapy (CBT) matters so much.

The guiding principle behind CBT is that our thoughts determine our feelings and behaviors, and so, in gaining better control over your mind, you will be able to change the way you feel and the things you do. It might seem like common sense, but it's actually harder than you think. Have you ever done something you knew you shouldn't have but couldn't stop yourself from, like lying or yelling at a loved one? Or tried to quit a bad habit like smoking or gambling, but found yourself struggling to do so? It's easier said than done, right?

Never underestimate the power of your thoughts. Positive thoughts can do so much to make your life better; it can lift your spirits and boost your confidence, making it easier to connect with others and enjoy yourself. On the other hand, negative thoughts can do a lot to harm us and our self-esteem. Over thinking, being pessimistic and worrying too much can cause us anxiety, fear, and if left unchecked, lead us to depression. A lot of the mental and emotional issues we struggle with are actually rooted in negative thinking and pessimistic beliefs. This is where CBT comes into play.

While there are many other kinds of therapy readily available to us right now, none have been quite as popular as CBT, largely thanks to its easy application and simple techniques. It integrates both behavioral and cognitive theories of psychology and targets our unrealistic thoughts and faulty ways of thinking, which distort our views and attitudes towards ourselves, our circumstances, and the world around us, and corrects them to help us become more emotionally and mentally well-adjusted.

All too often our problems and personal struggles stem from a negative view of ourselves and our situation. Our distorted thinking leads us to misinterpret things for the worse and makes it harder for us to cope with our stress and the challenges we face. With the help of CBT, you can finally learn how to overcome your anxiety, fears & phobias, obsessive thinking, and depression.

In this book, you will find a 21-day step-by-step program that will teach you all about Cognitive-Behavioral Therapy and how to practice it in your everyday life. It will show you over 30 different ways you can use CBT to overcome the hardships you face with simple, easy, and reliable tips and techniques.

However, it is by no means a perfect and absolute solution to all your problems. It can't cure your depression or rid you of your mental illness permanently and completely, but it can do a lot to make it more manageable, grant you relief, and improve your overall quality of life.

When I was a young boy, I was diagnosed with attention-deficit hyperactivity disorder (ADHD) and it's something I constantly struggled with, growing up. Because it was so hard for me to concentrate, I often did poorly in school and failed a lot of my classes. It was hard for me to make friends because everyone thought I talked too much to carry a normal conversation and no one could understand or empathize with my condition.

I felt embarrassed about my ADHD and I hated how it made me feel so isolated from everyone else, like I was going too fast and forever waiting for someone to catch up to me. I can't count the number of times I wished I had an "off" button for my brain, just so I could stop feeling stupid or different or wrong. So believe me when I say that I know what it's like to struggle with mental illness.

But then, after I started seeking therapy and counseling, I discovered cognitive-behavioral therapy, and it did wonders for me. Life got so much better once I started practicing CBT, so much so that I was intrigued enough to research about it some more and learn as much as I could so I could help others like me. Now here I am, writing this book.

So if you're ready to start living your best life today and want to learn how to better control your own thoughts, feelings, and actions, then come and join me on my journey to mental wellness through CBT.

© Copyright 2019 by Jacob Greene - All rights reserved.

This document is geared towards providing exact and reliable information in regards to the topic and issue covered. The publication is sold with the idea that the publisher is not required to render accounting, officially permitted, or otherwise, qualified services. If advice is necessary, legal or professional, a practiced individual in the profession should be ordered.

From a Declaration of Principles which was accepted and approved by a Committee of the American Bar Association and a Committee of Publishers and Associations.

In no way is it legal to reproduce, duplicate, or transmit any part of this document in either electronic means or in printed format. Recording of this publication is strictly prohibited and any storage of this document is not allowed unless with written permission from the publisher. All rights reserved.

The information provided herein is stated to be truthful and consistent, in that any liability, in terms of inattention or otherwise, by any usage or abuse of any policies, processes, or directions contained within is the solitary and utter responsibility of the recipient reader. Under no circumstances will any legal responsibility or blame be held against the publisher for any reparation, damages, or monetary loss due to the information herein, either directly or indirectly.

Respective authors own all copyrights not held by the publisher.

The information herein is offered for informational purposes solely, and is universal as so. The presentation of the information is without contract or any type of guarantee assurance.

The trademarks that are used are without any consent, and the publication of the trademark is without permission or backing by the trademark owner. All trademarks and brands within this book are for clarifying purposes only and are owned by the owners themselves, not affiliated with this document.

Chapter 1: CBT 101

The History of CBT

One of the leading forms of psychosocial intervention practiced by many counselors and mental health professionals of today, Cognitive-Behavioral Therapy (CBT) is a psychotherapeutic treatment that aims to help patients understand and control the thoughts and feelings which influence their behaviors, and ultimately, overcome the destructive behavioral patterns that result from their negative thinking and unrealistic beliefs.

As you might have already surmised from its name, CBT came about after rise and fall of both cognitive and behavioral theories of psychology. A brainchild of the 1960s, it emerged as the solution that addressed the criticisms and shortcomings of the two fields and integrated them into a single, cohesive practice.

The theoretical roots of CBT can be traced back as early as 1913, during the beginnings of behaviorism as pioneered by John B. Watson whose work laid the foundation for a lot of CBT's concepts. After that, it was also heavily influenced by the work of Albert Ellis on Rational Emotive Behavioral Therapy (REBT) in the 1950s as well.

With that said though, it's actually Dr. Aaron T. Beck that most consider to be the formal founder and first pioneer of Cognitive Behavioral Therapy (CBT). While working as a psychiatrist at the University of Pennsylvania, Beck discovered that the psychotherapy he had been using to treat most of his clients' depression had not been effective and that his experimental findings contradicted and disproved the fundamental concepts of Freud's psychoanalytic theory, from which the therapy was based off of.

Instead, what he observed was that most of his clients often had internal experiences (thoughts and feelings) that significantly impacted their behaviors and led them to develop a lot of the psychological distress and mental health problems for which they sought professional help for. This "internal dialogue", as he called it, impacted their perceptions and attitudes towards a certain person or situation in ways many of them did not realize. For example, a previously cooperative client might think to himself, "This is so hard. The therapy isn't working and I'll never get better," and thus, start to become more resistant, despondent, and apathetic towards both the therapist and their condition.

Because of this, Beck started to conceptualize depression in terms of the streams of impulsive, negative thoughts that his depressed patients often struggled (and failed) to overcome. He coined the term "automatic thoughts" to refer to this phenomenon and posited that people interact with the world through their mental representations of it (i.e., thoughts, ideas, belief systems). Thus, if a person's mental representation or reasoning is inaccurate or dysfunctional, then their feelings and behaviors may become problematic.

Realizing the importance of what he had discovered, began developing his own psychological theory and therapy. He investigated the kinds of automatic thoughts that seemed to be most common among his clients and categorized them as: negative ideas about the self; negative beliefs about the world; and negative views of the future.

With this, he got to work on how to identify and correct these automatic thoughts. This emphasis on thought processes was the reason why Beck initially labeled his approach as simply "Cognitive Therapy" instead of "Cognitive-Behavioral Therapy." Later on, however, he would rename it to CBT as he began to borrow heavily from previously established behavioral techniques to treat the negative mentality of his clients.

He helped his patients identify their own automatic thoughts and encouraged them to think more objectively and consider things more realistically. Once they corrected their underlying beliefs, it became easier for clients to stop their maladaptive behaviors and conquer their feelings of depression, anxiety, guilt, trauma, and negativity. This would eventually lead them to emotional relief and allowed them to function better as a whole.

With that said, however, CBT as a field of study has gone beyond the work of Aaron Beck and has now become an umbrella term for many different therapeutic techniques with the same fundamental elements and assumptions.

One example of this is Albert Ellis' Rational Emotive Behavior Therapy (REBT), which we mentioned earlier. Similar to Beck's CBT, REBT is a kind of cognitive therapy that seeks to resolve a client's emotional and behavioral issues through correcting their irrational beliefs. It was from Ellis' work that much of Beck's ideas originated.

Dr. Judith Beck, the daughter of Aaron Beck, is another important proponent of CBT as she did a lot to continue her father's work through her research and development of better CBT techniques. She also encouraged positive coping mechanisms in her clients. Now she is widely regarded as the foremost expert authority on CBT and one of the best and most skilled CBT therapists working today.

Currently, CBT is the most empirically validated and effective form of psychosocial intervention in the world of clinical practice. It has gone on to inspire more than a thousand research papers and has been used to treat a number of mental health problems and psychological disorders. Aside from that, CBT also owes a great deal of its popularity to its success in treating many of society's most prevalent mental disorders, such as eating disorders, anxiety disorders, mood disorders, trauma-related disorders, and more.

With that said, the field has certainly come a long way since it began over half a century ago, and it remains relevant and beneficial to this day. Many experts would agree that Cognitive-Behavioral Therapy (CBT) has undoubtedly become an integral cornerstone not just in clinical psychology and therapy, but in self-help and mental wellness as a whole.

How CBT Can Help

Now that you've been acquainted with a brief history of CBT and how it has developed and changed throughout the years, it's time to move on to the many different ways CBT can help people. Enumerated below are just a few of its many benefits and advantages, such as:

It can solve a specific problem

As we've mentioned before, CBT is actually a general term for a classification of a number of different therapeutic techniques, all of which are guided by the same underlying principle, and that is: when we change our thoughts, we change our lives. This makes CBT an incredibly versatile approach and enables it to address a wide range of issues just by identifying the maladaptive thought or behavior the client would like to correct the most.

For example, someone suffering from anorexia will need to change the way he/she feels about himself/herself and his/her body; whereas a patient struggling with social anxiety must resolve his/her feelings of insecurity and social isolation and target the thoughts that trigger them. These two clients have different presenting problems, but CBT can benefit them both because it can be tailored to fit any problem in particular, so CBT techniques can help just about everyone.

It is goal-oriented

It's been said many times that CBT is a goal-oriented therapy. This means that there is a clear and definitive objective in mind that the client and the therapist must define at the start of their relationship. During every session, they will work towards realizing this goal step by step, and both parties understand what it is that they ultimately want to achieve.

This is an advantage because it clarifies the purpose of the therapy and makes sure that both the therapist and the individual are in agreement about what they are looking to achieve. Sometimes, with other kinds of therapy like psychotherapy or behavioral therapy, this is not the case. In CBT, what the client wants to achieve is often what the therapist will do for them.

It gives the client more freedom

Similar to the previous point, another advantage that CBT has over other psychotherapeutic approaches is that it is more collaborative than most. CBT practitioners often work together with their clients to help them overcome their problems and alleviate their psychological distress. It is directive and focused, but it also allows the client more freedom and control over the therapeutic process.

CBT is also more interactive and requires mutual effort from both parties for the therapy to succeed. The therapist's role is to listen and guide them through their thoughts and experiences; while the client needs to be open, honest, and expressive. So while the counselor's guidance is important, the client's participation and involvement is equally as integral..

It deals with current problems

Unlike other therapeutic approaches, CBT mainly deals with present-day problems and experiences. It addresses thoughts and behavioral patterns that are currently detrimental to the client. It doesn't dig deeper into their past or analyze their childhood experiences and subconscious drives. Rather, it is firmly rooted in the here and now, and it emphasizes the client's current issues at hand.

This is part of the reason why it is the least time-consuming of all the therapeutic approaches, and also a factor for why it is so practical and efficient. Clients can start to see positive results and progress quicker because CBT helps them deal with their issues and improve their current state of mind. It doesn't waste time trying too hard to uncover the deeper or hidden meaning behind things.

It is faster than other forms of therapy

This brings us to the next advantage of CBT: it is a time-limited approach. As stated before, it is the least time-consuming of all the kinds of psychotherapy and takes only one to two months before clients can start to see some progress. On average, most clients will often need 20 hourly sessions on a regular basis, usually once a week, so the therapy can be completed in over five to six months.

This is why CBT is the most recommended form of therapy for clients looking for a simple and effective solution that can alleviate their psychological distress and better enable them to deal with their problems. It is quick and efficient, and most people have a good idea about what to expect.

Moreover, clients can also benefit from CBT in the sense that less sessions means it's less costly. It's a great help for people who are seeking professional help and counseling, but cannot afford to spend more than 6 months in therapy (be it due to time constraints or financial reasons).

It is easily accessible

CBT is perhaps the easiest to understand and apply of all the psychotherapeutic approaches. It's highly structured nature lends itself well to several different mediums, which makes it one of the most accessible and widely available forms of counseling. From individual counseling, to group counseling, to self-help books like this one — almost anyone can learn and practice CBT.

It can help with many different mental health problems

An evidence-based therapy, thousands of studies to date have documented and demonstrated the effectiveness of CBT in dealing with a wide range of mental health problems.

From clinical diagnoses like post-traumatic stress disorder (PTSD), generalized anxiety disorder (GAD), social anxiety disorder, borderline personality disorder, and eating disorders like anorexia nervosa and bulimia; to more common problems like overcoming addiction, recovering from substance abuse, dealing with depression, relationship problems, and anger management — CBT can help with quite a number of things, as you can see.

It helps you grow as a person

When you begin to seek help through CBT, it will promote positive behavioral change and personal growth in you. Through this process, you will be able to identify the root of your problems and understand your role in perpetuating your own unhappiness.

CBT can help you see the impact of your negative thoughts and beliefs, and once you do, you will begin to work towards changing them. This will make you more kind, forgiving, and accepting of yourself and your shortcomings, as you will start to correct your own negative self-concepts.

It will make you more positive

You might remember that earlier ago we said that Dr. Aaron Beck, the founding father of CBT, was able to identify three major kinds of automatic thoughts: negative ideas about the self; negative beliefs about the world; and negative views of the future.

In line with this, CBT is geared towards helping people overcome this negative mindset and instead, encourage them to adopt more beneficial ways of thinking and behaving. In this way, CBT can do a lot to help a person become more positive, as it addresses their negative views of the world and the future.

Cognitive-behavioral therapy (CBT) has the power to transform an individual's way of thinking, so they can replace their negative thought patterns with a more positive outlook on life. Clients will learn to stop jumping to conclusions, stop seeing things as purely all-good or all-bad, stop comparing themselves to others or blaming themselves too harshly for mistakes, and many other different kinds of maladaptive mindsets.

It promotes mental wellness

The main goal of psychotherapy is to promote mental wellness, and CBT is no different. It has countless of different benefits that can do this (many of which we've already named on this list). It can be as effective as medication in treating certain mental health disorders and doesn't put you at risk of dependence or can be helpful in cases where medication alone is not effective.

Other benefits include: helping a person reduce their stress, overcome their past trauma, stop over thinking or ruminating, calming their mind, and learning to regulate their emotions better.

The last part has become a focus of many psychotherapeutic efforts of recent years (such as positive psychology and mindfulness). It's important that a person knows how to control their thoughts and emotions instead of letting it control them.

It makes you more rational

In order for CBT to be successful in treating a client's psychological distress or dysfunction, the person must first learn to be aware of their own maladaptive thoughts in order to correctly identify the root of the problem and resolve it. They can do this through mindfulness training, meditation, and practicing emotional self-awareness, all of which helps them to become more objective and reasonable in their thoughts.

Cognitive-Behavioral Therapy (CBT) teaches your mind to see things from a new perspective and consider the truthfulness of your beliefs. It helps you think more clearly and makes you more resilient against negative thinking and feelings, thus allowing for better judgment and decision-making.

It makes you more empathetic

With the previous point in mind, CBT can also help you to become more empathetic by training you to be more level-headed in dealing with your problems. It encourages you to see past your own point of view and helps you see things better from other people's perspectives. You become better at distinguishing facts from irrational thoughts, and you gain more insight into the motivations behind the actions of others.

The last and most important way that CBT can help a person is by training them to become their own therapist. The ultimate goal of CBT is to guide its clients as they overcome their personal dilemmas and teaches them how to change their perceptions for the better, to see things more clearly and constructively.

It shows us how to approach our psychological distress with calmness and peace of mind, which makes us better equipped to handle negative or stressful situations. Moreover, the ability to resolve our problems on our gives us a better sense of control over our lives and builds our self-esteem and feelings of self-efficacy.

Cognitive-Behavioral Therapy (CBT) instills its clients with better coping strategies to help them deal with a wide variety of everyday challenges and overcome the hardships of life on their own. The skills you can acquire in CBT are useful, practical, and helpful in everyday life. It has also been proven to keep people from relapsing into their old, self-destructive ways and improve their overall quality of life.

Is CBT Right For You?

With all that said, now it's time to ask yourself whether or not trying Cognitive-Behavioral Therapy (CBT) is right for you.

With so many different options available when it comes to counseling and therapy, it's easy to feel confused and not know which one is best for you. Sometimes it's all a matter of trial-and-error, or simply asking your therapist for their professional opinion about which treatment option is suitable for you. However, if you can't afford to do either, then you can at least do some research and try to find out for yourself.

Thankfully, over here most of the research has been done for you. Now all that's left is for you to do some confirmatory checks and ask yourself the following questions:

What is my diagnosis?

Most of the people seeking therapy have been diagnosed with serious mental illnesses, and while it's not entirely necessary, it's best to ask for a psychological assessment from a trained professional to determine whether or not you have one, too.

In a nutshell, most mental illnesses are gauged on the level of the distress they cause the individual; how much they deviate from normal behavior; whether or not they cause significant impairment in a person's social, mental, or emotional functioning; and whether it makes the individual a danger to themselves or others.

Knowing your diagnosis can do a lot to help you figure out which type of psychosocial treatment is best for you. Each mental illness responds differently to each kind of therapy, so you should go for the one that's been proven to be the most effective in treating your specific diagnosis and symptoms.

However, if you don't have a diagnosis or feel that you don't have a serious mental illness, but rather, personal problems that you would just like to resolve, then CBT is the best answer for you. And as we've said many times before, it's also effective in treating anxiety disorders (i.e., GAD, social phobia), eating disorders (i.e., bulimia, anorexia), and mood disorders (i.e., bipolar disorder, major depression).

How serious are my problems?

Similarly to the last question, the seriousness of your mental health problems is an important consideration to whether or not CBT will work best for you. If you suffer from panic attacks, general anxiety, insomnia, specific phobias, substance abuse and addiction, relationship problems, anger management problems, or any of the disorders we've mentioned above, then CBT can help you.

However, if your problems are more severe or complex, then you might need a more long-term treatment plan, especially if you have multiple diagnoses or have a chronic or recurrent mental illness (like a personality disorder or an intellectual disability).

Are my problems rooted in my thoughts?

The fundamental idea behind CBT, as you already know, is that our thoughts direct our behaviors, so it's specially designed to treat problems wherein the individual's automatic thoughts play a crucial role in their problems. With the help of CBT, you will be better able to control and reframe your mindset ("I'm no good, I'm always messing up. Nobody likes me."), which will alleviate your emotional distress and help you eliminate your dysfunctional behaviors.

However, if your problems are not rooted in your thoughts, but rather your environment, physiology, or things that are out of your control, then CBT might not be the best choice for you. Someone suffering at the hands of an abusive partner or family, for example, can only be able change the way he/she feels and responds to the abuse, but still have to live with it. So as long as there is abuse, there will always be some degree of unhappiness in his/her life.

Do I have a clear problem to solve?

CBT is a solution-focused, goal-oriented therapy. Because it's only a short-term process, there needs to be a specific problem that you want to work on resolving. If you want to quit smoking or get over a bad breakup, for example, then CBT is a suitable option for you.

On the other hand, if you're just generally unhappy or dissatisfied with your life but can't think of a particular reason why (i.e., no past trauma, no abuse, no significant failures), CBT might not help.

If you're also interested in exploring your dreams and unconscious memories, or want to understand the meaning of life, then you're better off with psychoanalytic therapy than CBT, because CBT is more practical, direct, and focused on the here and now.

Am I ready to confront my personal issues?

Because you will be spending so much time analyzing and understanding your thoughts, you might learn or recall some uncomfortable things about yourself and your life. You will need to talk about your problems openly with your therapist in order for them to help you, as therapy cannot work if the client isn't ready to be emotionally vulnerable and confront their personal issues.

So before you go on, ask yourself: am I comfortable thinking about my feelings? Can I handle my emotions and my anxiety? It might be a bit upsetting at first, but if you really want to solve your problems, the best way is to face it head-on.

Can I dedicate time to therapy?

Even though CBT is quite a short-term process by most standards, 5-6 months is still a considerable period of time. You will have to go to hourly sessions once a week and sometimes even come home with homework and exercises for you to do outside of these sessions. This can be time-consuming, but you have to commit to the process in order to benefit from it.

Some people go to therapy and don't come back because they feel it wasn't effective or that it wasn't worth the time. People like this often expect therapy to happen overnight, but it doesn't. Not only will you need to dedicate your time to the healing process, but you must be emotionally invested, committed, and motivated as well.

So if you can't dedicate this time to allow yourself to get better and work through your problems patiently, then CBT will not be effective for you.

Do I believe in the power of therapy?

Before you try CBT, be honest with yourself first about whether or not you really believe that it can help you. If you're not at least open to trying it or willing to commit yourself to the process, then therapy is really not for you.

Therapy is a collaborative effort. Your therapist will help you get better, but they're not going to do the work for you. They're only there to guide you and help you through it. You need to be the one who wants to change and actually make an effort to improve your life with more positive thinking and healthier behaviors. If you don't, then you're just wasting your time. There really isn't any magic pill to be the cure-all for the mental distresses that we may face over the course of our lives.

So is CBT really right for you? It's a difficult question to grapple with. In summary, those who will benefit from CBT are generally people who: know what their problem is and want to fix it;

are willing to work hard and put in the effort to do so; and know that their issues can be solved with a more positive and constructive mindset.

Getting the Most Out of CBT

After you've pondered on all the questions above and have decided that CBT is the right choice for you, it's time to discuss how you can make the most out of it. Here are a few ways you can do that:

Embrace change

CBT is all about creating positive change in your life through your thoughts. Sometimes change can be hard — maybe even painful — but it's a crucial part of life. Trust in the process, even if you feel a bit of distress or discomfort. You have to understand that sometimes, things can get worse before they get better, just like how it always seems the darkest before dawn.

Set a time table for yourself

It's good to have goals and then set deadlines for yourself on when you want to achieve them. This gives you a sense of urgency and makes you more committed to getting better through CBT.

Be honest with yourself

It can be scary to think about your deepest fears and insecurities, but it can also deliver the best possible results CBT has to offer you. So no matter how painful it may be to think about what you're going through, you need to allow yourself to be completely honest and emotionally vulnerable in order for you to succeed in therapy.

Reflect on what happened

Everything you do in CBT has a purpose, so reflect on it. CBT helps you understand the dysfunctional thoughts, feelings, and behaviors you experience and redirect you towards a better, healthier way of life. Taking the time to ponder on what these problems are will give you a better idea on how to resolve them and enhance your therapeutic experience.

Integrate CBT into your life

Perhaps the best and most effective way to get the most out of CBT is by integrating it into your life. This ensures that, even after this book's 21-day step by step program with CBT is over, it can still create real and lasting change in your life.

You can do this by setting aside some time from your schedule to practice CBT techniques and methods on a regular basis or coming back to them every time you encounter a personal problem.

Remember everything you learn here and apply it as often as you can to yourself, your life, and even as advice to others. Only by doing so will you be able to reap all the benefits and rewards of Cognitive-Behavioral Therapy.

Chapter 2: Essential Things You Need To Know About CBT

How CBT Deals with things

Cognitive Behavioral Therapy is a well-known psychotherapy treatment that is notable for its positive results and feedbacks. It has helped thousands of individuals overcome different things and helps them regain control in their lives. It caters to different aspects on how a person responds to a certain situation or problem.

CBT is quite a complex and intricate method to understand. It is composed of several different aspects that should be understood before initiating the process. The three main parts of CBT are: thoughts, emotions and behaviors. These are all interconnected and can significantly impact one another.

Starting off with the chain, thoughts are one of the most crucial and important aspect wherein if negative thoughts are present, it may lead to negative emotions that can also trigger negative behavior. With that being said, everything lies within what the individual's train of thought is and how they deal with it.

Emotions are also crucial since this greatly indicates what and how a person might feel. Behavior deals with how a person interprets their thoughts and emotions and how they want to handle as well as express themselves in any particular situation. In this chain, behavior is mainly dependent on a person's thought and emotion. It deals with the cognitive aspect of a person as well as their behavior.

In terms of their train of thought, individuals will learn on how to accept the current situation they're in and, instead of choosing to think about the negative thoughts and emotions, they learn on how to focus more on the positive aspects in life. They try to see the silver lining in each situation and try to shed light on favorable emotions.

As for the behavioral aspect of CBT, it alters the way that different individuals react to various scenarios. When faced with a problem or situation, CBT allows them to take control of how they might behave and respond to it and lets them be a better person.

There are many different methods and tools of CBT. This type of treatment can be found in health centers wherein professionals can lead you through a rigorous process and help you on your way to wellness.

Some techniques in CBT include the following:

Cognitive Restructuring

Cognitive Restructuring is a common CBT exercise that can significantly aid individuals in dealing with their problems. This addresses the way an individual processes their thoughts and ultimately affects the emotions and behavior that follow.

How does it work? Well, CBT is specifically designed to allow individuals to recognize unfavorable thought patterns and find a way to alter them. Through this, it ultimately reconstructs the emotional system and gradually works through a person's depression, anxiety and other emotional and behavioral disorders. It involves identifying all the beliefs and ideas in one's mind and separates the positive from the negative ones.

Next to that, it assesses the unfavorable ideas and tries to turn it into favorable concepts. How? Negative ideas stem from over-thinking or reading too much into a situation. Through Cognitive Restructuring, it finds a silver lining under every situation and sticks to the positive side of everything. Unfavorable thoughts are eliminated and put to rest by replacing them with positive ideas that can essentially help the individual in the long run.

Cognitive Restructuring alters the ideas that a person thinks about when reacting to a situation from negative ones to positive ideas. The way an individual thinks in response to a situation will be turned into favorable ones by identifying unfavorable thought patterns then finding a positive alternative for this.

This can be done in a lot of different ways. First, individuals need to find general and automatic thoughts that are instantly recurring in our everyday experience. Then, we have to assess these thoughts if ever they are actually true and figure out if they are healthy or negative ideas.

Once they have made a decision, the individual has to replace these automatic thoughts with positive ones if ever they are negative in the first place, or keep these thoughts if they are creating good and positive impact in your life. When replacing them, they must create a better and much more favorable point of view that can essentially benefit them. Through this, they can create a good solution to eliminate the item that has been causing them distress.

For a clearer view of the process, let us start with an example. Say, a depressed person is often pessimistic and has little hope in life. This is a result from a negative loop between their negative thoughts which lead to negative emotions that produce negative behavior than can ultimately lead to other negative ideas and repeat the cycle again. This can be a problem for them to connect with other people and do normal things that can possibly lighten up their mood. With CBT, it works directly at the initial stage of the process and helps them alter their negative thoughts into positive ones to create a positive outlook for them. Ultimately, it can help depressed individuals become much more optimistic in life and have a little hope for the things to come.

Mindfulness Meditation

Meditation is practice that allows an individual to attain mental and emotional clarity. This technique uses strategies like mindfulness, breathing exercises, and self-awareness. Meditation can be done in a lot of different ways.

With that being said, there are several known types of meditation, each catering to a specific aspect that can essentially promote a clearer mind and soul. Breath awareness meditation pays attention to mindful breathing. This helps the individual focus more on the way they breathe and disregards all the thoughts that enter their mind. It benefits the individual by minimizing anxiety, worry, greater concentration and a better emotional state.

There are also other types such as Zen Meditation, Transcendental Meditation and Loving-kindness Meditation that can ultimately help individuals arrive at a clearer mind set and better soul.

Focusing more on mindfulness meditation, this particular type of meditation is also recognized to be an effective technique in promoting cognitive behavioral therapy. It can be used as a tool in aiding problems within the cognitive and behavioral aspect. Mindfulness is a type of meditation that coaxes individuals to be aware of the things happening within the present time and become more vigilant of their surroundings. This entirely disregards the past and focuses on the events we have at hand. It dictates that the present surroundings are the only things that matters.

This unique type of meditation can be practiced anywhere, at any time of the day. As an illustration, when individuals are waiting for a long line to purchase something or waiting for the bus at the bus stop, they can easily take note of everything that is currently happening around them. They become more aware of the things that surround them such as the different people, sounds and smell. They perceive what their senses perceive.

Mindfulness can be found in a majority of the meditation techniques. It can be extremely helpful in focusing on different matters. Breath awareness meditation is one example of where mindfulness is also incorporated.

Mindfulness meditation is known to be a great treatment for a lot of psychological problems, ranging from depression to anxiety and PTSDs. The benefits of mindfulness meditation includes lower fixation of unfavorable thoughts and emotions, better focus, sharper memory, reduced impulsive reactions and satisfaction in relationships. Mindfulness meditation can promote CBT because it also alters the way the brain works and how it processes information. It can reduce negative emotions, as what CBT also does, and boost positive ones to take their place. It lessens anxiety and helps us to change the manner we behave in certain situations to make us be better. Through mindfulness meditation, not only will the individual's mental health be enhanced but as well as their physical structure too.

Mindfulness pays closer attention to thoughts and emotions which are actually the 2 main and crucial aspects of CBT. Since it promotes a positive and desirable outcome for an individual's train of thought, it will most likely result to favorable emotions and better behavior.

Graded/ Gradual Exposure

Another viable technique for Cognitive Behavioral Therapy that individuals may utilize is graded/gradual exposure. This exercise is specially created with the intention of reducing fear and anxiety by slowly and progressively facing them and coming in contact with that object, place, situation or person. Graded/Gradual Exposure is actually perceived to be one of the most common and effective methods to take in overcoming a certain psychological problem. Professionals from all over the world have the same favorable results regarding this treatment and can say that it has really helped multiple individuals around the globe in coming to terms with the things they fear the most.

So, here's the story. Individuals tend to avoid the things they don't want or fear the most. As a result, their fear of that particular object, place, person or situation will only increase as they think about it. However, if they try to expose themselves to that particular fear in a gradual manner, they may be less inclined to fear it. This will slowly reduce their fear for that certain matter until will ultimately disappear.

To better understand it, here's an example. A person who is extremely afraid of being in closed and confined spaces, termed as Claustrophobia, will typically try their best to avoid being put in that certain situation. Through graded/gradual exposure, therapists will try to coax them into facing their fear little by little. Initially by putting them in a large yet close area, then gradually reducing the enclosed space through each session. With this method, they are slowly facing their fear and coming to term with certain facts and realities. At the very end of the treatment, most claustrophobic people would now be able to withstand and curb their fears and are no longer fit to be called claustrophobic.

Graded/Gradual exposure is connected to CBT and may actually promote it since it also does what CBT does. It alters the way that individuals think and how they perceive certain things.

With graded/gradual exposure, individuals are faced with their fears and shown what reality is actually like and different alternatives from their perspective.

Graded/gradual exposure also changes the way a person reacts, responds and behaves in a certain situation. It transforms the way they used to react since it is also connected to the way they think. Thoughts are the root of what stems from their behavior. Due to the fact that it changed their thoughts, it also ultimately made an impact on their behavioral aspect.

In CBT, an individual who has a fear of heights (acrophobia) will have to alter the way they perceive their fear. When placed in a situation that involves heights, they need to alter their negative thoughts and transform these into positive ones. Once this is done, their mind will relax along with their body and act more naturally instead of screaming in fear.

People with this fear are slowly exposed to different height ranges. As they gradually go higher while they progress, they will learn that their fear will slowly disappear. Once it disappears, their mind would have already been altered with favorable as well as positive ideas and their behavior towards the situation would have also changed from screaming or panting in anxiety to calm composure.

Activity Scheduling

This is a prominent Cognitive Behavioral therapy technique that is often regarded to be effective and efficient for individuals. This is also known to be very helpful for those who experience or deal with different psychological problems, especially depression.

People who are battling with mental disorders, such as depression, are often finding it tough to stay active and in fact, would then to lay on their bed throughout the entire day. So, in order to avoid being passive the entire time, activity scheduling is one of the many solutions they can use in order to solve their passive state and make an effort to become much more productive for the entire day.

Activity scheduling includes taking a part in different activities and behaviors that they normally wouldn't do as a result of anxiety, depression, and other psychological problems they might be currently facing. It entails a two-step process that can essentially help the individual be a lot better in the end.

Starting off, it begins with monitoring personal activities. Individuals have to take note of their activities throughout the entire week and see the different things they have achieved throughout the course of a week. This can show people that they can actually achieve a lot of things if they put their heart to it. Once the set of activities are listed and made, looking at it will improve the individual's mood when they realize the different things they were actually able to accomplish. Secondly, they would have to rate the intensity of the symptoms of depression they are experiencing alongside each activity. Through this, they can be able to identify the different activities that can actually be more helpful for them and keep their mind off of disturbing or depressive thoughts. If they look more into the pattern of activities that help them become happier and see the connection of each activity, they can devise an itinerary of things that can introduce wellness and possibly cure depression.

It is used to promote CBT since it caters to the way an individual acts in every situation. It monitors their movement and ways of behaving in a certain scenario. Through this, their behavioral aspect can be influenced and aided significantly. Activity scheduling is actually one of the many activities that can help an individual in their CBT journey.

Activity scheduling can be essential in pointing out the different activities that can promote wellness and happiness for an individual. In this process, they are given a specific tool to find out which ones are actually helping them overcome this illness and what makes it worse. Activity scheduling is often used by different therapists to treat depression from all over the world. When used effectively and accurately, it can lead to great results.

Behavioral Activation

Another Cognitive Behavioral Therapy exercise that can be used in treating several psychological disorders is Behavioral Activation. This technique enables us to get the deeper meaning and connection between a person's thoughts and behaviors. As mentioned before, thoughts and behaviors are interconnected with one another. Each aspect significantly impacts the other. Thoughts are deemed to be the root of everything. If a person has negative thoughts running through their mind, they will most likely tend to do negative acts and express negative behavior as well. These factors create a chain reaction with one another, if one aspect is touched or bothered, the other one will most likely follow in its way.

CBT is known to be extremely helpful for aiding different mental disorders. Behavioral Activation is one of the CBT skills that can ultimately help individuals overcome their psychological problems and create a better life for them in the future. Behavioral Activation is also noted by many therapists to be extremely useful in treating depression. It involves a long process that will ultimately lead to a better and fitter state of mind.

This process starts with getting to know your own feelings and coming to terms with the things you are currently experiencing. Individuals have to understand how they feel, where these emotions come from and what triggers them. Afterwards, they need to take note of the things they typically do on a daily basis. When this is done, they have to find out what they want to get out of life. They should see their goals and objectives. Then, their energy has to be directed towards wellness and motivation to do the things they want and accomplish their objectives. Ultimately, it all depends on having a good and positive change, even if it is little by little just to show progress in their activities.

For a greater understanding about behavioral activation, here's an example of how it's used. A man who deals with anxiety and depression often has different moods throughout the day/ week. There are days wherein he'd feel ecstatic and joyous and some where he feels extremely depressed. Then, when he actually takes note of the different things he has done throughout the day, he would have noticed that there are actually some activities that are considered to be emotional triggers for him. Since he is aware of the things that might potentially trigger him, he tries his best to stay away from those emotional triggers to keep a calm and collected vibe. He changes the way he acts towards these specific situations which evidently also would change his mood throughout the entire day. So, in this method he was able to identify the different emotional triggers he includes in his daily routine and was able to find a way to deal with those triggers.

Behavioral Activation is a useful and oft used tool in Cognitive Behavioral Therapy because it also deals with the cognitive and behavioral aspect. It helps a person to understand his/her situation and come to terms with their daily activities which may be impeding them from leading a good and normal life. It helps them figure out a way to negate their unfavorable thoughts and turn them into positive ones.

Problem Solving

Problem Solving is also another common and notable technique used in Cognitive Behavioral Therapy. In this method, individuals are taught on how to solve their issues, cope with the different problems they are faced with and try to regain better control over their lives. Problem solving uses a unique way in dealing with psychological problems. It directly deals with life's challenges and takes it head on. It immediately faces the problems with the use of cognitive and behavioral interventions.

This method teaches individuals how to have an active role when making decisions for an extremely difficult decision. As a result from repeated disappointments or chronic mood problems, some individuals may prefer to take the back seat and get a passive role during tough times. However, problem solving is here to teach individuals that they have to get more initiative and do whatever it takes to arrive at the goal they want.

This treatment gives one specific problem that may also apply to different situations in life wherein people can use that example problem and relate it with other real-life situations that may enable them to make better and more productive decisions all on their own. If an individual's problem solving skills are enhanced, it may lead to a surge of self confidence and other positive impacts on one's life.

When it comes to problem solving, there are actually four different core items that individuals have to take note of. The primary component of problem solving is distinguishing the problem orientation. Different people have different approaches to various problems. All these people have their own technique on how to solve a problem and how the way they think in order to address it.

So, knowing how you approach a problem, how you act towards it and the methods you take in order to solve it is very crucial in problem solving. There are some people who are much more comfortable in using the submissive approach. In this way, they can get rid of the problem immediately and not have to deal with it anymore. On the other hand, there are also different individuals who are much more strong-willed and outspoken, but do not take the problem into much consideration. They immediately jump to conclusions and speak their mind without processing all the information or thinking about the consequences. This aggressive behavior is a product of a compulsive approach.

The second item is clearly pinpointing the root cause of your problem. Misdiagnosing your own problems is quite a common thing to do. However, you must not be blinded by the things you feel but rather look at the situation clearly and see what the main factor is. As an example, you are having anxiety and stress at work. Some people might blame themselves and think it's their fault because they feel these things when, in reality, it's actually their work environment that's making them feel that way. The real problem in this equation is not their stress and anxiety, but rather the things they experience at work and the amount of tasks they have to accomplish per day.

The next core component of problem solving is brainstorming. Individuals must find different solutions and alternatives to solve their problems. After performing the two steps mentioned earlier, this step is actually the easiest yet most crucial step of all. Individuals simply have to find a positive solution to solve their negative problems. However, if they miscalculate the situation and end up doing more damage than good, then it might cause negative results in the end. Take note of as many solutions as you can and slowly eliminate each one to determine the best solution for you.

The last and most important step of all is Taking Action. All of the things you've done in the past will only go to waste if you don't take action. This step will determine the viability and effectiveness of your problem solving skills. It implements all the things you've planned out from the first step and will ultimately decide if your problem is actually solved in the end, or simply gotten worse. Taking Action is the key component in actually solving the problem and doing something to make a difference. Through this last step, you can clearly show all the things you've been trying to do and the effort you've placed into getting positive results. Every little thing you've done in the prior steps will all lead to you taking action in your life and doing something you think is right and what's best for you.

Problem Solving connects in with CBT because it manages the way a person thinks and behaves towards a situation. Through problem solving, individuals can first assess the things they are currently thinking and finding positive ones to replace the negative ideas in order to have a positive impact. After that, it manages the way we behave towards the situation since the individuals are looking for the best solution to solve the problem. A person's rash behavior is cancelled out because he/she must plan the things he/she must say and do to promote a better and positive result.

Chapter 3: CBT And Anxiety

30 Techniques on How CBT Handles Issues

Cognitive Behavioral Therapy can be useful in dealing with certain real-life situations. In fact, CBT is probably one of the most recognized treatments in the industry today. CBT handles the cognitive and behavioral aspect of a person which will essentially help change their entire outlook and treatment of life. Through this treatment, they can understand the deeper meaning of life and exactly how to tackle specific situations that require extra effort and consideration before taking action.

CBT is adaptable to many types of psychological problems. It has a wide range of specialties wherein it can be applied and made use of. This kind of treatment has treated a lot of mental disorders ranging from anxiety to depression and phobias. The techniques used in CBT are one of the key factors in making it helpful for a lot of illnesses. It can be used in treating many kinds of problems and is proven to be effective for most. CBT is identified to be one of the best and most positive treatment for patients with basic and complex mental disorders. Since this treatment touches on the cognitive aspect on an individual, it essentially causes a greater and more positive impact and follows through a change with their future emotions and behavior.

This portion shows 30 different ways how Cognitive Behavioral Techniques that can be applied to your individual life and possibly help you in achieving a better and more positive lifestyle. It shows you different types of methods on how to deal with certain situations or problems. Through CBT, you can learn different types of techniques on how to handle depression, anxiety, phobias or other mental disorders that may bother other individuals.

How CBT Handles Anxiety

Anxiety is the sense of uneasiness an individual may feel about a certain person, object, place or situation. Sometimes taking shape as fear or worry, anxiety is such a common feeling that comes and goes in everyone's lifetime.

However, there are some that develop certain kinds of anxiety disorders that can lead them to have extreme and irrational reactions or behavioral responses. Anxiety disorders are actually psychiatric problems that can make an individual feel extreme negative emotion that may lead to unfavorable circumstances.

There are six major kinds of anxiety disorders, all of which involve certain types of anxiety and different ways on how it is triggered and addressed. Cognitive-Behavioral Therapy (CBT) is actually widely regarded by many mental health professionals as the preferred psychosocial intervention for most of them.

Aside from its impressive effectiveness, it also helps the individual lead a better life even with the disorder, as it teaches them a lot of valuable skills that will help them cope with their conditions. Listed below are some of the anxiety disorders and how CBT can help individuals overcome each one.

Generalized Anxiety Disorder (GAD)

One of the most prevalent anxiety disorders around, Generalized Anxiety Disorder (GAD) is characterized by an excessive worry about almost everything in a person's life with no particular cause or reason as to why.

Individuals who have GAD tend to make a big deal out of everything. They become anxious about everything in their life — be it their financial status, work, family, friends, or health — and are constantly preoccupied with worries that something bad might happen. They expect the worst case scenario about everything and always try to look at things from a negative point of view.

With that said, it's easy to see how GAD can make it difficult for someone to live a happy and healthy life. It can come as a hindrance for their day-to-day life and become an issue with regards to their work, family, friends and any other social activities. Some of the most common symptoms of GAD include: excessive worry or tension, tiredness, inability to rest, difficulty sleeping, headaches, mood swings, difficulty in concentrating, and nausea.

Fortunately, however, CBT has worked wonders in treating all these symptoms and more. With the help of CBT, individuals suffering from GAD can change these negative thoughts into positive ones, which will ultimately change their behaviors for the better as well.

There are a number of CBT techniques that people with GAD can apply to better manage their symptoms. For example, if you have GAD and want to feel relief from all the muscle tension in your body, you can try yoga; whereas meditation can help you stop over thinking; and breathing exercises are good to practice when you start to feel yourself getting anxious again.

Yoga has been proven to help lower a person's stress, which in turn, relaxes their muscles as well. There are a number of different yoga poses and routines you can find on the internet tailored to relieving your stress and anxiety. Some examples include: the eagle pose, the headstand, child's pose, half moon pose, and the legs up the wall pose.

If you need help getting started with how to use yoga to ease some of the distress you may feel from GAD, here is a quick rundown of how you can do it:

- Go to the gym and sign up for their yoga class.
- Or if you prefer, you can stay at home and do yoga by yourself.
- It's often best to do yoga in the afternoon or at the end of the day, as a way to decompress.
- Set up your mat, and if you want, play some relaxing music.
- Breathe in and out, deeply.
- Be aware of your breathing as you move through each pose.
- Take your time going through all the movements.
- Most importantly, enjoy yourself and keep your mind clear.

On the other hand, if the most problematic symptom of your GAD is overthinking and emotional turmoil, not muscle tension and chronic pain, then meditation just might be the CBT technique for you. Here's how you can do it:

- Download some guided meditation videos online (there's plenty on YouTube).
- Listen to them on a regular basis, preferably everyday (as you wake up or before you go to sleep is the most ideal).
- Find a quiet place to do this, where you can be alone and away from distractions.
- Devote all your attention to these 10-30 minute mediations and do not think or worry about anything else while you're doing so.
- Make it a rule that once you start meditating, you need to forget about everything else going on in your life and just focus on the present moment.
- Repeat everything the instructor is saying in the guided meditations

By meditating, you are giving your anxiety a healthy and positive outlet and releasing your physical tension from your body. The more you do it, the more peace of mind you will feel, and the easier it will be for you to overcome your anxiety.

When using CBT, a person with GAD will have a much more favorable perspective in life. Instead of always worrying and thinking about the worst case scenario, CBT reinforces an optimistic and reasonable outlook on life, which will then have a positive impact on their behavior as well. Most of the time, they'll change from a tense and edgy person to a relaxed and easygoing one that doesn't assume the worst out of everything.

Social Anxiety

Another common type of anxiety is social anxiety, characterized by an immediate distress whenever you meet or interact with unfamiliar people. Affecting over 15 million different American adults, this can be considered to be one of the most prominent types of anxiety that in the country.

Also known as "social phobia", those with social anxiety often display visible signs or symptoms that indicate their discomfort towards the situation. Some of those symptoms may include blushing, stuttering, increased heart rate, sweating, being awkward or boring, and, worst case scenario, experiencing a full-blown anxiety attack.

If you are one of the many people suffering from social anxiety, than you'd understand how much of a disturbance it can be in your life. Because it hinders you from a lot of social interactions, you may have a hard time in connecting with other people and making new friends. This may also affect your personality, as it can keep you from enjoying yourself when you're out with friends since you don't really have the courage to stand up and talk for yourself. You fear becoming involved in social situations and you try your best to keep to yourself as much as possible and avoid interacting with other people at all costs.

Although individuals with social anxiety know that their reaction to the situation may be over-the-top or unreasonable, they just can't seem to keep the anxiety and emotions at bay. They often seem powerless when battling this emotion and sometimes, in the end, anxiety takes over their lives. Due to these symptoms, they may try their best to avoid situations where they might get pressured into socializing with other people at all costs.

In order to overcome social anxiety, many individuals have turned to therapy. Cognitive Behavioral Therapy (CBT) is one of the most common and used treatment for this certain problem. With an array of different methods and techniques, CBT can help you overcome your social anxiety by getting to the heart of the problem: your thoughts.

Everything we feel and do stems from our thoughts. So, CBT alters the way individuals process information and turns negative thoughts into positive ones. In turn, it generates positive moods that may also lead to favorable actions or behavior. When relating CBT to social anxiety, it tries to get rid of all the negative thoughts that may pop up into your mind when you're about to interact with other people.

For example, when you're meeting new people, you might instantly think that they might hate you or dislike the way you talk or act immediately. However, with CBT, it eliminates this type of thinking and keeps an open and positive mindset of the things that may happen. CBT can also help individuals calm themselves down when experiencing a panic attack or when having an inner conflict colored with anxiety.

There are some CBT techniques that are specially designed to help individuals overcome different types of situations. For example, Cognitive Restructuring can be used in treating social phobia. It can be crucial in understanding your triggers, controlling your mood swings and keeping a positive mindset on everything.

Typically, individuals would have to go to therapists for their own CBT treatment. However, there are some ways that it can still help you when you're on your own. You simply have to follow a series of steps in order to overcome the situation.

- Make an effort to calm yourself down before you interact with someone else.
- Look at the current situation you're faced with. Describe it to yourself.
- Assess how that particular situation made you feel and identify those feelings.
- Go through your thoughts about that certain scenario and scan through what your mind immediately thought of when you faced that situation. The first few thoughts that pop into your head are your "automatic thoughts."
- Narrow in on your negative automatic thoughts. Ask yourself what triggered these thoughts.
- Now, are these triggers reasonable? Is it your negative view of yourself or the situation justifiable? Be as objective as you can and try not to let your emotions get in the way.
- Soon, you will realize that your thoughts are only misguided and aren't actually true at all. They're just the lies you sometimes tell yourself which feed your insecurity.
- Work on erasing these thoughts from your mind by replacing them with the truth. For example, whenever you think, "Nobody likes me," automatically reply with "Hey! That's just not true! [This certain person] likes me!"

Cognitive restructuring can be extremely helpful for those individuals who are trying to control or assess the way they react to certain scenarios. It can help them lighten their mood.

As for those individuals who still need to calm their nerves whenever they are faced with a situation they dread so much, they can also try relaxation techniques. While we've already talked a lot about yoga, meditation, and breathing exercises to help you relax, here is another technique you can use to calm yourself down:

- Take a seat and sit with your back straight.
- Place one hand along your chest and the other one on your stomach .
- Inhale through your nose. You will notice your hand on your stomach area moves more while your other hand should only move slightly.
- Breathe out with your mouth. This will cause your stomach to move in while your chest will still move slightly.
- Repeat this process and count each deep breath you take. Imagine that with every exhale, you are releasing negative energy from your body.
- After a while, your muscle tension will decrease and you will feel a lot calmer than you were beforehand. Keep doing this until you no longer feel any distress or anxiety.

Panic Disorder

Panic attacks are characterized by out-of-the-blue emotions or feelings of trepidation when, in fact, there is no real reason to be afraid. Having recurrent panic attacks for seemingly no reason at all is what is known as a panic disorder. This is mostly found in young adults aged 20 and above. However, it can also be experienced by other children who also have panic-like symptoms.

Anxiety disorders can greatly affect a person's life. Always being at risk of spontaneous panic attacks may lead them to avoid going out, and thus, isolate themselves from others. Individuals with panic disorder typically live their lives in fear of getting another panic attack, so they try their best to control it or maybe even hide from other people.

Individuals with panic disorder often spend most of their time fearing the possibility of having another panic attack (a fear known as "agoraphobia"). Agoraphobia is when individuals stay on high-alert for potential panic attacks and always keep their guard up in case real danger arrives. This can cause them to avoid certain places like shopping malls, festivals, movie theaters, grocery stores, and the like.

With different types of indications, panic disorder typically includes symptoms like sweating, rapid heart rate, chills, trembling, or always sensing potential danger in every situation. In order to control symptoms like these, there are a lot of different treatments created for panic disorder. Cognitive Behavioral Therapy is also commonly used by therapists in treating patients with a wide variety of mental problems, including panic disorder.

As explained in previous chapters, CBT deals with a person's thought patterns, emotions, and behaviors. It deals with the cognitive and behavioral factors of psychological problems and seeks to transform a person's negative ideas and behaviors into more positive ones. When dealing with panic disorder, it is important for CBT to eliminate their constant fear of being in danger and replace them with the assurance that not all situations will lead to an untimely death.

There are several CBT techniques that can help individuals with panic disorder overcome their condition or calm themselves whenever a panic attack arises. Developing your calming skills is one of the most notable techniques. If you're struggling with panic disorder, try this basic guide on how to ease your mind and prevent a panic attack from escalating once you sense anxiety knocking on your mind's door.

- Take long, deep breaths.
- Are you anxious? Be honest with yourself about what you feel and identify your emotions.
- Work towards accepting these feelings, even the negative ones like fear.
- Once you've accomplished this, remind yourself that your thoughts only have power over you if you let them. Your feelings do not control you, but rather, you control them.
- Assess your thoughts and ask yourself if these are actually realistic or reasonable (much like what you did before, in dealing with social anxiety).
- Visualize a calming scenario and go to your happy place. This can be a pristine, white sand beach with the cool sea breeze in your face; or a lush, green mountain top overlooking a beautiful sunset. Wherever it is, go to it.

- Repeat a positive, self-affirming mantra in your mind. Examples include:

This is only a trick played by my brain; I am more powerful than these negative thoughts.

I am strong and powerful and I will not surrender.

I am getting stronger and healthier.

I can do this. I believe in myself.

No matter how terrible this feeling may be, it will pass. And I'll be okay again.

- Focus on the things on hand and the positive side of everything.

Obsessive Compulsive Disorder

Obsessive Compulsive Disorder, also known as OCD, is a psychological problem that involves uncontrollable ideas or thought patterns and behaviors that you feel obliged or the sudden urge to do. These are unwanted thoughts, obsessions or images that enter the individual's mind may serve as a great discomfort that will essentially turn into a hindrance between the individual's daily activities and their mindset. Afterwards, the individual will have no choice but to participate or perform repetitive acts and behaviors in order to control or deal with these thoughts.

OCD can greatly affect one's lifestyle. With these thoughts and compulsions, they will stop their day-to-day activities and try to engage or handle their thoughts. This type of mental problem can begin as early as the age of 7 and progress later on. Typically affecting male children over female ones, the rate of people with OCD will increase more on the women's side in the long run. There are different types of obsessions and compulsion when it comes to OCD.

For example, people who get easily worked up over getting in contact with dirt or germs often have this idea that it may get them sick; a type of OCD known as "contamination obsession." Other times, OCD can take the form of a need for symmetry in all things, which can lead individuals to arranging everything in a specific way and organizing everything because of an irrational belief like, "If this is not arranged by size, something bad will surely happen".

It can cause a great impact on their school, work, social and personal life. This can let them have a hard time getting to sleep, maintaining hygiene, forming friendships, uphold their grades or participating in any type of social or athletic performances.

There are different types of symptoms when it comes to OCD. Cognitive symptoms include constantly thinking "I am responsible for everything", "What if I'll get sick because of this?" and "I must know everything!"

There are also physical symptoms that may be identified, such as muscle tension, constant pain in the stomach, dizziness, headaches and feeling detached from your own body. For further implication that an individual has this type of psychological problem, there are also emotional symptoms that you can also check for, like anxiety, sadness, guilt, shame, and anger.

CBT is one of best and most recommended ways to treat OCD. Since it focuses on the cognitive and behavioral aspect of a person, it can be perfect to treat a disorder like OCD.

CBT tries to replace their unwanted thoughts and images with positive ones and gain a much more positive outlook in life. After working on the cognitive aspect, positive thoughts will then lead to positive emotions that will likely produce better behaviors towards situations. This can allow them to control the way they react to certain scenarios and handle their compulsion.

There are also some helpful CBT techniques that individuals may use whenever they feel those unwanted images creeping at their doorstep again or if they become unsettled by the emotions they're having. One of those techniques is by finding the root cause of your thoughts and emotions. This can be done by:

- Take a moment to stop and assess everything that is currently happening in this moment.
- Question the OCD and what it needs you to feel (e.g. be in control of everything or trying to make you feel safe).
- Come up with at least 3 other methods you can do to make you feel that way without paying attention to the OCD.
- If you can't, then write down what it is you're worrying about and set a time for you to worry about it later (for example, after you've finished your homework or project).

- Then, when you come back to it, you'll find that most of the time, you've lost interest in wasting your time and worrying about what it is your OCD bothered you with before, and you can go about the rest of your day in peace.

Another helpful technique is doing progressive muscle relaxation or PMR. This can be partnered with different deep breathing exercises to help release all the tension that builds up within your muscle and help you get to a calm and relaxing manner. This can battle OCD since it makes you feel uncomfortable whenever you feel the urge to do something. With PMR, you can relinquish those thoughts and feel relaxed at the same time. PMR starts with a process like:

- Sit in a quiet and comfortable room.
- Remove all unnecessary and tight clothing or items that may cause any uneasiness.
- Sit in a comfortable position.
- Take some slow, deep and even breaths.
- Pay attention to all your muscles starting with your face. Clench your muscles as you inhale and release the tension along your face muscles when you exhale while practicing your breathing technique.
- Repeat twice before proceeding to other areas like shoulders, arms, stomach, butt, legs, feet and repeat the process for each of them.

These techniques may just help individuals with OCD handle the tension in their body and fight off the unwanted images. However, professional help is also important. With long CBT sessions with your own therapist, you can overcome this problem and possibly live a better life.

Post-Traumatic Stress Disorder

Post-Traumatic Stress Disorder (PTSD) is a type of anxiety disorder that stems from traumatic, stressful or frightening events that may lead an individual to experience traumatic episodes that force them to relive that very same event.

PTSD is known to have a major effect on people's lives. This can impede them from trying certain things, going to different places, or socializing with other people normally. A traumatizing event (such as a car accident or a natural calamity) can lead individuals to constantly think of that occasion and experience horrific flashbacks, as well as nightmares. People with PTSD tend to avoid things that remind them of that experience. So, each time they see a trigger they experience panic attacks or flashbacks. This can restrain them from experiencing other things and will eventually isolate them from others.

This type of anxiety disorder should be treated as early as possibly to ease their psychological distress immediately and avoid any damaging, long-term effects. Symptoms of PTSD include recurring flashbacks of a certain traumatic experience, constant nightmares about it, and getting terrifying and negative thoughts relating to it. Along with this, people with PTSD also experience accelerated heart rates, profuse sweating, anxiousness, and at times, emotional numbness.

One of the top treatments recommended by therapists is Cognitive Behavioral Therapy. CBT helps individuals overcome the trauma and eliminate negative thoughts about that scenario and replace them with positive ones that can help them sleep better at night. It can also change the manner they react to a certain object, situation or person that might trigger their PTSD. Trauma-focused CBT can use a variety of techniques that will help individuals triumph over this mental disorder and find other healthier and more positive outlets to direct their energy towards.

There are some helpful CBT techniques that can aid those struggling with PTSD. Mindfulness meditation is one of the best CBT techniques in treating this particular anxiety disorder, as it allows individuals to calm their minds while also focusing on the present factors around them. This can be done by following these steps:

- Sit up straight on a chair or sit cross-legged on the floor.
- Take deep breaths, in and out. Pay attention to everything that happens to your body in this moment.
- Notice the way your body feels as you inhale and exhale. Focus all your attention on these bodily sensations.
- Afterwards, begin to redirect your attention on what's happening around you, like the sounds outside or the thoughts running through your mind.

- Take note and accept each idea without assessing if it's positive or negative.
- Whenever you find yourself judging them, return your focus on your breathing and start the process again.

This teaches a person to keep a calm and level head while reflecting on their thoughts and understanding what's going on inside them. For those afflicted with PTSD, it's important to stay focused on the present rather than the past, which is why mindfulness meditation is such an apt treatment for them.

It is important to come to terms with the things that happened to you in the past. However, it is not okay to allow it to ruin your future and all the good things that may still happen in your life by staying stuck there. PTSD is a serious condition, and only when you learn and accept the fact that you have to keep moving forward in life, can you truly heal from it. CBT can help you do this.

Chapter 4: CBT And Depression

How to Use CBT for Depression

The term depression has been thrown around so lightly in today's culture that it has now come to mean any feeling of sadness or lethargy. However, depression is much more serious with that, as those who struggle with it already know.

Called the "common cold of mental illnesses" because of how prevalent it is, depression greatly affects an individual's thoughts, emotions and behaviors in a negative manner. Living with depression is like coasting through life, feeling unmotivated to do anything and drowning in self-loathing. Most people who are depressed struggle to even get out of bed in the morning, much less do anything productive with their day. There are over six major kinds of depression, each with different factors causing its arrival.

There are a lot of ways on how to tackle depression. An individual can opt to undergo different types of therapy in order to take their mind off matters and try to heal. Depression is an extremely difficult and complex topic to touch on. With a variety of options to choose from on how to handle this type of psychological problem, one of the most prominent and effective methods used by multiple individuals and therapist all over the world is psychotherapy.

There are different types of psychotherapy but the most used and found to be most helpful for patients is Cognitive Behavioral Therapy (CBT). This particular form of therapy was specially designed to treat depression (as you might recall from reading the "History of CBT" segment in Chapter 1).

Handling the thought pattern, emotions and behavioral aspect of a person, it can allow them to get something greater in life and not dwell on the negative side of everything. CBT is a wide and complex treatment that is known to be helpful in treating a variety of mental illnesses, depression being one of them.

Listed below are some ways on how each individual can make use of Cognitive Behavioral Therapy when faced with different kinds of depression.

Major Depression

Major Depression is one of the most common types of depression. There are approximately 16.2 million adults suffering from it in the US alone. Also termed as "Major Depressive Disorder", "Unipolar Depression", or "Classic Depression", this kind of depression is characterized by feeling too much grief or gloom, being overly fatigued most of the time, having a hard time sleeping well at night, losing interest in activities that once excite you, not wanting to eat as much as you did before, feeling hopeless or experiencing anxiety, and perhaps contemplating about self-harm or suicide.

However, this type of depression does not typically stem from a person's surrounding or situation. A person could have everything one may dream of and still have depression. Major Depression can last for as long as week or possibly throughout one's entire lifetime. Causing a hindrance between their social and personal life, major depression can keep you from enjoying everything you love about life and isolate yourself from others. Negative thinking patterns may lead you to an unhealthy lifestyle. So how do you overcome it?

Cognitive Behavioral Therapy is one of the most common and effective methods used by therapists to help their clients overcome their depression. Enabling the individual to alter their thought patterns, Cognitive Behavioral Therapy (CBT) faces the problem head on and acknowledges the situation. This does not make any excuses or hide you from the truth, but rather allows you to accept the situation and think of a silver lining for it.

A lot of its success comes from the fact that CBT touches on the most important aspects of a person's life, which are their thoughts, emotions, and behaviors. CBT helps you eliminate your negative thoughts and replace them with more positive ones. As it alters negative thoughts into positive ones, it also impacts the emotions and behavior positively like a domino effect. It also deals with dysfunctional behaviors and changing them for the better.

There are some specific CBT techniques that can help individuals deal with major depression, but most experts would agree that the most suitable technique to apply here would be cognitive restructuring.

Depressed individuals tend to have negative automatic thoughts. Through cognitive restructuring, they can deal with this and replace it with more positive ones that can help them function better, mentally and emotionally. Here's a guide on how to use cognitive restructuring on your own:

- Assess the situation. Find the negative aspect that's upsetting you
- Keep track of your negative emotions. Describe them in your journal and rate the intensity of each emotion.
- Pay attention to all the things you automatically think of whenever you encounter a difficult situation and keep track of how much you believe in each of them
- Examine these thoughts and see if they are realistic or not
- Generate better and positive thoughts that are realistic and seems more likely to happen when compared to your automatic thoughts.
- Evaluate the process and repeat as much as necessary.

These techniques can be extremely helpful in dealing with a depressive episode on your own. However, it is important to remember that professional help can sometimes be the better option, especially when dealing with depression which can often leave the person feeling unmotivated at all to complete their therapy and hopeless about ever recovering from their mental illness.

Major Depression can be treated with CBT in different healthcare clinics. Individuals have to assess their own state of mind and once things becomes too hard for them to handle, they should talk to other people, like therapists, about their problems. This way, they can live a better life and slowly regain control.

Also known as "dysthymia" or "chronic depression", persistent depression is the most recurrent of all types of depression, typically manifesting in episodes that last as long as 2 years and return throughout an individual's lifetime.

It may not come as powerful as Major Depression but it may still take its own toll on the one that may be experiencing it. The feeling of being sad and hopeless, having second thoughts about yourself, lack of interest, and problem of being happy during joyous occasions may be a sign of this type of depression.

It can also change your perspective on how life works. Symptoms may fade out for a while before coming back as clear and powerful as ever, making it difficult for a person to feel like they have any semblance of control over their lives.

Therapy is one of the many ways in overcoming this particular type of depression. Cognitive Behavioral Therapy (CBT) can be essential in dealing with a long-term depression such as persistent depression. This kind of depression may be an occasional experience for some individuals. There are moments when they seem to be normal and happy, and other times wherein they just can't seem to see the bright side to anything. When dark moments come, it is important to use CBT in handling this situation.

CBT replaces negative thoughts with positive ones and changes the way one may behave around this kind of situation. It can possibly alter your trail of thought and behavior in order for you to see the better things in life. When people with persistent depression make use of CBT, it can be possible for them to get over this long-term illness and go on with their own life happily.

A common CBT technique that can help you get through persistent depression on your own is problem analysis. Also known as "situational analysis", it helps people see the problem objectively and find a positive solution for it. Problem analysis starts with:

- Finding the problem
- Understanding the problem and how it works

- Dividing the situation into smaller parts in order to understand it better
- Finding out what your goal is and what you want to work towards
- Finding positive ways to reach your goal and move on from the problem

Problem analysis can be helpful in treating persistent depression since it can help them overcome the problem in a positive manner. This CBT technique will aid them in triumphing over depression and help them on their way to recovery. It also teaches them how to respond to specific situations that may be complex to handle.

Manic Depression

Another term for Manic Depression is "Bipolar Disorder". This is composed of different periods called Mania and Hypomania. An individual's moods can be replaced between a state of feeling extreme euphoria and extreme depression. There are different moods for different periods, changing without any sensible reason.

Mania is a severe period that may last for around 7 days which is then followed by Hypomania, a less powerful experience that may still cause an impact onto an individual. There are different symptoms existing to distinguish this illness, most of which are similar to major depression. However, indications of the manic phase may be increased self-confidence, destructive behavior, high energy, less sleep, and a euphoric state.

When tackling something as complex as Manic Depression, CBT can do a great job in handling this illness. Directly impacting one's behavior, Bipolar Disorder can severely impact one's way of life and alter their actions and thought pattern. So, CBT can be a great method to undertake in order to manage one's behavior and positively impact their thoughts to induce better moods and feelings for an individual.

People with Manic Depression can overcome this illness through intensive CBT sessions and talking with other people in order to calm and control their mood swings. This can help them become better and gain better control over their life again. There are a variety of CBT techniques that individuals with bipolar disorder can make use of. One of the most helpful ways in dealing with this particular type of depression is by controlling your cognitive distortions, which you can do by making sure you are not:

- Overgeneralizing - jumping to conclusions because of a single instance (i.e., you miss the shot once and immediately think that you're a bad player and you can't play any sport well)
- Thinking All-or-Nothing – seeing the world in terms of absolutes, meaning people or circumstances are either all good or all bad
- Taking Things Too Personally – believing that everything bad that happens is because of you (i.e. "The teacher was mad at the class because I forgot my homework.")
- Minimizing the Positive – discounting the good things that happen because you believe they are by luck or something out of your control
- Maximizing the Negative – dwelling on your own failures and frustrations so much that they keep you from being happy

This can kind of cognitive reconstruction can help individuals with manic depression to overcome their depressive episodes as well as controlling their emotions. The process allows individuals to take control of their cognitive process and change their behavior. So, individuals with this type of depression can use this process whenever they feel the need to assess their thoughts and behaviors.

Perinatal Depression

Perinatal Depression is a depressive disorder known to be experienced by pregnant women during or after their pregnancy. Also called as postpartum depression, hormones produced during pregnancy can generate different mood swings and unusual behavior. This feeling can also be increased because of the difficulties a mother must go through after giving birth, such as lack of sleep and constant care of their newborn child. Symptoms that accompany this illness is the feeling of sadness, regular anxiety, worry regarding your baby's health, difficulty in caring for yourself or your baby, and possibly harming one's self or the baby.

Postpartum depression is extremely risky and dangerous when left untreated. This particular illness can possibly endanger the mother and child's health and well-being.

When dealing with Perinatal Depression, CBT can help mothers see a better outlook on life with new circumstances. This therapy can allow them to deal with their negative and unfavorable thoughts about their new life and replace them with positive ones that will allow them to see the bright side of things. Cognitive Behavioral Therapy will also allow them to adjust and change their behavior that may positively impact the situation they are currently in.

Through CBT, new mothers can see different methods on how to handle their every life and find out better options on how to address various situations favorably. CBT can help these women deal with the way they feel and the way they handle things. CBT is a wide and complex process which involves a lot of different procedures before actually arriving at the conclusion. With this notion, there are actually a lot of different CBT techniques that can help these individuals deal with their thoughts and behaviors better. One notable CBT process that is sure to assist mothers with perinatal depression is the Thought Challenge Exercise. The process starts with this:

- Look at the situation objectively
- Identify the feelings you possess regarding the situation and recognize them
- Challenge your thought patterns and the way you behave by seeing the evidences
- Alter these negative and unfavorable thoughts, emotions and behaviors into better ones by identifying them and looking for better solutions to handle things

Through this process, they can learn how to deal with things better and in a much more positive and realistic manner. This may allow them to avoid any type of potential danger within themselves for their own safety and for the baby. Although this can help them go through different situations on their own, it is still important to get everything treated by a therapist with the proper CBT procedure.

Atypical Depression

This kind of depression is not a long-term depression. It is actually a subtype of another type of depression, which is Major Depression. However, it regularly comes back whenever life seems to be getting down. Atypical depression goes away whenever good things happen and comes back when they don't. Don't let the name confuse you, the term "Atypical" does not signify its rareness.

It actually means it has different symptoms and signs when compared to other types of depression.

This can be challenging to address, considering that you might also seem baffled whether or not you're actually experiencing it. Symptoms that lead to Atypical Depression are increased appetite, insomnia, sleeping for more hours than usual, heaviness in your body, and sensitivity to comments and rejection.

The usage of CBT can be essential in battling this illness. In atypical depression, CBT can be used whenever these phases come back. Through this, individuals can positively change their train of thought and possibly replace negative ideas with better ones. This can give them a positive outlook in life and may allow them to be a better person.

There are various CBT techniques to help individuals go through this depression when they're on their own. A common one is by exercising. It is known to relax muscles, take your mind off of current matters (or from traumatic events), and maybe even allow the individual to practice staying relaxed and calm. There are some types that may help people with atypical depression in exercising to handle their depression. These are:

- Find a specific workout that you actually like
- Identify a specific workout goal that you would like to accomplish (something that is easy and attainable)
- Find exercises that also offers social support
- Make it part of your daily itinerary
- Find something that can be convenient to do
- Even if you feel depressed or out of the mood, do it anyway

In this method, they can also change their behavior towards different situation and learn to act better. When seeking help from professionals, CBT can be very effective. Talking to others about an illness is always brave, but trying to fix it is even braver.

Situational Depression may often look like Major Depression, however it is triggered by certain scenarios or situations in life. It is known to be as an adjustment disorder with depressed mood. It may be induced by situations like death of a loved one, a life-threatening event, abusive relationships, or financial issues. These situations may bring about situational depression along with its symptoms such as frequent crying, sadness, anxiety, social withdrawal and over-fatigue.

Situational Depression is becoming depressed over a particular event or scenario that happened, or is happening, in one's life. Through CBT, individuals may see a better way to cope with their situation and focus on a better and more favorable thought pattern. They may change the way they think about life onto a much more positive way and control the way they behave towards the situation.

This type of depression can be extremely hard to handle. When left without treatment, it may also progress into different types of complex and serious mental illnesses that will greatly impact one's lifestyle. There are various CBT techniques to choose from, in order to handle this problem. However, Journaling is known to be quite helpful and calming to do. It lets individuals assess their thoughts, improve their behavior and mood, and also attain a relaxed and calm feature that will essentially help them in the future. Effectively journaling your thoughts for depression can be done by:

- Changing your viewpoint to avoid any biases and to look at the situation objectively
- Writing down all your emotions and the way you feel about the situation
- Incorporating it into your everyday routine
- Attempt new things
- Stay focused on the positive side and ignore the negative side
- Jot down all the potential triggers for you
- List positive items on a daily basis

CBT can help these individuals achieve a better perspective in life. Simply by assessing your own self and talking to others when you have a chance can give a great impact to you. Talking about your own illness can help you rather than shame you. It is never wrong to be fighting battles of the mind.

Chapter 5: CBT For Fears And Phobias

How To Use CBT For Fears and Phobias

Fear is a natural biological response in humans. In fact, according to evolution, it is largely due to fear that human beings survived throughout the years and evolved to adapt better to their environments. Fear has become essential in our progress as a species and in our day-to-day survival, even when we are no longer fighting with wild beasts to survive.

With that said, while it's normal to feel fear towards certain objects or situations, sometimes this fear can get out of hand and become a phobia. Phobias are an exaggerated and recurrent fear response that's characterized by an active avoidance of a certain object, activity or situation. It typically develops during the formative years and persists into adulthood.

Often times, the person suffering from phobia knows that his/her fear is irrational and not proportional to the actual threat posed by the stimulus. This reasoning, however, doesn't do much to help them overcome their phobias. In some cases, the phobia isn't severe enough to require treatment, especially if the feared stimulus can easily be avoided. However, there are also others who do not have this luxury and may find their personal functioning and well-being impaired by their phobias.

With that said, a lot of people seeking professional help are looking to treat their phobias. Fortunately for them, the prognosis is generally good and success rates are high. Among the most common clinical treatments for phobias are: antidepressants, anxiolytics, beta-blockers, psychodynamic therapy, behavioral therapy, and of course, at the very forefront of this endeavor is cognitive-behavioral therapy (CBT). Through CBT, individuals can better manage, minimize, and sometimes even eliminate their fears and phobias altogether.

It's easy to understand why CBT would be the most ideal treatment method for fears and phobias. More often than not, specific phobias are deeply rooted in an individual's dysfunctional beliefs, which in turn influence their maladaptive behaviors regarding a certain stimulus. That's why CBT works best, because it focuses a lot on redirecting and controlling this problematic thinking and changing it to result in more functional behavioral responses.

If you're afflicted with a specific phobia and want to be free of your irrational fears, then CBT can definitely help you. So let's discuss the most common kinds of specific phobias and break down how to treat each and every one of them with CBT.

Arachnophobia

Starting off the list, the number one most common kind of specific phobia is arachnophobia (the fear of spiders and arachnids), which affects over 30.5% of the general US population or 1 in every 3 women and 1 in every 4 men.

Now, it's understandable why many of us would be afraid of spiders and scorpions, because of their unsettling appearance and venomous bites and stings. However, arachnophobic individuals experience a more intense fear than most, as merely the sight or image of a spider is enough to paralyze them with terror. So much so that it might keep them from being able to work properly, study well, sleep, or enjoy social activities.

What's more is, arachnophobia is quite unreasonable because only a minority of arachnid species is actually dangerous to humans, and most of them inhabit the wilderness or the desert. Yet, someone with arachnophobia will still search every room they enter to check if there are any spiders or scorpions. If they do find one, they will most likely keep a close watch on it the entire time and feel tense in its presence even if it's just a harmless domestic spider.

The CBT technique of choice in resolving arachnophobia (and all the other specific phobias mentioned on this list, you'll find) is exposure and desensitization therapy. Exposure and desensitization therapy, as I've explained before in the previous chapters, involves the systematic exposure of the individual to their object of fear until he/she eventually learns to feel less anxious about it and cope with their distress in a more functional way.

While I've already discussed the basics of how to conduct exposure therapy on yourself, I'll run through them again and contextualize it to this specific phobia.

- If you are afflicted with arachnophobia, work through your fear little by little in a series of gradual exposure exercises.

- At first, you might want to try simply thinking about a spider,

- When you do, resist your usual fear response (i.e., screaming, crying, tensing up).

- If this is hard for you to do, try meditating or repeating a positive mantra (i.e., "I am safe, I am okay, it's just a thought.")

- Try to do this for at least 5 minutes.

- Then, try it again the next day, but this time for 10 minutes.

- Repeat the process until you feel comfortable enough to move on to looking at a picture of a spider.

- Once you've conquered that, try using VR technology to simulate a spider.

- Finally, be in the same room as a spider without feeling any fear or dread.

Now, the key to all of these exercises is that you learn to recondition your mind to stop fearing the spider. Avoid cringing, crying, screaming, or running away when exposed to it, and instead, talk yourself through it. Challenge your fear and rationalize it until you've truly convinced yourself that there's nothing to fear.

Acrophobia

An intense fear of heights, otherwise known as "acrophobia", can be very disruptive in a person's life as most of us often face heights every day. Whether it's going to work in a high-rise building, looking out on our apartment window, or simply riding a train over a tall bridge, it can be difficult to avoid and terrifying to endure.

Luckily, many people suffering from acrophobia report that Cognitive-Behavioral Therapy (CBT) was able to effectively help them manage, and in some cases even eliminate, their specific phobia.

CBT is effective because it confronts a person's deep-seated fears and changes their way of thinking about heights. In controlling the anxiety-inducing thought patterns of an acrophobic individual and replacing them with more positive ones, CBT is able to effectively change the behavioral responses that follow.

- What you need to do first is relax your mind. Listen to some calming music or meditate and clear your head.
- Once you're in a good headspace, begin to imagine that you are somewhere high, like a mountain top overlooking a beautiful view.
- It's crucial that you do not allow yourself to feel anxious or afraid while you do this. If you do, focus on the music, calm yourself down, and talk yourself through it.
- It helps to have a mantra, so try saying, "I am calm and safe. It's okay for me to be around heights. I feel only peace of mind."
- Then, when you feel secure enough to allow yourself to imagine being somewhere high up, try to apply it in real life as well.
- Cross a bridge or ride an elevator going up and just enjoy the view. Stay calm and act as if you don't feel any fear at all.
- If you feel panicked, take deep breaths and close your eyes.
- Relax all the muscles in your body and try to focus on a single object, like your shoes and how your feet feel in them. Or better yet, imagine that you are in your happy place until you calm down.

If you keep doing this, over time you will recondition your brain to feel no fear at all towards heights, and thus, eliminate your acrophobia.

Aerophobia

Aerophobia is so common that, chances are, you probably suffer from it or know someone who does. This extreme fear of flying often keeps people from travelling and riding planes, which can cause them to miss out on a lot of amazing vacations and even career opportunities like attending international conferences and important meetings with foreign clients.

With that said, if you are one of the millions of people suffering from aerophobia, there's an effective solution to your problems: Cognitive-Behavioral Therapy (CBT).

Treating aerophobia with CBT is all about unlearning your maladaptive responses to heights, and in doing so, lessening your fears. Commonly, exposure and desensitization therapy is the technique of choice here, but since I've already talked about it so much, I'll teach you something else.

This technique is called "Socratic Questioning." Socratic questioning aims to help you determine how accurate and helpful your fears really are by exploring your thoughts and beliefs about them. Here is an example of how to apply this technique to treating your aerophobia.

- Start by proclaiming what you feel or believe ("I am afraid of flying and being in planes").
- Then, challenge that belief ("But why?") and answer as truthfully as you can.
- Never settle for "Just because," or "I don't know", but rather, really get to the heart of your problem ("Because I worry that it might crash. and the turbulence makes me uncomfortable").
- Explore the roots of your fears ("Why am I so afraid? I've never even been on a plane before.").
- Then, rationalize them ("Statistically speaking, the odds of being in a plane crash is 1 in 11 million" and "My friends and family fly all the time, and nothing bad ever happens to them.").

Socratic questioning helps you analyze and process a particular train of thought. With specific phobias, oftentimes there is actually no justifiable reason for them. Once you understand that there's really nothing to be afraid of, it will be easier for you to ride planes and fly, and the more you do it, the less frightened or nervous you'll feel.

Cynophobia

Next on the list is cynophobia, which refers to a severe fear of dogs. This one is particularly difficult to leave untreated, as dogs are generally seen as beloved pets. No doubt, you probably know more than a few people who have pet dogs. While it's normal to be a little bit afraid of dogs as a child, it's not normal to allow this fear to haunt you for the rest of your life and keep you from functioning well in your day-to-day life.

Someone with cynophobia is apprehensive or anxious about unfamiliar dogs, and in extreme cases, even familiar ones like a long-time family pet. This specific phobia makes it hard for them to even walk down a street without being afraid, because they worry that there might be dogs living in that certain neighborhood (and chances are, they're probably right, which only makes things worse).

Many believe that most cases of cynophobia develop from a traumatic early experience of being bitten or chased by a dog, a recent study revealed that majority of those with cynophobia have never even had any direct encounters with a dog at all. But if that's true, then how come people with this specific phobia find it so hard to overcome their fears?

Most experts believe that the answer lies in their negative thinking and misconceptions regarding dogs and the actual danger they pose, which is why CBT is their most recommended form of psychotherapy.

Similar to arachnophobia, cynophobia is also commonly treated with exposure and desensitization therapy. In fact, it applies the very same structure of the arachnophobia treatment we've discussed earlier.

- Start by thinking about dogs without fear.
- Don't move on to the next step unless you can overcome your fear of simply thinking about dogs.
- Next, imagine a dog — it's paws, it's bark, it's fur — without feeling afraid or uncomfortable.
- Then, look at pictures of dogs and remain calm.
- Try doing this with a friend, and then modeling their behavior. Most likely, they will say something along the lines of, "Awww! What a cute dog!"
- When you're ready, go to a pet shop and look at their dogs.

- The final step to overcoming your cynophobia is by petting or at least going near the dog without feeling afraid.

It also helps to learn better coping skills so that if you ever do feel afraid when doing exposure therapy, you'll know how to stop. Try to apply relaxation techniques like mindfulness meditation or progressive muscle relaxation (like what I've discussed earlier, when dealing with anxiety). Both have been proven to reduce anxiety and increase feelings of emotional well-being.

Astraphobia

Another common phobia is astraphobia, or the fear of thunder and lightning. As you might imagine, this can be a stressful affliction to have, especially in times of stormy weather. Sometimes even a darkening sky or light rain is enough to cause someone with astraphobia to start sweating, shaking, breathing heavily, and have their heart racing. Can you imagine being on the verge of a panic attack every time a bit of rain starts to fall down? It would make life very unpleasant, indeed.

Those with astraphobia often become obsessed with the weather and waste a lot of their time keeping track of it on a daily basis. They're also quick to take shelter or hide under the bed or inside a closet at the slightest sign of lightning or thunder. Some of them are so convinced that they will get struck by lightning when they go out that they're petrified of leaving their homes in times of bad weather.

If this sounds like you, then you can start treating your astraphobia with CBT by:
- Use biofeedback to recognize your fear responses. Be aware of your heart beat, breathing, and muscle tension so you'll know when you're starting to feel anxious.
- Then, moderate this anxiety using relaxation techniques like the ones I've mentioned earlier (yoga, meditation, breathing exercises).
- Calm yourself with deep breaths and clear your mind. Think of happy, positive thoughts and listen to some soothing music while closing your eyes.
- Let your emotions wash over you and detach yourself from them. Reassure yourself that you are safe and there's nothing to be afraid of.

- Psychoeducation is also good for treating specific phobias, so educate yourself on your condition so that you can better understand what it is and how to treat it.
- Learn as much as you can about astraphobia by researching it or talking to others who have it.

Doing all of these will give you more insight into yourself and your condition, and reestablish your sense of control in your life, which will improve your psychological well-being.

Trypanophobia

Similar to cynophobia, it's typical for children to be afraid of needles and injections, but over time, their fear should diminish as they mature. However, people with trypanophobia (fear of injections) still become paralyzed at the sight of needles and allow their anxiety to rule their lives. They wrongly believe that there's no need to treat their condition and simply resort to avoiding hospitals, doctors, and any medical procedures all together. This leads them to neglect their personal health, however, and may lead to some greater problems down the road.

That being said, those with milder trypanophobia are able to get injections, but they usually feel extreme dread, worry, and sometimes even pass out or have a panic attack because of it. No matter the severity of your condition, it's essential to your psychological health and personal well-being that you treat your trypanophobia.

Common ways to treat trypanophobia include: exposure and desensitization therapy, cognitive therapy, and mindfulness training. Mindfulness training is a cognitive strategy that enables a person to bring attention to their present and fully inhabit the moment they are living in. It's a good way to treat phobias because it stops the person from overthinking and becoming overwhelmed with their fears.

- In using mindfulness to treat trypanophobia, you first need to find a safe, quiet space for you to relax in.
- Sit quietly, close your eyes, and focus on your breathing.

- If you have a mantra (like "I am brave, I am fearless"), then repeat it to yourself silently.

- Focus on the stillness of your surroundings.

- Calm yourself by listening to your heart beat.

- Identify the emotions you feel upon seeing an injection or being injected without labeling them as good or bad.

- Detach yourself from these emotions and look at them objectively. Analyze if they are really reasonable or justified.

With mindfulness training, you're better able to control your emotional responses and regulate your fear. Being aware of your condition and how irrational it is will help you regain control over your thoughts, feelings, and behaviors towards injections.

Mysophobia

Everyone knows what a neat freak is, and chances are, most people have encountered one or two in their lives before. While most "neat freaks" often get teased for liking to tidy up after themselves and organizing everything all the time, more often than not, they are wrongly labelled as obsessive-compulsive germaphobes. In fact, most people probably don't even understand what a germaphobe really is, because if they did then they'd know it's not something you should joke about.

The proper term for it is actually mysophobia (fear of germs and dirt). Mysophobia is characterized by an obsessive fear of contamination in the form of illnesses, dirt, body fluids, or bacteria. Because the problem is rooted in a person's misappraisal of the danger posed by a feared stimulus, Cognitive-Behavioral Therapy (CBT) is really effective in treating mysophobia and has been the psychosocial intervention of choice for most cases.

As I've already explained exposure and sensitization therapy, socratic questioning, psychoeducation, and mindfulness training (all of which are common CBT techniques applied here), I think it's best if I introduce to you another useful strategy: Eye Movement Desensitization and Reprocessing (EMDR).

EMDR is particularly effective if your specific phobia is rooted in a traumatic experience from the past, because it's a therapeutic technique specially designed to treat the anxiety and distress caused by a certain memory. EMDR is all about working through your trauma and reconditioning yourself to respond to the feared stimulus in a different way (much like Exposure and Desensitization Therapy).

- The first step to using EMDR to treat mysophobia is to recall the specific traumatic event, your most painful memory regarding your mysophobia, and your most recent memory of an encounter you had with germs and bacteria.
- Then, you will need to imagine yourself in the future and picture yourself interacting with the germs or bacteria in non-fearful way (this is called a "positive cognition" with a "future template").
- Afterwards, you will need to picture yourself in that very same scenario, but this time, allow yourself to be afraid.
- As your terror and dread starts to resurface, focus on them and slowly put your hands on your upper forearms, making an X with your arms, and give yourself a hug.
- Close your eyes and gently tap your shoulders to calm yourself down.
- Go to your happy place in your mind and keep tapping yourself until your anxiety subsides.

This is called the "butterfly hug", which is a EMDR technique known as dual attention stimulation (DAS). It works by conditioning your mind to associate the feared stimulus with the calm and positive energy to transform your previously anxious and terrified state. There are many other EMDR techniques, but of the few of them that you can administer to yourself at home, the butterfly hug is by far the easiest, most popular, and most effective one.

So while specific phobias are among the most widespread of mental and emotional problems today, they are also one of the most successful and easy to treat, especially with CBT. Some of therapeutic techniques I've mentioned here, like Exposure and Desensitization Therapy, Socratic

Questioning, Mindfulness Training, and EMDR, are just a few of the many different options to choose from.

Each technique has its own strengths and weaknesses, and may be suited to some cases more than others. For example, if your phobia developed as a result of a traumatic experience, then EMDR will work for you; whereas a more general phobia could benefit from EDT or mindfulness training. However, all the aforementioned techniques are founded on the same principle: they aim to help correct your anxiety-evoking misconceptions and reduce your avoidant behaviors towards the feared stimulus so you can overcome your specific phobia.

With that said, the only person who can tell you what's best for you is yourself, because no one knows what you're going through better than you do. Although it's ideal, you don't need a professional therapist's opinion or help in treating your fears and phobias with CBT, as I've already taught you a number of different ways you can safely administer treatment to yourself. All you need to do is persevere and motivate yourself enough so you can successfully manage and eliminate your phobia.

Chapter 6: CBT And OCD

How to Use CBT For Obsession and OCD

We have touched on this somewhat in the earlier chapters, but I felt that this needed more space to give it its fair due. In recent times, OCD has become somewhat of a common term amongst every day society. The word is often thrown around lightly as a tease to someone who likes things a certain way or feels the need to be orderly and tidy. Most of the people who do this, however, don't even know the first thing about OCD or how serious it actually is.

Obsessive-Compulsive Disorder (OCD) is a chronic mental illness that affects over 2.2 million people in America. It is characterized by intrusive and unsettling thoughts, images, or urges that often compel someone to engage in repetitive, ritualistic behaviors or mental acts. Understandably, those suffering from OCD feel a great deal of distress over their condition because they feel as if they are slaves to their own obsessions and compulsions. In severe cases, it can even make it difficult for the person to think about anything other than their obsessions.

Another challenge that a lot of OCD patients struggle with is overcoming their need to enact their obsessive thoughts into compulsions. OCD is driven by anxiety, and people with this disorder often wrongly believe that the only way to alleviate their anxiety is by giving into their compulsions. While it does provide some relief, it's a maladaptive solution to a much more complex problem, as it can take away an individual's sense of control and freewill over their lives.

In the early days of psychotherapy, OCD was one of the most prevalent mental disorders in the world, but most psychologists didn't have the faintest clue on how to treat it. Many of them simply resorted to psychodynamic therapy, behavioral therapy, and antidepressants, even though it was proven to have little to no significant effect. Fortunately, in 1966, psychologists discovered the first effective psychosocial intervention for OCD: exposure and ritual prevention (EX/RP).

EX/RP is a CBT technique that proved to be so successful in treating the disorder that it went on to inspire the development of other similar treatments, most of which with successful outcomes.

Now, Cognitive-Behavioral Therapy (CBT) and its specialized techniques are considered the "golden standard" in treating OCD patients and alleviating their anxiety. It also helps them manage their obsessions and decrease their compulsions, which adds to a better quality of life.

So if you're suffering from OCD and looking to CBT to help you manage your condition better and ease your troubles, then you've come to the right place. In this chapter, I will be breaking down the different ways CBT can be used to treat Obsessive-Compulsive Disorder. But first, let's go over the different kinds of obsessive thoughts and compulsions.

Among the most common obsessive thoughts include themes of:

- *Orderliness and symmetry* - people with this kind of OCD often worry about the neatness and tidiness of everything
- *Contamination* - this leads someone to fear being contaminated with germs and bacteria
- *Rumination* - this means imagining a mistake that one has done or might do
- *Checking* - this type of obsession leaves the person wondering if they've already turned off the lights, turned off the stove, locked the doors, etc.
- *Dark Thoughts* - this induces a fear of even thinking about "sinful" or evil things
- *Violence* - a person with these thoughts often fears harming others, even though he/she does not want or intend to

As for compulsive behaviors, among the major kinds are:

- *Skin-picking*
- *Hair-pulling*
- *Hoarding/collecting*
- *Repeated hand washing or cleaning*
- *Repeating particular words or phrases*
- *Performing certain tasks repeatedly*
- *Constant counting*

As you can see, OCD can have many different subtypes and symptoms, depending on the particular obsessions or compulsions of the individual. But more often than not, an effective treatment for one type of OCD is actually effective for the rest as well. There is also the degree of the severity of OCD that needs to be put into consideration.

Now let's move onto the different CBT techniques that can help treat and alleviate obsessive thoughts and OCD and how to apply them into your life:

Exposure and Ritual/Response Prevention

As I mentioned earlier, Exposure and Ritual/Response Prevention (EX/RP) is actually one of the earliest CBT techniques used to treat OCD, and the first to produce successful results. As the name implies, this particular technique involves exposing the patient gradually to situations that can trigger their obsessive thoughts and compulsive behaviors.

It might seem counterintuitive, but with the help of the therapist, the patient is guided through it and taught how to respond more effectively to the situation. They are prevented from carrying out their ritualistic behaviors and forced to find new (and often better) ways of responding to the stimulus. As a result, it decrease the frequency of their compulsions and the intensity of their obsessions over time.

Now, the therapist is an integral part of the treatment process here. However, since this book is all about teaching you how to become your own therapist and administer CBT to yourself, here's how you can do it, too:

- Firstly, you will need to make a detailed description of all of your obsessions and compulsions, and then arrange them in order of least problematic to most (depending on how recurrent or distressing they are).
- Then, use this as a guide and start working on the least problematic of the bunch, as this will be the easiest to treat.
- With a particular obsession and/or compulsion in mind, try to figure out when the symptom most often occurs and what is most likely to trigger it.

- Once you know, expose yourself to this particular stimulus and avoid responding to it with a compulsion for a certain period of time.
- This can be difficult to do on your own, especially at first, so it's best to have a trusted friend help you through it until you eventually trust yourself enough to do it on your own.

To give you a better idea of how EX/RP really works, I'll use a concrete example. Let's say you have obsessive thoughts about orderliness and symmetry, which are often triggered by the sight of unclean or disorganized things. What you need to do is ask a friend to accompany you as you are exposed to certain situations where there may be unclean or disorganized things, like at someone else's house or office.

Of course, you know that you shouldn't go around touching other people's things without their permission but you feel the uncontrollable urge to tidy up after them - arrange all their pens by color or dust off all their books and stack them in a perfectly aligned pile. Try to refrain from doing this for around five minutes. Ask your friend to distract you or talk you through it. Then, when it gets easier, next time you see something dirty or cluttered, stop yourself for ten minutes, and then twenty, and then thirty...until it eventually gets easier and easier.

In time, you will stop needing someone else to keep you from acting on your compulsive behaviors. You might even stop needing to do them in the first place, because your obsessive thoughts have become so mild that they can now be easily ignored. This is especially true once you've learned how to redirect your thoughts onto something else.

Some good distractions that can help you through the "response prevention" process are: talking to a friend about something else (i.e., the weather, the news, etc.), meditating, writing down what you want to do, making plans, making lists, knitting, baking, and painting. All you need is any relaxing or leisurely activity where you do something productive. It also helps to have your friend or companion model what the appropriate behavioral response should be. In this case, it might be merely looking at the clutter and simply saying to the person, "You have a lovely home."

This works because your brain is repeatedly reinforcing that you do not need to carry out your compulsions to be rid of the anxiety brought about by your obsessions. You will come to realize that it's okay to stop giving in to them, because nothing bad actually happens when you do. On the flip side, you might have saved yourself suffering from the burst of outrage from the home owner due to the touching of his stuff without permission.

Cognitive Therapy

The next CBT technique we will be talking about is Cognitive Therapy. While Exposure and Ritual/Response Prevention (EX/RP) was all about changing your dysfunctional behaviors for the better, Cognitive Therapy focuses on reframing your way of thinking. This will help you identify which thought patterns of yours cause you anxiety or stress and how to modify them.

Cognitive Therapy is all about challenging your thoughts and finding more functional ways of thinking. This includes strategies like self-talk, thought stopping, and relaxation training — all of which I will be breaking down for you. But first, let's contextualize everything with an example.

Say for instance, you're an elementary school teacher with OCD who has obsessions with violence. Sometimes you find yourself wondering, "What if I set one of my students on fire?" for no apparent reason. The thought surprises you and you feel immensely guilty about it because you worry that just thinking about the act in itself is already evil. Cognitive Therapy can help you with this using self-talk.

Self-Talk

Self-talk is a powerful tool for managing your OCD. Although you might not know it, you're constantly practicing self-talk everyday. It's that inner voice that monologues everything you do and think as you go on about your day, from the moment you wake up to the moment you go to sleep. However, in terms of Cognitive Therapy, self-talk refers to positive, encouraging affirmations that you give yourself as you interpret and process your personal experiences.

- In the scenario stated above, you can overcome the intrusive thoughts with self-talk by reminding yourself that you are not your disorder. It's your OCD that's making you think all these terrible things, and not at all a reflection of who you are as a person.

- Remind yourself that you are more than your condition. Find things about yourself that you love and show some appreciation to your own strengths, accomplishments, and positive characteristics.

- Allow these intrusive thoughts into your mind but don't let them affect you or dictate what you do in any way at all. Simply observe them, say to yourself, "This is how I am feeling, but it's only a feeling. It doesn't control me."

- Moreover, you can try repeating a mantra like, "These thoughts do not hurt anyone. I do not want to hurt anyone. I am kind and caring and compassionate, but I have OCD and sometimes these thoughts get inside my head. Just because I think something doesn't mean I want it or agree with it. I am in control of my thoughts, not the other way around. It's okay. Everything is fine. Everything is good."

Habit Reversal Training

Habit Reversal Training or HRT is one of the most used types of behavioral therapy in treating OCD. With the name itself "Habit Reversal", it reverses the habit formed by individuals that are typically performed in certain situations and help them to overcome the urge to do it.This is also helpful in treating different behaviors caused by a variety of conditions, like Tourette's syndrome.

HRT is seen to be highly effective in helping people with unwanted behaviors or habits, such as hair pulling, tics, repetitive behaviors or nail biting. When treating OCD, it is highly recommendable to use this type of behavioral therapy since it helps them get rid of the urge to follow the OCD and minimize or possibly stop their repetitive behavior. This training is made up of five different parts that can help individuals overcome their disorder. It starts with:

Awareness Training

If you want to minimize or put an end to your behavior, it is important to know it and accept it beforehand. How can you put an end to something if you are not aware about it? Same goes with this, you can't stop your behavior if you aren't even aware of its presence. Through awareness training, individuals can pay attention to their behavior in order to work a way in diminishing it.

This step allows you to figure out when you typically perform this particular behavior, what are some triggers and signs before you actually do it. Awareness training helps individuals know and understand their behavior more deeply and find out some things they never knew before.

Identifying and strategizing

This step identifies the problem in your behavior and partly continues the work you've done in the first step. Once you've identified all the triggers and urges you have, it is time to strategize a new behavior or a way to combat your urge. This new behavior will replace the old one. It is important to practice this new behavior and be aware. Whenever you want to go back to the old behavior you have been so used to, you can try to do this instead. For example, if your typical behavior in response to nerve-racking situations is by biting your nails, the new behavior you'll have to do is to purse your lips instead.

Finding your own motivation and sticking with your plan

When doing something difficult, we tend to find a source of motivation to keep us doing or to remind us why we're here in the first place. Same goes with habit reversal therapy, there will be some instances where you'll question what you're doing or why you're even doing it in the first place. This is why you need to write down a list of all the reasons why you want to go through HRT and make this a source of your motivation. Find all the people you want to do this for and all the problems that you've had because of your unwanted behavior. After finding you motivation, it is important to stick with your HRT and try to comply with it until the very end.

Reducing and Relaxing

These unwanted behaviors tend to show up whenever a person's body is put under a great amount of stress. So, it is important to reduce your stress level and eliminate any triggers that may induce your tics. Relax your body more and give it enough time to rest. In this part, it is important to know different relaxation techniques. There are some that also coincide with the CBT techniques such as deep breathing exercises, progression muscle relaxation, mindfulness meditation and the like.

Testing and Training

After all the different processes you've went through, it's time to test out and practice your new skills and behavior and see how you respond to different situations. You may be placed in front of triggers and it is important to train yourself to get rid of the urge to go back to your old habits. This is the most crucial step of all because it displays all the work you've done in the past. Once you've practiced this new behavior enough, it will soon become an automatic response for you and successfully replacing the old behavior you once developed.

These steps can help individuals overcome their unwanted tics. With a little effort and concentration they can possibly get through and develop a new behavior. Here is a situation example for deeper understanding.

An individual has OCD and tends to bite their nails off whenever they're under stress. So, to overcome this unwanted behavior, they have to become aware of their habit and understand it. Afterwards, they need to find a different behavior to replace that, let's say pursing their lips. When this is done, they need to practice this behavior until they get used and more accustomed to it. HRT can be done on your own. However, it is still more advisable to seek professional help in order to fully eliminate your old behavior.

Imaginal Exposure (IE)

OCD is a complex and wide psychological problem. With a lot of different types and subtypes, it can be difficult to assume which treatment is best for each one of them. There are some treatments that require a lot more intensive procedures than others. There are also others that cannot be applicable for some. Let's look at Exposure and Response Therapy for example. This type of therapy can be applicable for people who have OCD about physical things like about getting germs from touching a doorknob. The simple ERT procedure would be to let them touch multiple doorknobs without letting them wash their hands. However, it cannot be applicable for individuals who have more complex OCD behaviors. For example, individuals who are afraid of losing loved ones cannot perform ERT. So, as a substitute for this, they can undergo Imaginal Exposure or IE. Through IE, individuals will experience visualization of different scenarios that expose them to their fears or OCD. Imaginal Exposure will expose them to seemingly real-life situations and train them on how to react to these particular situations.

Imaginal Exposure is for more complex and hard to handle OCD problems. There are some who opt to go through visualizing different scenarios while others choose to write imaginal exposure stories. Through visualization, patients are asked to undergo this process:

- Think of a particular situation that triggers your OCD (like losing the ones you love)

- Once you've identified the situation, start imagining yourself in the scenario (you may be facing it by standing or looking at it)
- Afterwards, try to picture that specific scenario over and over again until it will not induce any visible or emotional trigger in you
- After being exposed to it several times, try your best to come back to that scenario until you can accept that it isn't reality and it will not always be like that. This will reduce your negative emotions and change your behavior towards different circumstances

Through visualization, individuals can easily access their minds and visualize their OCD triggers. By confronting their worst fears, they can slowly diminish their level of anxiety and reduce the intensity of their emotions.

There is also another way to use Imaginal Exposure and that is through writing imaginative stories. These stories entail your greatest fear and you finding a way to confront these emotions. Through writing your fears, you can let out everything you feel and expose yourself to the different OCD triggers within you. The short story that the individual will write will consist of their obsessive thoughts taken to the worst case scenario. Individuals with OCD may not be too keen to begin or go through with this type of therapy. However, it can be very crucial in allowing them to overcome their greatest fears and face their negative thoughts once and for all.

Here are some tips on how to write your own imaginal exposure short story to get the best results and to really impact your thoughts, emotions and behaviors:

Make Your Story From Your Perspective

As you are trying to overcome your own fear, it is important to write things from a first person point of view. This is so that we will actually feel the things we "did" in the story and keep it as close to our heart as much as possible. This will allow the writer to see the consequences of their action and actually feel the story. In the cognitive aspect, the brain will process the information as if it was their own doing, therefore making the therapy effective.

Always keep it realistic

It is important to not go beyond the bar. There is a fine line between reality and imagination so it's important that you should not go beyond that line. Keep things around the aspects that you think may happen if ever you would do a certain act. Don't go far from the actual topic and try to keep things as realistic as possible.

Use Authenticity

Be authentic about the thoughts you're currently thinking about and the emotions you're currently feeling. Only talk about the things that are bothering you. If it isn't actually a problem, then don't bother to write about it.

Focus on the now and write in present tense

Write your story in the present tense so that you'll actually feel you're living in it, in the exact same moment. Don't go and write about it like it happened a year ago, write things as if they are fresh and currently happening as we speak.

Keep it concise

When writing, it is important not to beat around the bush. Keep things as short and concise as possible. If it isn't actually important, then don't bother to write about it. Don't waste your time writing about things that doesn't actually keep you up at night. Rather, focus on things which detail the most important and vital part of your illness. Of course, for those with a flair for the language, it is alright to give free rein to your creative expression. Just stay on point while doing it.

Go the limit

Take your fear to the worst possible scenario. Make it out to be the worst thing that could every happen to you in your entire life. In this way, you can become exposed to the worst things and learn how to cope situations like this, or maybe even lighter ones.

Imaginal exposure can be of great use for individuals who cannot undergo ERT. It can also be extremely helpful for OCD since it exposes them to different made-up scenarios that also resemble real-life situations. Through IE, individuals can touch on both their cognitive and behavioral aspect which will in turn produce positive thoughts and better behavior.

Chapter 7: CBT And Those Bad Habits

How To Use CBT For Bad Habits

Everyone has a bad habit; something they know isn't good for them but they can't help but do anyway. However, no matter how much enjoyment we may think we feel from these bad habits — whether it's swearing, spending too much, or drinking too much coffee — we understand that they're called bad habits for a reason.

These maladaptive behaviors disrupt our lives and often make us feel like we don't have any control over ourselves, especially when they get out of hand. They hinder you from attaining your goals and jeopardize your physical and mental health. Not to mention, they're also often a waste of time and energy.

So if you came to this book looking to break a bad habit using CBT, then you're in luck. We've listed down below some of the most common bad habits and how to overcome them using different CBT techniques.

Stress Eating

Everyone feels stress from time to time, and most of us often deal with it in our own ways. Some common ways to de-stress include exercising, dancing, gardening, baking, painting, journaling, or listening to music.

However, sometimes people find comfort in eating when they're stressed, which can quickly become problematic if left unchecked. This maladaptive behavior is called "stress eating", which refers to the compulsive need or desire to eat large amounts of (often unhealthy) food whenever a person feels unhappy, anxious, or distressed. Think chocolate and ice cream.

Most of the time, people don't stress eat because they are physically hungry, but rather, because they feel momentary happiness and relief from their emotional emptiness and distress. However, this relief is fleeting and can often leave the person feeling guilty, disgusted, or hating themselves instead in the aftermath. This emotional dependency on food can have a negative effect on your body and weight, as it often results in an overwhelming sense of guilt, nausea, and obesity.

Fortunately, Cognitive-Behavioral Therapy can help with those struggling to break this vicious cycle of stress eating. Most commonly, the CBT technique applicable to treating it include journaling, which we will flesh out below to let you have an idea of how to actually go about doing it.

- Reflect on your stress eating and try to figure out what triggers it.
- Avoid these triggers at all costs.
- Keep a food journal so you can keep track of your diet. Record everything you eat in this journal and monitor your caloric intake.
- Regularly read this journal and assess your patterns of problematic eating.
- Then, with the knowledge you have gathered in your food journal, figure out how you can overcome these triggers. For example:

If you tend to stress eat the most when you are bored, keep yourself busy. Find a new hobby (i.e., exercising, origami, writing poetry) and devote your time to mastering it.

If you stress eat the most after a hard day of work, find other ways to decompress. Do yoga, drink some tea, watch a movie, take a walk, have a drink with a friend, or play with your dog. Understand that there are better, much healthier ways of relieving your stress.

If you stress eat when you're feeling down or depressed, look for other outlets to deal with your sadness. You could try talking to a friend, spending time with your loved ones, journaling how you feel, or even crying it out.

Watching Too Much TV

Television has been called "junk food for your brain", and perhaps for good reason too. Most of us have probably adopted the bad habit of watching too much TV at some point in our lives. While it may seem relaxing and enjoyable at first, it can turn into an incredible waste of your time if done in excess. It's okay to do it every once in awhile, especially after you've had a long hard week and want to kick back and reward yourself with a few episodes of your favorite show, but mindlessly consuming too much entertainment and staying on your couch all day to channel surf is actually very bad for your brain.

Numerous studies have shown that people who watch more than 3 hours of TV a day often neglect their personal health, hardly exercise at all, feel unmotivated in life, and find it hard to do anything productive or enjoyable. They've reached that certain point where watching TV no longer gives them any enjoyment or engagement at all, so why do they find it hard to stop thoughtlessly pressing the remote and just zoning out in front of their televisions?

Some believe that it's because watching TV is simple, easy to do, and requires little to no mental effort at all. Others say that it's because television gives them a false sense of connection when they're lonely or bored. Whatever the reason may be, if you're struggling to break your bad habit of watching too much TV, you can try using CBT techniques like activity scheduling and systematic positive reinforcement to help you quit.

Just follow these simple steps and reclaim your life from your addiction to TV:

- Set a certain amount of time for you to watch TV, and then do your best to stick to it.
- Then, once you're done, schedule activities for yourself to do. It can be something as simple as doing the chores or your homework, as long as you do something other than watch TV all day.
- Then, as the days go by, lessen your time in front of the TV and schedule more and more activities for yourself.
- Gradually increase the level of difficulty or time for your activities, like going from washing the dishes, to baking brownies, to hanging out with your friends. (yes, for some folks who have watched too much tv, interacting with actual living humans may seem to be a herculean task)
- Every time you complete a certain task or activity, reward yourself with something other than watching television.

These techniques work because they teach your brain to associate the positive feelings you get from your rewards with not watching TV. Gradually cutting it out of your life also helps to make you feel less withdrawal symptoms and more of a certain sense of purpose in your recovery process.

Procrastinating

Everyone's tried procrastinating from time to time. If you don't know, procrastinating means putting off something you often don't want to do but need to, and leaving it at the very last minute. However, while you're out there enjoying yourself and distracting your mind, trying to forget about all the work you need to do, deep down inside, you're feeling bad and there's a constant sense of guilt hanging over your head.

If you turn procrastination into a habit, you will suffer from diminished performance, poorer mental and physical health, and more feelings of stress, worry, and guilt over time. Procrastination is a maladaptive, self-defeating behavior that gives you short-term benefits but at a pricier, long-term cost. So why do so many of us procrastinate anyway? And why is it so hard to stop?

Some researchers theorize that people procrastinate because they wrongly believe it to be a form of "self-care"; while others believe that we've learned to procrastinate from our role models; and some say that we procrastinate because of a deep-seated fear of failing and feeling like we're not good enough to do the tasks which we are supposed to do. Because there are so many different reasons why we procrastinate, there are also a variety of different ways you can stop doing it. Examples include:

- Practice positive self-talk. Tell yourself something like, "I know it's hard, but we have to do it. So please, let's just start it. I believe in you. You're going to do great."
- Find new role models you can look up to, who do everything on time. Follow them around for a while and ask them to help you understand why it's so much better not to procrastinate.

- Develop your skills. Whatever it is you're putting off, if you feel insecure and unsure of yourself and think you won't be able to do it well, then work on your skills. This will boost your self-confidence and motivate you to procrastinate less and do better at the task.

Choosing Bad Partners/Relationships

Everyone knows what a "bad relationship" is. It's the kind of relationship where you don't feel valued or heard, where your partner doesn't treat you as an equal. This can mean that they're unfaithful to you, or they feel embarrassed to be seen with you, or that they only ever want to talk and never listen. Sometimes, bad relationships mean unrequited love; being with a partner whom you love but doesn't love you back. Whatever kind of bad relationship you've been in, the end result is always the same: you feel heartbroken and hating yourself for being so stupid.

If you've had a string of bad relationships like the ones I just described, then perhaps it's because you have a bad habit of choosing the wrong partner. Oftentimes, this stems from an attraction towards people you can't have or don't reciprocate your feelings, either to the same degree or at all. Author Stephen Chbosky once wrote, "We accept the love we think we deserve," and this is exactly why some people constantly find themselves in one bad relationship after another.

If that person is you and you're looking to change your self-defeating ways, then some Cognitive-Behavioral Therapy (CBT) can help you with that. Your goal here should be towards building your self-esteem and developing a more positive relationship with yourself, which you can do through journaling, positive self-talk, and mindfulness training.

- Write down at least ten things about yourself that you love. It can be either personality traits or physical features, as long as it is positive.
- Now, read out loud these positive statements to yourself, and afterwards, try to add some more.
- Whenever you're feeling down about yourself, say something positive like, "I know you can get through this, you're strong," or "Just because other people can't see your worth doesn't mean you don't have any. I love you. I think you're amazing."

- It also helps to start each day with positivity, so write down these messages on your wall beside your bed or somewhere you can see when you wake up. (try the toilet wall mirror too, you can look at it every single day when you brush your teeth)
- Then, set aside 10-20 minutes each day for you to meditate. Recall your day as you're meditating and try to identify the emotions you've felt.
- Ask yourself why you felt that way and if it was reasonable or justified.
- If ever you did something wrong or embarrassing, forgive yourself.
- Get comfortable being alone for now. Learn to enjoy your own company.

All you need to overcome your self-defeating habit of being in bad relationships is really to just practice more self-love and boost your self-esteem. Once you do that, you will start choosing partners who are right for you and stay in healthier relationships.

So all in all, while bad habits may not seem like the most pressing of psychological problems, they still need to be addressed. Little things like watching too much TV can quickly turn into TV addiction and, before you know it, you've wasted months or years off of your life just by staying in the couch all day, unable to let go of the remote.

Procrastination is also particularly harmful to students or anyone with a demanding job that requires them to give it their all. It can significantly impede their performance and cost them a lot of great opportunities in life, as well as lower the quality and standard of their work, which will give others a bad impression of them.

There are lots of other bad habits that we didn't mention here, but a lot of the same techniques we've detailed above can be applied to quite a number of them. Cognitive-Behavioral Therapy can help you break the vicious cycle of wasting your time with unproductive things by reconditioning your mind and changing your maladaptive behaviors.

Chapter 8: A Little Bit Of Structure And Hand Holding Never Hurt Anyone

The 21-Day Step-by-Step Guide

Now that we've wrapped up our discussion on all the major problems and issues Cognitive-Behavioral Therapy (CBT) and its many techniques can deal with, it's time to apply all that knowledge on how to solve your particular problem in mind.

If the issues you are dealing with right now weren't covered in the earlier chapters, don't worry. I've created this comprehensive, 21-day step-by-step guide on how you can deal with almost any difficult situation using CBT and come out the other end a better, happier, and more emotionally well-balanced person. Be guided by these steps and keep them in mind on your journey to mental wellness with CBT.

- **Day 01 - Know what your problems are**

Before anything else, you need to sit yourself down and figure out what it is you've been struggling with lately. Get a pen and paper or make a list in your journal about all the problems bothering you right now. No matter how big or small, write down every single problem you're experiencing that you can think of.

- **Day 02 - Sorting out your priorities**

Next, what you should do is look through your list and figure out for yourself which problems are causing you the most distress. Rank them from most difficult to deal with to the least, and from there, start with the last entry on your list. This way, you start with the easiest challenge and work your way up over time, as you gain more understanding and better mastery over how to use CBT.

- **Day 03 - Understanding the problem**

Now, with a particular problem in mind, focus on that and devote all your attention to understanding it. This stage of the process is known as guided discovery. A common CBT and counselling technique, guided discovery is all about reflecting on how you process information.

So go through the problem in your mind and try to recall how it came about and the ways in which you responded to it. Understand as much as you can about what caused the problem and what is perpetuating it. Consider the situational, social, mental, emotional, and behavioral factors involved.

- **Day 04 - Identifying your obstacles**

Following that same train of thought as the last point, identify the obstacles getting in the way of your path to mental wellness. Think of all the things that make it harder for you to resolve your particular problem and brainstorm ways in which you can overcome these obstacles. This is a crucial step in the process because if you overlook this or fail to do it, then it will simply keep coming back to haunt you and hinder your progress every step of the way.

- **Day 05 - Set goals for yourself**

Now that there's nothing getting in the way of you resolving your problem anymore, it's time for you to set goals for yourself. Know what it is that you want to achieve and break it down into simpler, more manageable goals. For example, if you want to quit smoking, then smoke 1 less cigarette than your usual today, and then 2 the next day, and then 5, and then 10...until eventually, you quit smoking all together. Remember you have to walk a tight line between setting unassailable goals and goals which are too lax. The goal has to be achievable at each given state of your being. Referencing to the cigarette example, smoking one less cigarette than you usual could be deemed as achievable in your present circumstance, while asking you to jump from smoking daily to totally cutting out smoking immediately would be deemed as one of the unassailable goals I was talking about. Progression from cutting one cigarette to two and more, would entail you having to be honest with yourself and go about setting challenging but achievable goals.

- **Day 06 - Figure out your thoughts on the problem**

Take your journal out again and write down every single thought you have regarding this particular problem. How does it make you feel? What are the beliefs and assumptions you have surrounding it? Does it affect the way you feel about yourself or your life? Be as honest as possible with yourself and really take the time to ruminate on these questions.

- **Day 07 - Identify your automatic thoughts**

As I mentioned before in the introduction of this book, automatic thoughts refer to the thoughts that occur in response to a certain trigger or event. These are reflexive and unconsciously done, but can greatly impact a person's life. So whenever something happens to you — no matter how big or small — quickly write down or record the first thought that pops into your head.

- **Day 08 - Practice more positive thinking**

Here you can use cognitive restructuring to recondition your brain and change those negative automatic thoughts into more positive ones. Similar to guided discovery, cognitive restructuring will allow you to change the way you process information because it asks you to challenge your thoughts and the emotions and behaviors that they elicit. Once you've identified the unfavorable thought, try to change it in a way that finds a positive aspect in it.

For example, if you think to yourself, "Nobody likes me," you need to challenge it by thinking about all the people who actually do like you. Afterwards, you can think about all the reasons why you don't need people to like you. So now, every time this negative thought pops into your head, challenge it with "These people like me," and "I don't need others to like me, because I already like myself."

- **Day 09 - Reaffirm yourself**

Self-affirmations can help enhance your likelihood of succeeding in resolving your problem with CBT by boosting your self-esteem and increasing your motivation. I've already talked about it a lot, especially in dealing with anxiety, depression, and OCD, but the change that it can have on your life really is astounding. If practiced daily and devotedly, these positive statements are powerful enough to change the way you feel about yourself and the world for the better, along with minimizing your anxiety, stress, and negative thinking.

I've shared several affirmations and positive mantras you can speak to yourself in those chapters I mentioned before, but you can also make one for yourself! Just be positive and strive to see yourself and your situation in the best possible light you can.

- **Day 10 - Know how you feel about the problem**

Practice mindfulness when thinking about the problem at hand. Describe the situation and how you feel about it. Go into detail about the things it made you think and the way it made you feel. What was the first thought that popped into your mind? How did you feel? Identify these emotions and refrain from labelling them as "good" or "bad" and reacting to them in anyway at all.

- **Day 11 - Manage your emotions**

Now that you've already dealt with your problematic thought patterns, it's time to move on to your negative emotions. Do some more reflection and ponder on what certain situations or objects trigger unwanted emotions in you, and until you figure out why, try to avoid them at all costs. Keep your emotions in check by practicing meditation or other relaxation techniques like breathing exercises and yoga.

- **Day 12 - Overcome your negative emotions**

Next, you need to work on overcoming whatever negative emotions you might have. Sadness, stress, doubt, jealousy, shame, frustration, or guilt, positive self-talk can help you deal with it. Like I previously mentioned in the chapter about OCD, positive self-talk is a powerful tool in working through your negative emotions.

Simply reassure yourself that everything is fine and well, and think of as many reasons as you can to support that claim. You don't need to resort to lying to yourself; just practice genuine gratitude for all the good things in your life and remind yourself of all the great things about you.

- **Day 13 - Overcome your fears**

This step is optional, but if your fear is a big part of your problem, then you need to deal with it correctly. The techniques I've mentioned in the chapter about specific phobias can all be applied to resolve just about any fear you might have, so give it a try. You could use graded exposure, relaxation training, mindfulness training, socratic questioning, psychoeducation, and even EMDR if the fear is especially traumatic.

- **Day 14 - Identify your maladapative behaviors**

After you've addressed the dysfunctional patterns in your thoughts and emotions, let's proceed to your maladaptive behaviors. Sit yourself down again and reflect on all the habits and behavioral responses that you feel are bad for you and want to stop doing. Write it all down in your journal. It could be something like lying, sleeping in, saying sorry all the time, procrastinating, and so on.

- **Day 15 - Overcome these negative behaviors**

Once you've already identified the negative behavior you would like to stop doing, the next step is to overcome it. You can use aversive conditioning, wherein you pair the behavior with an aversive stimulus to recondition your brain into no longer wanting to do it. One common example of this would be flicking your wrist with a rubber band every time you say something mean or rude.

You can follow the steps listed in the chapter dealing with bad habits and behaviors. They would be helpful in shoring up the resolve to overcome these negative aspects, while at the same time emphasizing on the positive steps which you are taking.

- **Day 16 - Replace them with positive behaviors**

Now that you've successfully rid yourself of those maladaptive behaviors, it's time to replace them with more positive ones through systematic positive reinforcement (SPR). Applying the same principles of behavior as aversive conditioning, SPR works by rewarding yourself with something every time you do something positive.

For example, buying yourself some ice cream every time you overcome your fear of public speaking or do well on a test. This will encourage you to keep doing those positive behaviors more and more over time, even when the reward is no longer there, because your brain has already learned to associate it with those positive feelings.

- **Day 17 - Accept the things you can't change**

But what if there are certain things about your problem that you can't resolve or that you have no control over? For example, in dealing with a breakup or being rejected for a job or college that you want, a lot of the situation is largely out of your control. The best thing for you to do would be to simply accept it and come to terms with it.

Doing meditation as well as in depth mindfulness training can really be of help when faced with situations that seem to be totally out of your control. As they always like to say, change is the only constant and the only thing you can control is yourself.

- **Day 18 - Work through any past trauma**

At this point of the process, your journey should be coming to a close. You've resolved all your dysfunctional thoughts and behaviors, and learned to control your emotions better. However, if there is still some lingering trauma from your past regarding the problem, then you need to deal with it as well.

It might be that you need to forgive someone who hurt you or come to terms with yourself about the things you did or didn't do. If your trauma runs deeper than this, you might want to try EMDR, the therapeutic treatment we've mentioned in treating specific phobias like mysophobia.

- **Day 19 - Be proud of all the progress you've made**

As our journey is nearing its end, it's important that you take the time to look back on all the progress you've made and feel proud of how far you've come. It was certainly a struggle, but you've made it. You've done your best and now you're ready to move on from your problems. Pat yourself on the back. You deserve it.

- **Day 20 - Ending treatment & maintaining change** (tips from Chapter 8)

Now it's finally time to end your treatment and close this chapter of your life. The problem that made you seek this book for help is now resolved, and all that's left for you to do is go on with your life and continue to be the better person that you are. While the hardest part is certainly over, you need to work hard to keep going and do your best not to fall back on your old, dysfunctional ways. Maintain the positive change in your life by following the tips I've listed down below, later on in this chapter.

- **Day 21 - Apply what you've learned**

As the famous American pastor Joel Osteen once said, "Every day, we have plenty of opportunities to get angry, stressed or offended. But what you're doing when you indulge in these negative emotions is giving something outside of yourself power over your happiness. You can choose not to let little things upset you."

Bearing in mind those wise words, all of the things you've learned and the progress you've made would be useless if you didn't apply it to your life. Your journey with CBT has been all about learning to be your own therapist, so use all the skills you've developed and knowledge you've gathered from this book and apply it to whatever challenges you face next. The more you cultivate it, the easier it will be to apply, and the better your life will be.

Other Ways You Can Live Your Best Life

Along with this 21-day step-by-step guide, there are plenty of other positive habits and practices you can incorporate into your every day routine to improve the overall quality of your life. This is ideal because it reinforces your learnings and sees to it that even when you're done with the program, everything you've worked hard on and all the progress you've made still stays with you. A few additional ways you can continue living your best life is through:

1. **Meditation**

We've said it time and time again: meditation is good for your mental and emotional health. An integral facet of relaxation training, which is used to treat anxiety, obsessive thoughts, OCD, phobias, and maladaptive behaviors, meditation in and of itself can be greatly beneficial.

Just in case you needed reminding, meditation helps relieve your stress, facilitates better sleep, reduces muscle tension and body pain, reduces blood pressure, boosts your immune system, deals with your worries and anxieties, clears your mind, increases positive emotions, and promotes greater focus, awareness, and emotional control.

Millions of people from all over the world attest to how practicing meditation daily has changed their lives for the better, so why not do the same? Set aside 10-20 minutes a day to meditate and sit in tranquil silence. Find a comfortable, safe space - be it, in your room or on your bed - and set your timer. From the moment it starts ticking to the moment it stops, try to think about nothing but your breathing. Get to work on identifying your emotions and releasing all the negativity you feel. Find some peace of mind, and when you're done, go on about your day with a better, more rational mindset.

2. Nature Therapy

If you feel that sitting in silence for a few minutes a day and doing seemingly nothing is really not for you, then nature therapy is a good alternative you can try. Nature therapy (sometimes also known as "eco therapy") is all about reconnecting with Mother Nature. It is founded on the belief that all human beings are a part of the circle of life here on Earth and that our souls all yearn to be at peace with our natural environments.

Doesn't it feel good to go outside, breathe in the fresh air and bask in the sunshine? Don't you feel a certain serenity wash over you when you enjoy the beauty of the great outdoors? In the modern age of technology where humans have become more urbanized and screen-driven than ever, nature therapy provides a calming, therapeutic effect because it reminds us of place in the natural world. Practicing nature therapy can give you a sense of balance and harmony in your life.

So make time in your busy schedule to spend a day at the beach, go camping in the woods, or take a weekend trip to the lakehouse or golf course. Leave behind all your worries and stresses for the day, and your emotional and mental wellbeing will be all the better for it.

On the other hand, even if you live in a bustling city and work a strenuous job you just can't leave behind, you can still find the beauty in nature in small ways — like going for a walk in the park or tending to your garden in the backyard. Anything that gets you outdoors and brings a sense of purpose-ness to your experience is already nature therapy in and of itself.

3. Stargazing

Similar to nature therapy, stargazing has also been found to be very therapeutic to our mental health, perhaps because it satisfies our innate human need for connection and meaning in life. Looking up at all the vastness and beauty of the inky, black night sky and its twinkling stars reminds us that we are not alone in the Universe; we are all living on the same cosmic plane, under the same beautiful sky.

Even the ancient Greeks as early as 750 B.C. gazed up at the stars and looked to the night sky for guidance. When it's just you and the stars, time seems to stand still. You'll find that your thoughts tend to clear and your connection with the world around you strengthens. It can make you feel imaginative, inspired; or calm, hopeful, and at peace with yourself and the world.

With that said, it's important that you go out on your roof or look out your balcony window every once and a while to marvel at the night sky, because it can do a lot to help you find peace in your life and give you a new perspective. It helps you slow down every now and then and contemplate the greater meaning of life. When you're with others, it also provides the ideal ambiance for having deep, meaningful conversations and making great memories.

4. Physical Activity

Next, another way you can improve your life — and perhaps the most obvious of all the ones listed here — is by becoming more physically active. For those of you out there already rolling your eyes and hating the thought, I implore you to listen: you don't have to go to the gym every day, but regularly engaging in exercise and making sure you work up a sweat every other day or so will do wonders for your physical, mental, and emotional health. This is especially important if you work a desk job or have a sedentary lifestyle.

Some alternatives to working out at the gym include: jogging, biking, swimming, dancing, boxing, hot yoga, wall climbing, horse riding, gymnastics, or playing a sport like basketball, football, soccer, badminton, tennis, volleyball, field hockey, or even fencing. There are so many other ways you can get active and take care of your body; choosing the right one for you is all a matter of what you enjoy and whether you'd like to develop your stamina, strength, flexibility, or coordination.

We all know that exercise is good for you, because it keeps your muscles working, burns calories, and allows us to release toxins from our body in the form of sweat. Aside from that, exercise also releases endorphins in our brain, which create positive feelings and help us feel less pain. It also relieves feelings of depression, anxiety, and stress, as well as promote muscle growth and bone strengthening. It boosts your energy, clears your skin, fights against antioxidants, and minimizes the risk of chronic illness. It's also been shown to help you relax more and sleep better, which brings us to our next point.

5. Better Sleep

Getting a good night's sleep does a lot to improve a person's overall functioning. Most adults need 7-9 hours of sleep every night, but the quality of sleep that they're getting matters, too. Sleep promotes better heart health and better blood flow. It reduces stress, makes you more energized and alert, improves your memory, facilitates weight loss, enhances the collagen in your skin, and allows your body and your organs to repair itself.

However, not getting the needed amount or quality of sleep on a regular basis puts a person more at risk of developing depression, heart disease, diabetes, and even certain cancers. It weakens your immune system, impairs your cognitive functions (i.e., memory, decision-making, reasoning, problem solving), promotes wrinkles, and lowers your metabolism. So it's not hard to see why you need to make sure your body is getting the amount and quality of sleep that it deserves.

You can do this is by improving your sleep hygiene. Try to go to sleep and wake up at the same time every day, to regulate your body clock. Resist the urge to sleep in and stick to a strict sleep schedule. It's also good to have a nightly routine of things to do before you go to bed, like reading, brushing your teeth, or listening to music. Put your phone away and don't look at any electronic screens like your TV or computer monitor at least 1 hour before you go to bed, because it makes it more difficult for you to fall asleep. For the same reason, avoid drinking any caffeinated drinks like coffee or soda 3 hours before bed, and take naps between 11 AM to 3 PM for not more than one hour.

6. Healthy Eating

Finally, another way you can take better care of your mental and emotional wellbeing is by eating healthier and having a well-balanced diet. Observing proper nutrition helps a person lose weight, regulate their metabolism, fight against chronic disease, keep their heart healthy, strengthen their bones and teeth, improve their memory, and puts them in a more positive and energized mood.

Still, in spite of all these benefits, many of us still find it difficult to eat healthier because our cravings for pizza, burgers, donuts, soda, chocolate, cookies, and candy. While these foods may be delicious and addictive, they are also low in nutritional value and negatively impact our health. The first step towards change may be the hardest, but over time, it'll get easier and easier to do, and your body will thank you immensely for taking care of it.

Some tips to help you start eating healthier are: drink herbal tea instead of soft drinks or juice; have at least 1 day a week where you don't eat meat; gradually quit eating fast food; eat fresh fruits when you're craving sugar or candy; avoid food that's high in saturated fat (like pizza and burgers) or processed sugar (like milkshakes and ice cream). A nutritious diet is one of the foundations of good health — physically, mentally, and emotionally speaking — so make sure you take good care of yourself by following these tips.

Chapter 9: To Sum It Up

We've officially finished our journey together to mental and emotional wellness with Cognitive-Behavioral Therapy (CBT).

Recapping Everything

The introduction began with an explanation of why CBT is important, especially if you consider yourself a pessimistic thinker or have been struggling with negative feelings and self-destructive behaviors. I introduced CBT to you as an effective solution to your troubles and elaborated on its guiding principles, mainly: our thoughts control our emotions and behaviors.

In Chapter 1, I included a brief history of CBT and outlined how it came about and how it changed and developed throughout the years. I listed down all the major benefits you could get from letting CBT into your life, as well as all the factors to consider when deciding whether or not CBT would be the right choice for you. There were also ways on how to make the most out of CBT and this book mentioned.

Chapter 2 was all about the basic tools of CBT, wherein I discussed the importance of journalling, mindfulness meditation, behavioral activation, and affirmations, as well as a guide on how to do them.

Next, Chapter 3 introduced the 30 different ways CBT handles issues and how it could help with specific problems. It was largely devoted to dealing with many different kinds of anxiety, like GAD, social anxiety, panic disorder, and PTSD.

In Chapter 4, you learned all about how to use CBT in treating your depression. There were several techniques discussed, as well as the different kinds of depression like major depression, manic depression, perinatal, atypical depression, and situational depression.

Chapter 5 is where you learned how to use CBT to treat and eliminate fears and specific phobias, such as the fear of heights, thunder and lightning, flying, spiders, dogs, injections, and germs.

You also learned how to manage different kinds of obsessive thoughts and compulsions with CBT in Chapter 6, where techniques like EW/RP, cognitive therapy, and more were introduced.

Chapter 7 did the same, but for maladaptive behaviors. It discussed all the most common ones, like stress eating, watching too much TV, procrastinating, eating junk food, being tardy, and so on.

Once all the major areas of psychological distress and dysfunction CBT could resolve were already addressed, Chapter 8 outlined a comprehensive 21-day, step-by-step guide on how to use all the different CBT techniques into dealing with more general problems that weren't mentioned earlier. Some additional tips on how to continue improving your life even after your treatment process with CBT has ended were also discussed.

Thus, that brings us to Chapter 9, the final chapter of the book dedicated to taking stock of everything. Now that you understand the importance of CBT, its different techniques, and how to apply it in resolving your personal problems, it's time to look further into the future and ask yourself: what's next?

Life After Cognitive-Behavioral Therapy

Now that you've learned all about CBT and successfully applied it to dealing with your own personal difficulties, it's time to finally move on with your life. The hardest part is over, and what waits ahead for you is a brighter future.

Ending your therapy can be difficult, because often times people just can't believe that it's over. While some feel a sense of fulfillment or emotional closure when they're done, others don't, which can make it harder to say goodbye. However, bear in mind that just because this journey is over doesn't mean you should forever close your door on Cognitive-Behavioral Therapy. Problems are a natural part of life, and so, you can expect to apply everything you've learned here later on again in your future.

What's more, even if you don't have any problems to deal with at the moment, it's still good to practice some of these CBT techniques in taking care of your mental health. So keep journaling, keep meditating. Always think before you act and be critical of your thoughts and emotions. Unlike a lot of life's endings, ending this journey that you've had with CBT right now shouldn't be a sad one, so be happy and keep all your learnings with you as you move forward into the future.

Conclusion

And that brings us to the end of our journey together. Hopefully, you will have successfully accomplished the 21-day step-by-step program we've outlined here in the earlier chapter for you or, if I've already covered your specific problem in the chapters about anxiety, depression, OCD, and bad habits, applied some of the CBT techniques I've mentioned there.

Thank you for coming along with me on our journey with Cognitive-Behavioral Therapy. I hope you learned a lot about CBT and that it changed your life for the better. I also hope you've achieved all that you've wanted from these programs as well as techniques, and that it has helped you effectively overcome whatever struggles or challenges you were dealing with, in a healthy and functional way.

If you've followed all the steps correctly and devotedly, and integrated these additional tips we've provided on how you can keep promoting mental and emotional wellness in your life, then you should be well equipped by now to deal with whatever life throws your way next. Congratulations, and best of luck to you!

Here's to a happier and healthier you. Here's to becoming the best version of yourself and creating positive change to start living your best life today, all with the help of Cognitive-Behavioral Therapy (CBT).

Bonus Extra!

Bonus Extra On Meditation

I have also seen fit to add in this extra segment on meditation because I find that it is helpful on both a personal as well as professional level. It also acts as both a complementary, as well as an integral part of the CBT process. Alright, enough talk and let's dive in to the meat and potatoes of the matter.

Breath Meditation

The kind of meditation that I would like to talk about at this juncture would be dealing with the breath as the principal object of focus. This means when we attend to our meditation sessions, the thing that we will bring our mind and awareness to will be the simple in and out of our breath.

Why the breath?

Well, because we all have to breathe right? Somehow or another, every one probably has to breathe, either through the nose or through the mouth. Hence the breath makes for a very handy and easily accessible object of focus which we can depend upon just about any place, any time. Think about it, if you were on a plane with absolutely nothing to do, or commuting on the daily train, you can just sit or even stand comfortably and start focusing on your breath. Easy peasy.

How to do Breath Meditation

You would have to find a comfortable space for yourself. A note here. You do not have to be in the traditional meditative pose, which is most often cast as sitting cross legged on the ground and having your back erect and eyes closed. In this situation, finding a comfortable space for yourself could easily just mean getting to a less occupied area on the bus or train, your own table in the office or even doing meditation whilst standing up. (it can be done, you just need practice)

Of course, for the absolute beginner, or for just about anyone who is easily distracted by all the hum drum that life has to offer, going to a quiet spot like your home, a park, by the sea or in the mountains would be doing yourself no harm if you were looking to derive maximum benefits from meditation. For me, I would recommend that you choose somewhere that is very easily accessible. You may know a perfect spot deep in the mountains, with picturesque views and cool, fresh air. Yet if you were to only go there for one or two weeks per year tops, it really isn't some place for you to consider as the spot to do your daily meditation. Most folks would be doing it at home, or somewhere easily accessible from home.

You would want to try and ensure that it is weather proof, which means you don't have to cut short your session every time there is a rain cloud. Fresh air would be a relatively good alternative to the air conditioned air we are constantly exposed to these days. Minimize the number of bugs in your meditative space so as to cut down on the potential distractions. Try focusing while having a fly attempting to crawl up your nostril. You get the idea. Once you have the constant space settled, then we move on to the posture.

The meditative posture. To be fair, the classic cross legged sitting on the floor with your back erect and eyes closed position is really one where most meditation centers and courses would adopt. You can use that as the benchmark which you would strive to attain, but that does not have to be your starting point.

You can begin meditation by sitting comfortably on a chair, just do not slouch. You do not want to compress your stomach and intestinal areas because you might limit your air intake, which would then affect your breath and focus. You can also begin meditation by lying on your back. Some folks do it on their beds, but a word of caution. Most times, people find that they would drift off to sleep just because it is their bed. As the human body is so sensitive and conditioned to anchors and cues that by just being on the bed, the urge to sleep would automatically kick in. Meditation does not equate to sleeping. That much has to be made clear at this point. For folks who find it needful to lie down, it would be best done on a harder surface. Perhaps a wooden floor or a thin mattress laid on the ground. The firmness of the ground would reduce the tendency for the body to fall into sleep mode, though I personally would like to state here that sitting up would still be one of the better postures to be in so that you would find it easier to concentrate.

Focus on the Breath. Now with all the sundry duties settled, it is time to get down to the actual process of meditation. Your primary focus will be on your breath. You would be paying attention to your nostrils as you take in the breath, and again to your nostrils as you breathe out. Always breathe through your nose, which is another reason why sitting up is good because most folks would be able to do nose breathing whilst sitting up. You will pay attention to your nostrils expanding slightly, and the coolness of the air on the intake, and you will pay attention to your nostrils puffing out slightly, and the hotness of the breath on the exhalation. All your attention and focus should be centered on your nostrils.

During this practice, thoughts as well as images would tend to come into this personal space which we are trying to create for ourselves. It is all well and easy to just give you a simple - ignore them, but it doesn't quite work that way does it? Our primary focus is our breath, so what should we do now that images and thoughts are dragging our attention away from the breath and onto them?

At the start, you can give those thoughts and images the attention that they crave. If you start thinking about what to eat later, or what movie to watch on the weekend, you can actually allow your consciousness to pay attention to them. Try to build up your awareness such that you seem to be looking at those thoughts with a sort of detachment. It is as if you are looking at someone else's thoughts instead. You give these thoughts the attention, but you try to build up that detachment where you look at these thoughts through the lens of a third party. Then you want to watch these thoughts as they spiral away after initially demanding your focus and attention. As they fade off, you will refocus your awareness and concentration on the breath.

This focus on and focus off the breath due to the interruption from our mental thoughts would be a pretty constant occurrence in the earlier stages of meditation. Some of the learned folks would compare your mind to a monkey, and your focus on the breath as a chain tied to a stout post, which is binding the monkey. At the initial stages, the mind or monkey would jump up and down, but after exhausting its energy, there would be periods it would just lie still. Those are the times where you find yourself being able to focus on the breath for a protracted period. Just to be clear, there is no hard and fast rule to what is termed as a protracted period. It all depends on every individual. For a person who has a hyperactive mind, having five or ten seconds of focus on the breath can be termed as a protracted period.

As the meditation practice grows, you will find that the monkey tends to disturb lesser. Even during the incidences of disturbance, you would tend to be able to make it go rest in a shorter amount of time than before. With the growth of your concentration on your breath, you will find that your sessions will start to stretch. From ten minutes to twenty. From half an hour to the full hour.

During the course of the session, your entire focus will still be on your breath. There is no need to bring in any thoughts or imagery which may be troubling you.

I will not be expounding any of the benefits that breath meditation will bring, but I would rather leave it to yourself in experiencing them. As a parting word, I can say personally a calmer approach to life seems to be something which I have experienced.

To a fulfilling meditative journey. Please start.

A Way of Helping Out

At the end of this book, would you be able to think of 1 or 2 things which you have learnt and are able to share with the folks on amazon?

Please Go ahead and share that 1 best thing which you have learnt

It would be a great help to other folks in letting them know of your beneficial experience

And it would be helping me out as well because reviews mean quite a big deal

Thank You Very Much!

www.ingramcontent.com/pod-product-compliance
Lightning Source LLC
Chambersburg PA
CBHW062017090426
42811CB00005B/880

9781733238335